Learning to be Prejudiced

Learning to be Prejudiced

Growing up in Multi-ethnic Britain

Alfred Davey
Reader in Applied Social Studies
Department of Social Policy
The University of Newcastle-upon-Tyne

with the assistance of
P.N. Mullin
M.V. Norburn
I. Pushkin

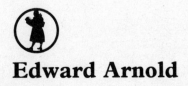

Edward Arnold

© Alfred Davey 1983

First published in Great Britain 1983 by
Edward Arnold (Publishers) Ltd, 41 Bedford Square, London WC1B 3DQ

Edward Arnold (Australia) Pty Ltd, 80 Waverley Road, Caulfield East, Victoria 3145, Australia

Edward Arnold, 300 North Charles Street, Baltimore, Maryland 21201, U.S.A.

British Library Cataloguing in Publication Data

Davey, Alfred
  Learning to be prejudiced.
  1. Prejudices
  I. Title
  303.3'85   HM291

ISBN 0-7131-6402-6

Text set in 11/12 pt Plantin
by Colset Private Limited, Singapore
Printed and bound in Great Britain by Richard Clay (The Chaucer Press) Ltd, Bungay, Suffolk

Contents

Preface

The research which forms the basis of this book was carried out in collaboration with the late Isidore Pushkin, better known as Push, Paul Mullin and Veronica Norburn. It was made possible by a grant from the Social Science Research Council to Alfred Davey and Isidore Pushkin. Although each member of the group laboured more on some parts of the project than they did on others, the final results were the product of group planning and a genuinely integrated team effort.

As a team we are indebted to each other in all sorts of ways but jointly our thanks are due to the teachers, parents and children who so willingly took part in the study. They cannot be named because of the demands of confidentiality, but we would like them to feel that their cooperation was valued and appreciated. We should also like to acknowledge the help of Diane Kearton and Anita Henderson in the initial stages of the project.

The present book is not a collective effort in the same sense as the research itself. It contains a great deal of other people's research as well as that of the team. The selection of other people's work and the use to which it has been put as illustrative or supporting material, no doubt displays the interpretational biases of the author, Alfred Davey. It is he, therefore, who must bear the responsibility for the judgements which have been made as well as for the way in which the team's research has been presented. At the same time, the book has greatly benefited from the team's sifting of our data, their scrutiny of draft chapters and their critical and supportive comments.

Paul Mullin has written the statistical appendix and he has also been responsible for reducing the quantitative data to a manageable tabular form for the book. The team owes a considerable debt to Paul Mullin's statistical ability and computational skills.

Finally, the warmest thanks are due to Pat Bertram and Maureen Hordon, both for their accurate typing and for their unfailing patience and helpfulness in the preparation of the manuscript.

1 Introduction

Immigration is not a new phenomenon for Britain. In the last 500 years a variety of groups of people have settled here either because they were too bad or too good for their own countries or because they thought Britain offered them an escape from poverty and the opportunity of a new way of life. In the seventeenth century, substantial numbers of French Huguenots came to Britain to avoid religious and political discrimination as did large numbers of Russian and European Jews in the nineteenth century. Political refugees from Nazi Germany began to enter the country before the Second World War, and after the war large numbers of displaced and stateless people were rehabilitated in Britain.

However, if immigration into Britain is not a new phenomenon neither is the insularity of the British outlook. Historically there has always been a conflict between the publicly espoused notions of justice and fair play and the various legitimations that have been used to justify class, national or racial superiority.

The arrival of a relatively small number of Jewish immigrants at the turn of the century provoked a blatantly anti-semitic campaign to end immigration. The same objections were raised again in the 1930s when an attempt was made to appease anti-semitism by denying asylum to Jewish refugees from Nazi Germany. It was predictable, as Lester and Bindman (1972) have observed, that if a small number of European Jewish immigrants, similar to the British in appearance and cultural traditions, aroused opposition, then a substantial settlement of Asian and Afro-Caribbean peoples, different in pigmentation and culture, would meet with considerable antagonism.

The flow of immigrants into Britain was greatly accelerated in the immediate post-war years. Industry was changing over from war-time to peace-time production and the great production growth of the 1950s began. Immigrants from the West Indies and the Indian sub-continent were sought in order to meet the growing demand for unskilled and semi-skilled workers, especially in those industries where working conditions were uncongenial and shifts at unsocial hours had to be worked.

The current estimate of Britain's black population (people of Asian, Afro-Caribbean and other New Commonwealth ethnic origin) is around

1

1.85 million, which constitutes 3.4 per cent of the total population. About half the present adult population of Asians and West Indians had settled here by June 1962 when for the first time entry was restricted by the Commonwealth Immigrants Act.

Since the newcomers were predominantly young people, the minority groups contain a comparatively large proportion of children. (It is estimated that approximately 40 per cent of the total black population in 1976 were born here). Furthermore, since the newcomers tended to settle in concentrated communities, primarily in London and the South East, the West Midlands, the North West, Yorkshire and Humberside, the proportions of children of Asian or West Indian parentage rose in some schools to 50 per cent or more. The teachers found themselves in a state of cultural shock and in need of new skills, new knowledge and new attitudes. The response of the colleges and departments of education was, however, painfully slow. In 1972, Townsend and Brittan made a study of various organizational aspects of 230 multi-ethnic schools. They reported that of 596 teachers they questioned in their first year of teaching, only 66 had had any preparation for teaching in such schools and, of these, six had received only one lecture.

It is, therefore, not surprising that in later phases of the research, it was found that some teachers resolved their professional problems either by rationalizing them out of existence or by denying that they existed at all. For example: 'Having worked in a school with a large proportion of immigrants I wonder if too much emphasis should be given to racial differences. Children are children the world over. They meet and play on equal terms. Constant discussion of racial differences might lead to embarrassing situations'. Head teacher (Townsend and Brittan, 1973, p. 15). Another head teacher was much less hesitant: 'I do not consider it the responsibility of an English State School to cater for the development of cultures and customs of a foreign nature. I believe our duty is to prepare children for citizenship in a free, Christian and democratic society according to British standards and customs and that any sectarian needs should be met by denominational foundations supported by the people of that particular sect' (ibid, p. 13). Similar views were also reported as prevalent by Jelinek and Brittan (1975): 'In my opinion most primary school children have no thoughts of race and I think it would be most unwise to put thoughts of racial differences in their heads', (p. 46).

It would be wrong to suggest that such views, although found to be common in widely different parts of the country, are shared by all teachers. In particular, they are widely divergent from the beliefs of the many teachers who organized themselves into such self-help organizations as the National Association for Multi-racial Education and the All-London Teachers Against Racism and Fascism, in order to advance a more positive and informed approach to education in a multi-ethnic society. Nevertheless, these teachers would be the first to admit that their views are not always readily accepted by some of their colleagues.

Brittan's analysis of teachers' opinions in the third phase of the study (Brittan, 1976) reveals that 94 per cent of the sample of primary and secondary school teachers believed that 'Schools have a responsibility to promote good race relations amongst pupils.' However, there was considerably less support (62 per cent) for the suggestion that, 'School syllabuses should be revised to include lessons on the culture and countries of origin of immigrants', and only 46 per cent thought that 'Schools should adapt their ways to accommodate the different cultural traditions of immigrant pupils.'

Commenting on the response to the questionnaire as a whole, Brittan concludes that taken in conjunction with the earlier evidence (Townsend and Brittan, 1973) it would seem to be beyond doubt that many teachers believe assimilation – that as far as possible black children should become as white children – should be the objective of multi-ethnic education. Suggestions for curricular and organizational changes in schools which recognize that a transformation has taken place in British society during the last 30 years are not likely to get support from those who feel that differences between groups do not matter or are best ignored. 'Perhaps,' writes Brittan, 'it is felt that the passage of time will sort out those issues as black and brown pupils become indistinguishable from white ones except by the colour of their skin.'

For those teachers who hold such views or who believe that racial issues can be tidied away out of the lives and education of young children, the results from the investigation which form the major part of this book, will prove a disappointment. The study aimed to assess what effects growing up in a multi-ethnic society had on the ways children perceived themselves in relationship to others. Did the children see themselves as belonging to discrete social groups? If so, what markers did they use to differentiate one group from another? What were their feelings towards those who were seen as belonging to groups other than their own, and did they make friends across the group divisions?

The results provide good evidence that racial and ethnic distinctions are extensively employed by primary school children in the process of adapting to a multi-ethnic society. By the age of seven or eight they have not only learned the standard classification system but also what attitudes should be adopted to people classified in a particular way.

But why does colour and ethnicity play such a prominent part in children's relationships with each other? Why is it that so many children appear to learn the same kind of things about other groups in their socio-cultural milieu? The short answer must be that the categories which children employ to simplify and understand their world are not their personal inventions but those which Durkheim (1964) might have described as 'external, coercive and collective'; in other words, constructs which are readily and culturally available.

However, the reason why the pattern of attitudes and discriminatory behaviour towards the same outgroups persists across generations requires a rather more complex explanation. Initially children do not learn the values, attitudes, knowledge and skills appropriate to their culture from the community at large; they learn them as a member of a specific group which stands in a particular economic and social relationship to other groups in that community. A child may learn, for example, how he is expected to behave towards others and how he can expect them to behave towards him, as a white middle-class Jewish boy in Glasgow or as a black working-class Muslim boy in Bradford.

As a result of their group memberships children do not perceive each other and react towards each other solely as individuals but as members of recognizable social collectivities. Moreover, their evaluation of themselves will come to depend on a process of social comparison between their own group and other relevant and socially contiguous groups.

As Bhiku Parekh expressed it in his BBC lecture (1978) on Asians in Britain:

> Their relationships are structured and mediated by the wider relations between the groups to which they belong. Joe, a Christian, does not relate to Joseph, a Jew, as one unique individual to another. They approach each other against the background of the history of their respective groups. (p. 36)

The relationships between blacks and whites in contemporary Britain have evolved from a variety of forms of colonial social structures. But it would be a gross over-simplification to imagine that the present state of inter-group relationships can be explained simply in terms of the residual beliefs from the days of Empire. There are real and ascertainable inequalities in the social status, living standards and in the access to authority and political resources between blacks and whites which mirror the unequal economic and political relationships of colonialism. Colonialism was characterized by a master–servant relationship which at best was paternalistic. In today's Britain there are no black members of parliament and, more significantly despite their high concentration in some areas, very few black local councillors. Minority group workers are clustered in the low-status, uncongenial, poorly paid jobs. Their cultures are negatively evaluated and they are under constant pressure to adopt British habits, customs and values which they are assured will make a better way of life for them.

It matters little, therefore, if children or even their parents, lack historical memories, since the long-established patterns of dominance and subjection, power and powerlessness between blacks and whites persist.

To say they persist is perhaps to understate the case. There is a constant process of action and reaction between the beliefs and images that one group entertains of another and the way in which its members behave towards the outgroup. Rex and Tomlinson (1979) speak of a cumulative principle:

> . . . whereby the existence of racist beliefs, once they are established, lead to discrimination, and this discrimination produces conditions which justify the beliefs. Thus, the British image of the West Indian, Indian or Pakistani is not now simply that of a colonial savage, but additionally of a man in the ghetto, or a young man in trouble with the police. (p. 287)

This dialectical process finds a synthesis in the social learning of the children. They are socialized into a concept of themselves within the context of the preferences and biases which exist in their society. Any awareness that their perception of others may contain a projective and pejorative element derived from their own group and its position in the established structure of group relationships in their community will be lacking.

Later learning, mediated through the shared assumptions and practices of their groups, is likely to be congruent with early learning. Such is the consistency in the continuing process of enculturation that in later life, they will be unable to recognize, without a conscious striving for new perceptives, the part played by the socioeconomic structure in creating the images of the outgroups. They will probably cite them as the reality which confirms their independent evaluations and judgements.

Thus, the children's beliefs and perceptions, on which our research has focused, may stand in both a dependent and a causative relationship to the structure of the multi-ethnic society into which the children are being initiated. On the one hand, the children's subjective constructions of the world in which they live provide vivid indications of what is happening within our social environment. On the other hand, if the children's preferences and biases continue to be reinforced and eventually crystallize into adult attitudes, they will make a crucial contribution to the future pattern of intergroup relationships.

The learning and utilization of a society's system of social classification and the differential pattern of values related to it constitute a critical part of the subjective experience of the relationships which exist between minorities and the dominant group. But beliefs and values are intimately related to the social conditions in which they arise and in which they are subjectively validated.

The next chapter, therefore, examines in general terms the interaction between the socio-cultural determinants of intergroup relationships and the personal and motivational factors which influence the way in which such relationships are experienced and understood.

The following chapter looks at the concept of human equality and considers how far this ideal has been in evidence in the recent history of ethnic minorities in Britain. In examining the social inequalities which form part of the day-to-day context in which children are learning about each other, particular attention will be paid to the part played by the immigration and nationality laws in legitimizing racial distinctions. If governments define some people, primarily identifiable by their pigmentation, as problems or as unwanted and relegate others to a class of sham citizenship, then their best intentioned policies for racial equality are unlikely to carry conviction.

Chapter 4 sets out the theoretical orientation of the study. The view is taken that the genesis of ethnic prejudice in children cannot be understood independently of the normal and progressive process of packaging the environment into meaningful units, or categories, in order to make sense of the world. After a discussion of categorizing as a means of simplifying and managing the physical and social world, we consider how children may acquire their intergroup attitudes via the processes of social comparison and social differentiation.

Chapter 5 sets out the plan of the study, describes the schools in which it took place and gives some preliminary background information about the children's parents. The parents' views are discussed in detail in Chapter 11. The children's responses to the different tasks with which they were presented, are set out in Chapters 6–10.

In the last chapter, the various aspects of the investigation are brought together and the implications of the findings for the education of children growing up in a multi-ethnic society are considered.

Finally, since the field of community relations represents a verbal minefield for the unwary, it is perhaps as well to make clear the way in which the terms 'white', 'Asian' and 'West Indian' have been used in this study to denote the different groups of children taking part. The term 'white' refers to indigeneous children with two white parents. No children of mixed parentage were included in the sample. 'Asian' refers to children whose parents had migrated from India, Pakistan or Bangladesh: children whose parents had migrated from East Africa were not included. 'West Indian' denotes children whose parents were of Caribbean origin but children of East Indians who had migrated from the Caribbean were excluded. Both the Indian sub-continent and the Caribbean are areas of great cultural complexity and the terms 'Asian' and 'West Indian' should not be taken to imply that the people within each group share an identical culture. The terms are used merely to indicate the broad geographical origins of the groups concerned.

2 Prejudice and group conflict

Despite the enormous amount of research activity which has been devoted to the investigation of prejudice and intergroup relations by social scientists, we are still far removed from an agreed model of explanation. However, two main streams of thinking can be seen to have influenced the study of prejudice and intergroup relations. One school of thought has emphasized the role of individual motivations, frustrations and needs, while the other has minimized individual factors and insisted that prejudice and discrimination are a product of conformity to group demands which in turn are determined by the friendly or hostile relationships between the political, economic, religious or cultural groups to which individuals belong. As Pettigrew (1958) puts it: 'One strongly emphasizes the personality of the bigot and neglects his cultural milieu; the other views intolerance as a mere reflection of cultural norms and neglects individual differences (p. 29).

Of course, few investigators would want to put the dichotomy between the two broad groups of theories as sharply as this. Most would agree that prejudice and discrimination are rooted both in the socio-cultural environment and those psychological processes which direct an individual's conduct in it. Their disagreements concern the priorities they accord to any set factors. Although for the analysis of a particular case of prejudice or conflict it might be useful to pay more attention to either the personal or the social causes, it has become clear as research has become more refined that for an explanation of discrimination and intergroup hostility in general the two approaches cannot be considered to be independent of each other. For example, competition for status or limited resources can lead to discriminatory behaviour, that will create attitudes of prejudice and hostility, these feelings and beliefs will find expression in fresh discriminatory behaviour which will in turn create further economic or social discrepancies.

The interdependence of the types of causation can be seen in the much publicized incident at Crawley in May 1976. A reporter from the *Sun* newspaper discovered that, by a piece of bureaucratic stupidity, two Asian families from Malawi had been temporarily lodged in the four-star Airport Hotel by the West Sussex County Council. The Asians were British passport-holders, had been issued with entry vouchers, were looking for work and had repeatedly asked to be transferred to simpler accommodation. But these were not the facts which were fastened upon by the people who shouted at them in the street, made abusive phone calls or sent them National Front leaflets. Nor were these points much emphasized by the press. 'Migrants here just for welfare handout', said the *Daily Telegraph*. 'We want more money, say £600 a week Asians', reported the *Daily Mail*. Criticism which could have been directed more accurately at the administrative procedures of the County Council was transformed into hostility towards the immigrants' alleged misuse of the social services.

If we were to treat this as a single event we might be tempted to explain this example of intergroup prejudice in terms of the prior existence of racialist attitudes amongst a vociferous and deviant section of the population. The Asians, ably aided by the press, had innocently activated a syndrome of preformed judgements. 'I never heard in Malawi', said one Asian, 'that the English people had anything against us, I thought with a voucher that would mean we were welcome'.

On the other hand, an explanation could be offered in terms of historical, economic and demographic factors which makes little reference to personal and psychological determinants. It can be argued that the relationship between the native Britons and the Asian immigrants can best be understood against a background of the past colonial relationship.

For centuries Britons had a master-servant relationship with their colonial subjects in different parts of the world. Not only was the relationship economically and politically exploitative but Britons convinced themselves that the subjugation of other cultures was a moral necessity. Now, having laid down the white man's burden, it is still thought natural for whites to expect preferment over blacks, and the disadvantaged position of the non-white immigrant is taken as natural. However, despite tight entry controls the fear persists that Britain will be overwhelmed by large numbers of poor, unskilled immigrants and their descendants, who will compete unfairly for jobs, lengthen the queue for council houses and make disproportionate demands on the social services.

Thus, it can be argued, that the response to the Asians at Crawley represented a genuine conflict of interests brought about by a previous social system and the current state of affairs in the United Kingdom. The hostile and discriminatory attitudes of individuals can neither account for the origins of the competitive situation or for its persistence; they are a product of it.

As in most conflicts of their kind the case of Crawley is but the latest incident of a prolonged reciprocation between the socioeconomic and the personal determinants of intergroup attitudes and behaviour. It would be difficult to accord causal precedence to either set of factors. Nevertheless, some attempt must be made to comprehend the dynamics of this interactive process, if the contribution of the two approaches is not to be lost in futile debate. Although the competitive, hostile or cooperative relationships between groups might be best explained in terms of their history and the objective socioeconomic situation, it is equally true, as Henri Tajfel (1969) has observed, that 'such situations have their effects on the motives and attitudes of millions of individuals, and these motives and attitudes in turn determine in part intergroup behaviour.'

Both schools of thought can point to evidence which supports its assumptions and perhaps the simplest way of delineating the dimensions of the problem is to summarize the main findings, first from a study which demonstrates the contribution of individual motivations to prejudice and discrimination and follow this by an influential investigation based on group conflict theory.

The prejudiced personality

As defined by most psychologists, prejudice is a negative attitude. That is to say, it is a relatively enduring predisposition to evaluate objects, persons or events in a particular way. An attitude represents the residues of past experience which have been unified and ordered to give the individual a commitment to a point of view. Once formed, a prejudiced attitude is difficult to change since it acts as a filtering mechanism for incoming information. There is a tendency to deny, distort or ignore new facts which may upset the existing attitude and to actively seek and select out information which will support it. This process has the effect of rapidly gathering objects, people and events into categories for which a practised response is readily available.

For those psychologists who favour the personality approach to prejudice such attitudes are primarily a property of the inner dynamics of individuals. The range of theories which seek to explain the genesis and patterns of prejudice in individual terms is very extensive indeed. However, a common feature of all these theories is the functional need-fulfilling character of prejudice for the individual, whether this be the maintenance of self-esteem (Fromm, 1941; Rogers, 1951), the working-out of inner conflicts by displacement, as in the various versions of the frustration–aggression theory (Berkowitz, 1962; Miller, 1941), or performing other utilitarian and social adjustment functions for the individual's personality (Katz, 1960).

One of the most influential investigations in this group is undoubtedly Adorno *et al.*'s *The Authoritarian Personality* (1950). This research arose directly out of concern over the Nazi persecution of the Jews and probably no work on prejudice has been subjected to such meticulous and methodological scrutiny (see for example Christie and Jahoda, 1954). Data for the study were collected from some 2,500 Americans in various walks of life.

The investigation found that highly prejudiced people rarely have a specific bias against one particular group such as the Jews but were antagonistic to a wide variety of minority groups. They tended to idealize the groups to which they belonged and to be derogatory and hostile towards groups in which they had no membership. This pattern of behaviour the researchers described as ethnocentrism.

These intensely ethnocentric people were found to have a cluster of personality characteristics. First, and foremost, they were authoritarians. They had a strong emotional need for submission to authority and wished to see society ruled by powerful autocratic leaders to whom they would give unquestioning obedience. Secondly, they were rigidly moralistic and believed that all deviations, especially sexual deviations, from the conventional code should be severely punished. There was also a tendency towards self-glorification and an avoidance of introspection. They conceived of others in rigid categories: 'good' and 'bad', 'like me' and 'not like me', and were unable to tolerate ambiguity. However, undesirable traits which they were unable to admit in themselves were readily perceived to exist in Jews, blacks, foreigners and other immoral outgroups.

When the investigations turned to an examination of the childhood of these authoritarians it was found that they were frequently the children of harsh, unrealistically demanding parents who were preoccupied with problems of social status and who exacted rigid obedience to their rules and values. The researchers argued that fear and dependency discouraged the child from conscious criticism of his parents but the hierarchical family structure left him with a hostility towards authority which he dare not express. Instead it is directed towards Jews and other minority groups which the parental values had led him to perceive as relatively unprotected by the authorities for which he has such an overt respect.

Despite numerous methodological criticisms *The Authoritarian Personality* remains an impressive and plausible study. Moreover, later research has established that the syndrome is not confined to members of majority groups. Jews, for example, may be ethnocentric, authoritarian and anti-semitic (Radke-Yarrow and Lande, 1953), and black American authoritarians, according to Grossak (1957) exhibit similar attitudes and personality mechanism as American whites.

The study goes a long way towards explaining the psychological mechanism by which certain child-rearing practices produce low frustration tolerance, repressed hostility and status anxiety which is expressed in ethnocentric and racialist attitudes. Nevertheless, although there may be good reasons for believing that some people who have been severely frustrated in their life histories may become more intense in their intergroup prejudices, it is quite another matter to attempt to explain large-scale social aggression, such as that against the Jews in Nazi Germany or the attempts at genocide in some African states, on the basis of individual frustrations.

It is of course possible to avoid making the implausible assumption that millions of people had identical childhood experiences by postulating that children come to share their parents' attitudes as part of their induction into a particular society.

Conceivably, in authoritarian cultures such as existed in pre-war Germany and Japan the strategies for coping with one's inner impulses, as described by Adorno *et al.*, would be mediated through the traditional family structure and educational institutions and become widely shared. Nevertheless, it is still necessary to make a speculative leap from individual emotional problems to uniformities in group behaviour.

The group approach

It is simpler, and more convincing, to postulate that widespread consistencies in prejudice and discrimination are not rooted in individual motivations and frustrations but in the shared experience of group membership, the relationship between groups and the perceived legitimacy of that hostility. For the most part individuals do not interact with each other in *ad hoc* ways but as members of social collectivities, national, ethnic, religious or socioeconomic entities, in circumstances which are not of their own creation.

Those theorists (see, for example, Sherif, 1966; Coser, 1956) who reject individual explanations maintain that what determines the functional relationships between two or more groups is the reciprocity or conflict of their interests in the competition for scarce resources. Whether the issues at stake are economic or political interests or matters of status and prestige, the shifting pattern of alliance or conflict between groups inevitably has repercussions on the way in which the in-group members perceive and evaluate the outsiders. For example, close contact between ethnic groups facing a common threat as was the case in mixed black and white American units during World War II lead to a favourable reappraisal of the others' characteristics (US War Dept, 1947). Conversely, although the British recognized the Sikh regiments as a splendid fighting force during the war, some municipal corporations later found it difficult to accept that a male immigrant wearing a turban could be an efficient bus conductor.

There is a considerable amount of evidence which indicates that intergroup attitudes are relatively independent of individual personality dynamics, and closely associated with group norms and expectations. In an early study of children's racial attitudes Horowitz (1936) found that white children in the northern United States were as prejudiced towards black people as those in the south. He concluded that the children's negative attitudes were 'chiefly determined not by contact with Negroes but by contact with the prevalent attitude toward Negroes'.

In a cross-national study in two areas of the world where interethnic conflict is intense and the cultural sanctions of intolerance explicit – South Africa and the southern United States – Pettigrew (1958) was able to demonstrate that the degree of individual prejudice was more closely related to a tendency towards conformity than any personal compulsion towards ethnocentricity or authoritarianism. As Pettigrew comments:

> Susceptibility to conform may be an unusually important component of prejudice in regions where the cultural norms positively sanction intolerance. In addition, there is no indication in either of these samples that there is any more externalizing personality potential for prejudice in these areas than in more tolerant parts of the globe (p. 40).

Perhaps the best evidence for the interdependence of group attitudes and group relationships comes from the series of large-scale studies carried out by Muzafer Sherif and his co-workers (Sherif and Sherif, 1953; Sherif, 1966). The object of the research was to investigate under controlled conditions the effect of conflict and cooperation on the formation of intergroup attitudes and stereotypes. The project was a longitudinal one and its significance lies in the skill with which Sherif managed to create the complex phenomena associated with the historical development of intergroup behaviour in the natural setting of boys' summer camps.

In the first stage camp activities were arranged to get the boys acquainted with each other. In the second stage they were randomly assigned to two groups, Bulldogs and Red Devils, except that the researchers saw to it that friends should find themselves in different groups. Activities within each group put a premium on cooperative effort, e.g. preparing the group's meals or improving the group's swimming facilities.

Once a strong sense of group identity had developed the researchers set up a series of competitive activities between the groups. Prizes were awarded to increase the tension and there was never any ambiguity as to which group was the winner and which was the loser. In addition situations were devised which put one group at an unfair disadvantage. On one occasion, for example, it was arranged that the Bulldogs arrived late for the camp party at which there was a vast contrast in the attractiveness of the various food. The Bulldogs found they were left with unappetizing and damaged food. A name-calling and food-throwing riot ensued.

The fourth stage was devoted to the reduction of hostility but the researchers found that once the aggressive attitudes and derogatory stereotypes were formed hostility continued to escalate even when the groups were engaged exclusively on benign, non-competitive activities. Good intergroup relationships were eventually restored by engineering problems which created a state of mutual interdependence, that is to say, the task was urgent and compelling but neither group could manage without the participation of the other. For example, it was arranged for the camp truck to break down and in order to get it going it was necessary to pull it to the top of a steep hill which neither group could manage alone.

A number of generalizations pertinent to the present discussion can be drawn from these experiments. Foremost amongst them is the fact that the boys who took part were socially well adjusted and had not experienced any notable personality traumas in their life histories. They felt, thought and behaved as they did as a result of the intergroup relations which were imposed upon them.

Secondly, when the interaction between groups is repeatedly of the competitive win-or-lose type changes take place in social relationships both within and between the groups involved. Feelings of antagonism arise and unfavourable stereotypes of the outgroup and its members become standardized in the group, even though the boys in the two groups were more or less evenly matched in social background and in personal and physical characteristics. The performance of the outgroup is derided and all its activities viewed with suspicion. Simultaneously, self-glorifying and self-justifying attitudes towards one's own group develop and within – group cohesion is strengthened.

In the same way as hostile attitudes and behaviour are a product of intergroup relationships so is the reduction of antagonism. Contact between groups in non-competitive situations was not in itself sufficient to bring about a change. Such occasions tended to be used for the exchange of blame and invective about the status quo. The history of the conflict distorted the groups' views of each other and effectively routinized the hostility.

The friction was reduced and the unfavourable stereotypes amended, over a period of time, by the introduction of a number of tasks which were too compelling for either group to ignore but which could not be accomplished without the coordinated efforts of both groups. These general results and conclusions have received a considerable amount of empirical support from Blake and Mouton (1961) working with adults in industrial settings.

Collectively these studies provide powerful evidence for Sherif's contention that the problems of intergroup behaviour which are so crucial in human affairs are not primarily problems of the deviate personality. They are problems of membership in national, racial, ethnic and social groups and the pattern of interaction between groups.

The interaction between individual and group factors

There are, then, potentially two broad groups of factors involved in the prevalence and persistence of prejudice and discriminatory behaviour. First, there are the broad socio-cultural, economic and political factors which determine the cooperative, competitive or hostile relationships between groups and prescribe the appropriate conduct for the respective members. Secondly, there are the personal, cognitive, emotional and motivational factors which influence the manner in which the relationship between groups are experienced, understood and utilized by people in their daily lives.

Neither set of factors can be ignored as they are closely interrelated. No one's attitudes, negative or positive, are purely personal affairs uncontaminated by the social context in which they have developed. No matter how much we reason, choose and act for ourselves we do so within a network of historically transmitted relationships.

On the other hand, not all our friendly or aggressive acts towards others are pure products of intergroup relationships. It would be a mistake to think of people as victims of their social environments. Individuals are not necessarily coerced by the social, political and economic biases of their society. Tradition may prescribe what is customary but people contrive to fulfil what they consider to be their obligations in ways which suit their own needs and purposes.

In South Africa, for example, racial discrimination is enforced by the policy of apartheid. The official norms for intergroup behaviour are explicit and reinforced daily in the lives of black and white alike, yet the students in Pettigrew's study varied markedly in the rigidity of their adherence to the official code. Their compliance appeared to be associated not only with different patterns of group affiliations but with individual aspirations. Predictably, students who supported the dominant National-ist Party were more intensely anti-African than those who were not members of the party but Pettigrew also found that students whose fathers were manually employed were more conforming than those whose fathers were professional workers. Presumably, these students had to be especially careful to think and behave appropriately if they were to rise in the social hierarchy.

In other words, in the same way as a policy of ethnic differentiation can perform many useful economic and political functions for a society, so individuals may find their prejudices to be personally rewarding. Our prejudices not only help us to identify suitable scapegoats on which to vent our frustrations but, used with care in the appropriate contexts, they can facilitate entrées to admired groups, buy us friendship, win us respect and smooth the way to social and occupational success.

It is perfectly obvious, therefore, that although every individual is, willy-nilly, a member of many groups and, further, that every group has its own outgroups, a great deal of our social behaviour is carried out in circumstances in which group commitments are disregarded. A satisfactory theory of prejudice and intergroup relationships should be able to make some predictions as to what kinds of situations are likely to evoke interpersonal behaviour and which are likely to be perceived as causes for intergroup behaviour.

Tajfel (1978) has suggested that differences in social behaviour can be conceived as lying on a continuum ranging from the 'purely' interpersonal to 'purely' intergroup, the absoluteness of both extremes being somewhat hypothetical. What is meant by interpersonal behaviour is an exchange between two or more people predominantly in terms of their individual concerns and characteristics. Conversely, when individuals belonging to different social categories interact in terms of their group identities, we have an instance of intergroup behaviour.

Although there are extreme outgroup haters, as described by Adorno *et al.*, who are likely to perceive nearly all social situations as involving an 'us' and 'them' dichotomy, the vast majority of people regularly engage in interaction at different points of the continuum. The nearer the situation is interpreted as being towards the interpersonal end the more variability will be shown in the behaviour towards members of outgroups. On the other hand, the nearer the situation is seen to be to the intergroup extreme the more uniformity will individual group members show in their behaviour towards out-groups. There will be a readiness to categorize individual members of the out-groups on a fraction of their attributes such as their gender, their language, their religion, their ethnicity or their pigmentation, and respond to each complex individual as if he or she were a perfect example of the group as a whole.

The basic conditions for the emergence of predominantly interpersonal or intergroup behaviour can also be arranged along a continuum which Tajfel describes as moving from one extreme which he calls 'social mobility' to one of 'social change'. The former he defines as an individual's belief (usually shared by others) that group boundaries are flexible and permeable, that he can, in principle, move from one group to another and, in many important ways, improve his position by his own individual efforts. 'Social change' denotes the belief that the divisions between groups of whatever kind, socioeconomic, ethnic, religious and so on, are immutable. Therefore, the only way open for an individual to improve his or her conditions, or resist deterioration in conditions, is to act with the group as a whole.

A good example of the effect of such an interpretation of a situation is provided by the attitudes, stereotypes and discriminatory behaviour which emerged in Sherif's boys' camp experiment. In such an intense competitive series of exchanges it was not difficult to believe that one's fate was bound up with the fortunes of the group as a whole while the idea that one could change sides was almost inconceivable. Indeed, when a member tried his hand at a lone peace-making mission he was rejected by the other group and called a 'traitor' by his own group.

Sanctions, both overt and implicit, against certain kinds of individual mobility exert a powerful influence in all cultures. When rigid group boundaries are interpreted as illegitimate and alternatives are conceivable, if not immediately obtainable, as is the case with black minorities in this country, then smouldering discontent may become open social conflict.

Conclusions

In outlining the problems involved in the explanation of prejudice it has become clear that a comprehensive account must embrace a great deal more than a study of individual motives and frustrations. While there is good reason to believe that some people may 'need' prejudice as others 'need' drugs to cope with their emotional problems we cannot legitimately move from the individual's inner states to the explanation of intergroup conflict, which appears to be endemic to human societies. Rather, causation should be seen as running in the opposite direction since, for the most part, discriminatory behaviours and associated attitudes are to be understood in terms of the individual's experience as a group member, and the interactions and reciprocities between groups.

Research on intergroup relations must logically entail a study of the problems of institutionalized power and the control of complex organizational systems for the production and distribution of resources. But this does not eliminate the necessity to investigate the subjective experience of in-group affiliations and the consensual interpretations by members of a group of their relations with members of other groups.

A sharp division between groups may be all that is necessary to push subjective perceptions and beliefs towards the intergroup–social change extreme of Tajfel's continua. Nevertheless, it will always be in some individuals' interests to attempt to structure the perception of others so that impenetrable social dichotomies are created, as is evidenced by the often repeated saying that if the Jews had not existed Hitler would have had to create them.

3 Equality and race

'Every statement about the nature of social discrimination is based, more or less explicitly, upon an idea of the equality of human beings'. (Lester and Bindman, 1972, p. 73). The idea of human equality which, in Europe, has evolved from the Judaeo-Christian belief in the Fatherhood of God, would be subscribed to in one form or another by most people in Britain. Many, however, would argue that this ideal sits ill with our policies and practices towards minority groups.

The purpose of this chapter is first to examine the notion of equality and then to consider how far this ideal has been pursued in the social treatment of ethnic minorities and the laws which specifically apply to them.

Since individuals are patently unequal in their skills, intelligence, strength and virtue in what sense can they be said to be equal? The reply is likely to take the form: they are equal in the sight of God or that all people are born equal. In other words, it is not claimed that people are equal in their endowments or accomplishments but equal by virtue of the fact that they share a common humanity. Now as Bernard Williams (1962) observes, if all this statement does is to remind us that people are human this is tantamount to saying that people are people. Nevertheless, he goes on to argue that even if this claim for equality is a very weak one, even tautologous, it can serve a useful purpose. It reminds us, for example, that all who belong to the species *homo sapiens* speak a language, live in societies, interbreed despite alleged racial differences, feel pain and experience affection for others. The assertion that all people are alike in the possession of these, and other characteristics, while indisputable, is not trivial. For we know that there can be certain political and social arrangements which systematically treat people as though they do not possess these characteristics and neglect the moral claims which necessarily arise from them.

It is not difficult to demonstrate that the case for equality based on the universality of human characteristics has rarely had the force of a moral imperative. The notion of the brotherhood of man has, from the time of St Paul, coexisted in Christendom with slavery, serfdom and more subtle forms of human subjugation. On the other hand, the existence of such ideas has both provided the grounds for attacking inequality and forcing into the open the justification for treating people unequally.

In one way or another these justifications have taken the form, not of denying the moral claim which arises from the human capacity to feel pain, experience affection, etc., but of asserting that some people possess this capacity in a lesser degree by, for example, being of diminished responsibility, invincibly ignorant, underdeveloped or childlike. By virtue of this restricted capacity their claims to equality can be disregarded.

Biological equality

Justifications of unequal consideration have always been found to be more persuasive when people do not interact as individuals, but as members of groups or social categories in predetermined roles, for instance, rulers and ruled. During the past 300 years, as Europeans penetrated the New World, Asia and Africa, and encountered people of different appearances and cultures, they repeatedly convinced themselves that various features of other groups were manifestations of restricted human capacity and that these were perfectly congruent with certain population boundaries. By the mid-nineteenth century the natural superiority of Europeans was a matter of received wisdom. Technological superiority was considered to the outward and visible sign of biological superiority.

The recurrent and continuing attempts to provide scientific evidence for propositions on the inequality of the biological endowments of varieties of peoples who are differentiated from those of European origin by virtue of their pigmentation and other physiological attributes have received little support from contemporary biologists. In 1947, 1951 and again in 1964 the United Nations Educational Scientific and Cultural Organization (UNESCO) assembled a group of world experts in the biological and social sciences, to give an authoritative opinion on the biological aspects of race. The signatories to the final statement (reproduced in full in Baxter and Sansom, 1972) declared:

1. All men living today belong to a single species, *Homo sapiens*, and are derived from a common stock.
2. Biological differences between human beings are due to differences in hereditary constitution and to the influence of the environment on this genetic potential. In most cases, those differences are due to the interaction of these two sets of factors.
3. There is great genetic diversity within all human populations. Pure races – in the sense of genetically homogeneous populations – do not exist.
4. Since the pattern of geographic variation of the characteristics used in racial classification is a complex one, and since this pattern does not present any major discontinuity, these classifications, whatever they are, cannot claim to classify mankind into clear-cut categories.

Differences between individuals within a race or population are often greater than differences between races or populations.

5. Certain physical characteristics have a universal biological value for the survival of the human species, irrespective of the environment. The differences on which racial classification are based do not affect these characteristics, and therefore it is not possible from a biological point of view, to speak in any way whatsoever of a general inferiority or superiority of this or that race.

New statistical techniques which combine all the available information on biochemical polymorphism make it possible to quantify the extent of genetic differentiation within and between human populations and give a new insight into the nature of race. In a recent article in *Nature* Jones (1981) reports that analysis shows that by far the largest component of the total genetic diversity of mankind – about 84 per cent – arises from genetic differences between individuals belonging to the same tribe or nationality. About 6 per cent arises from differences between tribes or nationalities. Only about 10 per cent of the total biological diversity of mankind arises from genetic divergence between 'racial' groups (classified as European, African, Indian, East Asian, New World and Oceanian). In other words, the genetic differences between the so-called races of man are only slightly greater than those which occur between nations within a racial group, and the genetic differences between individuals within a local population are far greater than either of these. Far from being divided into a number of discrete 'racial' types, mankind as a whole is a fairly homogeneous species.

It is clear, then, that in whatever way biologists choose to classify the diversity of mankind for the purposes of their morphologies, these classifications cannot be used to justify unequal treatment on the grounds that one 'race' or population is inherently or genetically inferior to another. Any justification for assertions that this or that group has a greater or lesser entitlement to consideration must be sought in the social and political relationships within or between societies rather than in the state of knowledge concerning biological differences.

Thus, the anthropologist, Manning Nash (1962) argues that racial ideologies – systems of ideas which rank races as superior or inferior – are not a product of the state of scientific knowledge but a response to social conflict and crisis. They flourish, he points out, where the participants in the conflict have hereditary, visible and physical badges of difference and, in particular, where the parties are not only physically but culturally different. The form which a racial ideology assumes will be related to the factors which give rise to it and the particular social system in which it is embedded but, in general terms, it will serve the following purposes:

1. Provide a moral rationale for systematic disprivilege;
2. Allow members of the dominant group to reconcile their values with their activities;

3. Discourage the subordinate group from making claims on the society;
4. Rally the adherents to political action in a 'just' cause;
5. Defend the division of labour where it is structured on racial and ethnic lines.

A successfully propagated ideology will, for the dominant group, both rationalize the inequalities between the privileged and the disprivileged and conceal the contradiction between affirmations of theoretical human equality on the one hand and the policies and activities necessary to subjugate and deprive another group, on the other.

Intelligence and ethnicity

Despite repeated authoritative refutations of pseudo-biological fallacies concerning innate and immutable differences between populations or categories of person, racial ideologies have shown considerable resiliance. In part, their longevity is attributable to their plasticity, which has enabled their proponents to put them forward in transformed and more sophisticated guises. Recently, educationalists are most likely to have become aware of propositions regarding biological inequality of superficially discrete categories of people as a result of the controversy concerning the differential performance of black and white children on standardized tests of intelligence.

The relative contributions of the genes and the environment to ethnic differences in intelligence-test performance is an extremely controversial topic which has produced a great diversity of research data of considerable complexity, which cannot be conveniently summarized here. Davey (1973) briefly reviewed the evidence and considered the effect of the controversy on teachers' beliefs and attitudes. A comprehensive review of the evidence will be found in Loehlin *et al.* (1975) *Race Differences in Intelligence*, and Vernon (1979) *Intelligence: Heredity and Environment*. It would, however, be useful at this point to consider the fundamentals which need to be kept in mind when considering such data.

Let us begin by accepting the fact that there are many reasons for believing that there are genetic differences between one individual and another and very few for believing there are not. We can infer this, for example, from the fact that siblings, even chronologically very close siblings like non-identical twins, can differ quite strikingly. If intellectual differences were due entirely to environmental differences then siblings, reared together, should be more alike than they actually are. Nevertheless, we do not inherit our intellectual abilities. Our genetic endowment is only the necessary condition for development not a sufficient one. Development depends on a sequence of environments, pre-natal and post-natal to which the growing organism is exposed.

The assumed inherited potential for intellectual development cannot be seen and it cannot be measured. It can only be inferred from the way people act, speak and think. In other words, a person's intelligence can only be expressed through the medium of acquired skills and knowledge. It follows, therefore, that valid comparisons of intelligence between individuals or groups of individuals can only be made when all have had an equal opportunity of acquiring those skills.

On the basis of his review of several lines of evidence Jensen (1969) in his now notorious paper, 'How much can we boost IQ and scholastic achievement?', concludes that some 80 per cent of the variation in intelligence-test scores is due to hereditary rather than environmental influences. By applying his heritability estimate to the frequently reported difference of some 15 points of IQ between the score of the average American white child and the average American black child he argues that 'genetic factors are strongly implicated' (p. 82). His hypothesis is supported, he maintains, by the fact that even when comparisons are made between blacks and whites at the same socioeconomic level a substantial, although reduced, difference persists.

By Jensen's reasoning, if genetic inheritance totally controlled the outcome with environmental factors held constant, the IQs of blacks and whites should still differ. On the other hand, if the environment were the sole determinant, the difference should disappear. The results, in fact, show that with the principal socioeconomic variables of parental occupation, income and education equated the difference is reduced by about a third. The remaining disparity can, therefore, be attributed to either genetic factors or uncontrolled environmental differences. If one is satisfied that by equating education, occupation and income, like is being compared with like, then the genetic argument will be favoured. But the truth of the matter is that it is impossible to match the environments for groups of blacks and whites since pigmentation itself influences the individual's environment. Whether the residual difference is due to being black genetically or black in a culture which traditionally despises blackness remains open to doubt.

An alternative approach to estimating the genetic contribution to intellectual performance is to approach the problem from the opposite direction that is, by comparing identical twins, individuals with the same genetic programme, brought up in different environments. Identical, or monozygotic twins, account for only 2 per cent of the populations; if one adds the further condition that the identical pairs should be reared separately it is obvious that evidence of heritability from this source will be scarce.

In fact, only four sets of separated identical twins have been located and tested in the past half century: 19 pairs were assembled by Newman, Freeman and Holzinger (1937) in the United States, 53 pairs were studied by Burt (1966) in Britain, a further 44 British pairs by Shields (1962) and 12 pairs were reported on by Juel-Nielsen (1965) in Denmark. Jensen (1969) originally used only the first three of these studies for his hereditability estimate and his paper places particular stress on the Burt data, since it is based on the largest sample. In addition, although Burt's separated twins were spread over the entire range of socioeconomic environments, of all the investigations their test scores showed the highest degree of agreement. Unfortunately for Jensen's argument, Burt's data were subsequently found to be fraudulent (Beloff, 1980).

This line of evidence, therefore, rests on 75 pairs of identical twins, seen over a period of nearly 50 years, and tested at a variety of ages between 12 and 60. Nonetheless, although these data from opposite sides of the Atlantic would yield different estimates of hereditability if considered independently, they agree in so far that in each study there is a closer relationship between the test scores for the identical twins reared apart than for the non-identical twins reared together. This is fairly conclusive evidence for believing that some portion of the variation in measured intelligence between one individual and another is genetically determined. It does not mean, however, that an estimate of hereditability can be derived from these studies, either individually or collectively, which has universal application.

Each set of data is derived from white samples living in a relatively homogeneous range of environments. The separated twins were not placed randomly but put into approximately similar homes selected by relatives or adoption agencies. If the children had been placed in a diversity of homes, ranging say from black working-class to white upper-class the proportion of the score variation attributable to the environment might have been different.

The fact of the matter is, there can be no general answer to the proportion problem, as geneticists have repeatedly emphasized (See, for example, Lewontin, 1974). Estimates of hereditability depend on the extent of the environmental and genetic variation that exists in a particular population at a particular time. If we are comparing individuals within a small homogeneous community the proportion of score variability attributable to environmental factors is likely to be small since their effects will be roughly equal for all. Alternatively, if we are comparing individuals within a large heterogeneous population then the amount of variation which can be explained by environmental influences is likely to be large. By extending his hereditability estimate, derived entirely from within white populations, to racial differences Jensen is, in effect, arguing that the environmental variability between ethnic groups is comparable to the environmental variability within them.

A further objection to generalizing estimates derived from these studies across ethnic groups arises from within these data themselves. As we have said, the scores of the identical twins reared apart show a greater similarity than the scores of the non-identical twins reared together, but the investigators also compared the results from the separated twins with identicals reared together in order to estimate the contribution of environmental factors. Although the IQs of monozygotic twins usually show a close relationship they are rarely identical. Newman *et al.* (1937), for example, derived their data from 50 pairs; 24 of which showed individual differences of five points or less, but eight pairs had differences of between 10 and 20 points. Genetically, the pairs were identical so the differences between the individuals must be due to uncontrolled environmental factors. Since, however, the magnitude of some of the differences is of the same order as those recorded between blacks and whites, one might legitimately question whether these too are not environmental.

Kagan (1969) in the following issue of the *Harvard Education Review* summarizes Jensen's paper as, 'a pair of partially correct empirical generalizations wedded to a logically incorrect conclusion' (p. 274). The partial facts to which Kagan refers are, as we have seen, first that the more closely related two people are, the more similar their IQ scores, suggesting there is a genetic contribution, and second, that black children generally obtain lower IQ scores than whites. Jensen combines these to draw the logically faulted conclusion that there are genetic determinants behind the lower IQ scores of black children. Kagan demonstrates the error in Jensen's conclusion by an analogy with the changes in average height of children. The heights of children in many areas of the world have increased considerably in the last 30 years as a result of better nutrition and immunization, not as a result of changes in genetic control. Yet a person's height is still subject to genetic control. 'The essential error in Jensen's argument is the conclusion that if a trait is under genetic control differences between two populations on that trait must be due to genetic factors'. (p. 275).

By extension from Kagan's argument it would be more useful to think of intelligence not as a genetically fixed capacity, but as a generic term for an individual's set of strategies for processing information and problem solving which have crystallized out of a complex interaction of upbringing, schooling, sex and ethnicity. It follows from such a conception that a well-constructed test of intellectual ability could be useful, within the fairly precise environment in which it has been standardized, not because it measures this or that proportion of innate potential ability but because it can be used diagnostically to ascertain an individual's strengths and weaknesses in the linguistic, conceptual and manipulatory skills which are necessary for all-round efficiency in that environment.

What part genetic factors play in the development of these skills and stratagems is uncertain and is likely to remain uncertain in the absence of some totalitarian experiment designed to control human mating, reproduction and child rearing practices and which systematically varied living conditions. We do know, however, that the defective linguistic skills, disfunctional patterns of conceptualization, depressed motivation and academic disenchantment which so often characterize the low IQ scorer are closely associated with poverty, social disorganization and social isolation. (See, for example, Wiseman, 1964; Davie, Butler and Goldstein, 1972.)

If intelligence were thought of as a syndrome of culturally valued cognitive skills we would be less likely to be asking questions about the possible genetic basis for racial differences and more likely to be devoting our investigatory efforts to identifying the remediable environmental impediments to cognitive development.

Suppose we were to accept Jensen's figures at their face value. What we are talking out is a difference of some 15 points of IQ which reduces to around 10 points when some environmental influences are equated. The difference, which it is claimed demonstrates a genetic and inalienable gap between blacks and whites, is no more than the variation which might be found in a normal family and infinitesimal when compared with the range of differences within ethnic groups (Jones, 1981). The gross disjunction between the social conditions and social expectations of blacks and whites in both Britain and the United States at least gives cause to doubt that differences of this magnitude in the distribution of measured intelligence are the critical determinants of their respective life chances.

Now consider the opposite proposition. What would follow if it could be proved incontrovertibly that blacks and whites had, on average, the same capacity to do well on tests of cognitive ability? Socially and occupationally probably nothing would follow. The data reviewed by Jencks (1973) show blacks and whites with equal test scores still have very unequal occupational statuses and incomes.

Mathematical estimates of genetic differences do not explain social inequality. Society distributes its opportunities for advancement unevenly. Those who are privileged will prefer to retain their privileges and will contrive to believe they are deserved. Equality is a social and political ideal not a matter of biological concordance. If all individuals are to have an equal opportunity for self-actualization then political effort will be required to initiate social policies which aim to reduce not only psychological and educational disadvantage but also the economic and social inequalities which underlie them.

Equality of opportunity

Let us summarize the argument so far: We have argued that 'races', identified by some obvious physiological characteristic such as skin colour, do not represent genetically homogeneous groups of individuals. Further, the assumption that some 'races' so defined can be regarded as superior to others is a nefarious one. We also argued that the hypothesized genetic differences between ethnic groups does not explain their differential accomplishments.

If the environmental differences between groups were narrowed then the various heritability estimates used to predict intellectual potential would change. Consistent variability in the achievements of groups of individuals within a society which coincide with ethnic boundaries, are more likely to be explained in terms of belief systems which sustain a stable hierarchy of groups and the differential consistencies in the respective groups' social and economic environments.

Attempts to reduce the amount of variation in people's environments, or at least to remove the obvious impediments to their development, are usually described as policies to provide equality of opportunity. The term, however, is not without ambiguity.

Bernard Williams (1962) suggests that equality of opportunity 'might be said to be the notion that a limited good shall in fact be allocated on grounds which do not, *a priori*, exclude any section of those that desire it' (p. 125). But as Williams points out, this formulation is not altogether satisfactory since *a priori* exclusion, that is exclusion on grounds which are unrelated to the good in question, can work in subtle ways.

For example, following the introduction of the 1944 Education Act, a policy of educational expansion was initiated, in order that every child should be educated according to his or her 'age, ability and aptitude'. Secondary education was expanded, fees abolished and university provision substantially increased. It was intended that there should be no *a priori* exclusion on the grounds of wealth but that everyone, regardless of their social and economic position, would have an equal chance of receiving the type of education which was appropriate for their abilities. Nevertheless, the association between educational achievement and social class continued to be a feature of our educational system, whether judged by the proportion of children from professional and managerial families who continued their education beyond the statutory school leaving age, the proportion of them who were admitted to the maintained grammar schools or the number which entered the universities (Halsey, Sheehan and Vaizey, 1972). The educational services remained inegalitarian in their effects despite the reorganization of secondary schools and the expansion of the universities because there was a failure to appreciate that there was a marked correlation between social background and educational attainment even amongst children of similar measured ability (Wiseman, 1964; Douglas, 1964). Indeed, as the influential studies of the National Children's Bureau have shown, the educational chances of some children in low socioeconomic groups may be pre-empted even before they enter school. The national sample studied by Davie, Butler and Goldstein (1972) revealed that the risk of perinatal death is 30 per cent higher than the national average for infants born to women in social class V. The surviving children were more likely to be living in overcrowded conditions than the rest of the sample and to be living in premises which lacked basic amenities. They were less likely to be seen at post-natal clinics, least often to be found in play and nursery groups and least often to be seen at dental clinics. By seven these children were likely to show signs of retarded physical development and to be failing in school. The chances of a seven-year-old class V child being a non-reader was 15 times greater than that for a child in class I.

Given then a relationship between social deprivation and educational attainment, it cannot be said that the same educational opportunities are being offered to x and y if x is living in debilitating conditions which could be rectified by some form of social action and y is living in developmentally favourable conditions. In this case it is not only necessary that there should be no *a priori* exclusion from a particular form of education on the basis of wealth but that access should be free of remediable environmental impediments.

The Plowden Committee (1967) recognized the pressure for some evening-up of conditions by recommending the creation of Education Priority Areas. Subsequently research (Halsey, 1972) demonstrated that a variety of forms of pre-school programmes could improve children's attainment in areas where social conditions were poor.

Policies which distinguish between people's circumstances and as a result treat people differently obviously depart from the conservative version of equal opportunity which seeks to treat everyone alike. Such policies are more correctly described as what Jencks (1972) has called 'compensatory opportunity'. If, however, we are agreed that individuals whose opportunities are to be equalled should in some way be compensated for certain features of their social and family backgrounds we are forced to consider the question raised by Williams (1962) 'Where should this stop?' (p. 128). Should the process stop at the boundaries of ethnicity?

Any race-specific policy would, of course, be contrary to the universalistic philosophy which has informed the provision of social services in Britain since the beginnings of the Welfare State. As Jones (1977) has observed, the essence of the Welfare State was that it catered for social need irrespective of extraneous social, cultural or economic personal characteristics.

> To treat or even record coloured immigrants differently for no other reason than because they were coloured immigrants seemed to strike at the heart of this philosophy and constitute a form of colour discrimination which whether it was intended to be positive or negative in the first instance, seemed a highly dangerous and unwelcome precedent. (p. 193)

The various social services agencies have therefore seen it as their duty to ignore race, insofar as it is possible, by responding to the needs of the new settler groups only insofar as they shared vulnerabilities with other needy people.

The Department of Education and Science adopted a similar approach by repeatedly insisting that educational disadvantage be defined in non-racial terms. It recognizes that many children, including those of ethnic minority groups, experience educational difficulties, and that such children merit special attention from the educational service. No programme directed specifically towards minority groups is, however, required since all who suffer from educational disadvantage have common needs. Minority group children it was claimed would 'benefit increasingly from special help given to all those suffering from educational disadvantage' (DES 1974).

What lies behind this philosophy of universalism is the fear, born in the pre-war years of economic depression, of the socially divisive effects of means-tested benefits and the reflexive self-stigmatizing effects that selective provision has upon the applicant for that provision. 'Selectivity can mean many different things', wrote Richard Titmuss (1976), 'but to most critics of "Welfare Statism" it denotes an individual means test; some enquiry into resources to identify poor people who should be provided with free services, or cash benefits; be excused charges, or pay lower charges' (p. 115). While universalism was originally concerned with avoiding differentiation by social class, his attack on the American 'War on Poverty' campaign which initiated a policy of 'positive ethnic discrimination' makes it clear that he thought it not only an inappropriate way of attacking black poverty, but one which forced the black community nearer to the margins of society. He saw it as providing two standards of service, one for the black and one for the white which he regarded as even less acceptable than two standards of service for the poor and non-poor. 'The American failure has been due to the belief that poverty was the problem, and that the advance of the poor negro could be presented as a pro-negro enterprise; it has not been seen as a universalist problem of inequality, social injustice, exclusion' (Titmuss, 1976, p. 114).

There is a genuine tension between the universalist philosophy on which the provision of social services has been based and proposals for more selective services which a race-specific approach to need would arouse in a particularly acute form. Ethnic minority groups are not the only section of the community who are poor and socially and educationally disadvantaged; therefore, to single them out for special consideration would predictably arouse antagonism. As an American (Kirp, 1979) observing what he calls the 'British dilemma' has written, 'The dilemmas of social class were familiar; the unique dilemmas of race were not generally acknowledged' (p. 23). Nor is it possible to see how the possibility of stigmatization, which so concerned Titmuss, could be avoided. 'Aiding racial minorities might just reinforce the long-standing British impression that these groups are, after all, inferior' (Kirp, 1979, p. 61). Although a race-specific policy might help the immediate needs of the minority groups, it has been argued, ultimately it could be to their detriment. Better therefore, to avoid charges of favouritism and the possibility of stigmatization, by diminishing the significance of race and providing extra resources for areas for special need, as in the case of the EPAs, on the assumption that in this way local authorities would be able to benefit minority groups less ostentatiously.

The policy of universalism appeared to envisage a society in which there is a fair and rational distribution of resources and services according to need without stigma or condescension. There would seem to be, however, formidable historical and psychological obstacles between the aspiration and its realization. The Political and Economic Planning Report (PEP) summarized by Daniel (1968) provided ample evidence that black people experienced discrimination in comparison with white people in their search for work, in their attempts to rent or buy accommodation and in education. Furthermore, there is little evidence that the position of the Asian and West Indian communities has improved over time. Smith (1976) reported that in terms of job levels and earnings immigrants who have been in Britain for a comparatively long period are no better off than more recent immigrants. Nor was there any change in the pattern of high concentrations of immigrants in areas of poor housing. There was an increase in owner occupation between the two surveys in 1968 and 1976 but the houses purchased were so inferior, in terms of location, age and structure, that they represented a poor investment even if bought at a low price.

However, it is in the area of seeking work that black people appear to be at the greatest disadvantage. Research carried out in the 1970s by PEP (Smith, 1974) has shown that members of black minority groups tend to have lower job levels than white people and to have lower earnings. Field experiments also showed that the minorities were subject to direct discrimination in recruitment, and indirect discrimination through the insistence on requirements which were discriminatory in effect and irrelevant to the job. Analysis of Department of Employment figures demonstrates that not only has unemployment among black people increased considerably in the last few years, but that in times of high unemployment the minorities are more vulnerable than the whites. For example, between November 1973 and February 1980 total unemployment doubled, whereas the number of black people on the register quadrupled. There is evidence to suggest that a large proportion of this figure is to be accounted for by the rapid rise in unemployment amongst young black people aged from 16 to 24 (Runnymede Trust, 1980).

Overall the evidence suggests that members of black minorities are more likely than members of the white majority to be unemployed, to have more difficulty in obtaining work, more likely to be in low-paid jobs, and more likely to be living in sub-standard housing in disadvantaged inner-city areas. In short, they suffer from a degree of multiple deprivation which is not found to the same extent amongst other dwellers in deprived urban areas. It is perfectly obvious, therefore, that any policy which aims to cater for social need 'irrespective of "extraneous" social, cultural or economic personal characteristics' (Jones, 1977 p. 193) cannot possibly be effective until some form of equality of respect has been established.

The notion of equality of respect is a valuable one in this regard. Respect is owed to each person as a rational and moral agent and since all are equally such agents respect is owed equally to all. Williams (1962) points out that the notion cannot be taken to mean that all people are the same, 'But it does mean that each man is owed an effort of understanding, and that in achieving it each man is to be (as it were) abstracted from certain conspicuous structures of inequality in which we find him' (p. 118). In other words, the notion of equality of respect demands that we look beyond the labels and *categories* of people which are the accompaniments of political and social inequality and let our actions towards them be guided by consideration of their *individual* views, purposes and needs.

Equality and the law

The existence of racial discrimination and a concern for equality of respect was the reason for the introduction of successive Race Relations Acts in 1965, 1968 and 1976. Each expanded the scope and strength of the law against discriminatory practices.

Now, equality of respect, as we have defined it, is an attitude of mind and the most commonly stated objection to legislation of this kind is that you cannot change peoples attitudes by law. In one sense this is true. Attitudes are a predisposition to feel for or against something and we do not stop feeling because we are ordered to do so. But if the State cannot act directly against prejudice, it can act against discrimination and ensure that the possibility of equality is kept open. If discrimination is officially condemned and effective measures are undertaken to curtail it in the various institutions in society, then a new set of public standards and expectations are set up and one of the supports for prejudice is removed.

Nevertheless, no legislation against discrimination can be effective unless a considerable proportion of the population is disposed to support it. But the effectiveness of any popular support for the Race Relations Acts has been seriously weakened by the tensions and contradictions between them and the immigration and nationality laws. Whereas the Race Relations Acts seek to affirm that people share a certain communality of humanity and are deserving of respect irrespective of ethnic origins, the immigration laws have progressively fragmented the notion of a common citizenship and introduced racial distinctions between one British subject and another. The origins of this double-edged policy are to be found, on the one hand, in our image of ourselves as a tolerant liberal-minded people and on the other, in anxieties regarding access to jobs, welfare and other resources, coupled with the assumption that white people, especially those born in the United Kingdom, have a prior right to such resources. As Bhikhu Parekh (1978) wryly remarks, '. . . attitudes developed during the imperialist era did not vanish simply because the colonial natives, now settled in Britain, were fully fledged British citizens rather than colonial subjects' (p. 47).

The series of laws concerned with the interlocking questions of British nationality and immigration control are quite complex but a brief survey will serve to demonstrate how in practice they have introduced racial distinctions between different kinds of British subject and created unequal categories of citizenship. (A more extensive and technical review will be found in Liu, 1977.)

It is convenient to begin with the British Nationality Act (1948) which established a common status for 'citizens of the United Kingdom and Colonies'. Any person born in the Commonwealth or a British colony was automatically a citizen of the UK and Colonies. They could enter Britain without restriction, and once here they had the right to find employment, vote and hold public office.

Yet even within the general category 'citizens of the UK and Colonies' there was a subtle difference between citizens of sovereign Commonwealth countries and colonial British subjects. The discrepancy arose because under the Act the Home Secretary delegated his authority to the Governor of a colony or a protectorate for the registration of Citizens of the UK and Colonies. But the colonial status of a British subject could be amended, on application and at the discretion of the Home Secretary, to one enjoyed by all Commonwealth citizens after the subject had been resident in Britain for four years. The amended registration also entitled the person to a passport issued in Britain for the purpose of travelling abroad. In contrast, Commonwealth citizens, as well as Irish citizens, were entitled to UK citizenship and a British Passport of UK origin, if they had been resident in Britain for only 12 months.

The distinction had little effect on immigration, especially as during the 1950s and 1960s most of the British colonies acquired independence and joined the ranks of the Commonwealth countries. Even so, British subjects from the Colonies were made to feel inferior, probationary citizens by virtue of the discriminating basis of their acceptance. Moreover, as later events were to show, this was to be the beginning of the attempts by British governments to create an exclusive United Kingdom citizenship out of the general category of 'Citizens of the UK and Colonies'.

Whatever popular support there may have been for the concept of a multi-racial Commonwealth it certainly did not extend to the reality of a multi-racial Britain. With increasing immigration into areas already suffering from neglect and decay, it was almost inevitable that the new settlers would be scapegoated for every social inadequacy to be found in such areas. There were sporadic outbreaks of racial violence in Notting Hill and Nottingham in 1958 and fears were publicly expressed that Britain was being swamped by unskilled, ill-educated, non-white migrants who would compete unfairly for jobs, lengthen the queue for council houses and make excessive demands on the social services. The political leadership of the country, which as a result of its *laissez-faire* attitude, had totally failed to anticipate or deal with the transitional problems of migration, gave way to, and sometimes even promoted, the popular clamour for immigration control.

The Commonwealth Immigrants Act (1962) took the next step towards extracting an exclusive United Kingdom citizenship from within the general framework of British nationality by introducing for the first time the category of 'United Kingdom passport holder'. Henceforth only those citizens of the UK and colonies whose passports had been issued in the United Kingdom, or on behalf of the United Kingdom government by a High Commission abroad, would have an unrestricted right of entry. All other Commonwealth citizens, along with aliens, would only be admitted if they had first obtained an employment voucher from the Ministry of Labour.

A further twist of the discriminatory screw was given by the Commonwealth Immigrants Act 1968, which narrowed the category of UK passport holders who were exempt from immigration controls to those who had a 'close connection' with the United Kingdom. 'Close connection' was defined as; birth in the United Kingdom or descent from a parent or grandparent born in the United Kingdom, naturalized or legally adopted in the United Kingdom or a registered citizen under the British Nationality Acts.

The Act was designed to serve two purposes. First, a large number of the second and third generations of white Commonwealth settlers were neither UK passport holders nor born in the UK, and had therefore been subject to the restrictions of the 1962 Act. In future, white Commonwealth stock would not be lumped together with Asians and West Indians for the purposes of immigration control. Secondly, the Act was intended to restrict the inflow of British Asians from Kenya and Uganda who had fallen victims of the policy of Africanization in East Africa. As citizens of the UK and Colonies and holders of UK passports and for whose welfare the UK government had assumed responsibility when Kenya and Uganda became independent, it was only natural that they should seek to exercise the right of abode in their adopted country. Under the new Act they were unable to meet the 'close connection' or patriality requirement, but the

Government declared it would meet its moral responsibilities by issuing these UK passport holders with special entry certificates and vouchers outside the normal quota system instituted under the 1962 Act. This, in fact, amounted to operating a double standard for a single category of UK passport holders. In future there would be two categories of UK passport holders, one exempted from immigration control, the other dependent on the issuing of a voucher before the right of abode could be exercised.

The Act was the subject of complaints to the European Commission on Human Rights. The Commission declared the complaints to be admissible on the grounds that 'publicly to single out a group of persons for differential treatment on the basis of race might, in certain circumstances, constitute a special form of affront to human dignity'.

The UK government admitted to the Commission that the Act was discriminatory in intention but did not change its policy; indeed, the Immigration Act (1971) made yet finer distinctions between 'citizens of the UK and colonies'.

The 1971 Act extended the parent and grandparent patriality clauses of the 1965 Act to citizens of the UK and Colonies who have been resident in the United Kingdom for five years or more. Thus, those UK and Colonies citizens who had established their right of abode would be treated as patrials. This concession compares favourably with the terms of the previous Act but the fact remains that the patrial clause confirmed that there should be two classes of citizenship of the UK and Colonies. Non-patrial citizens, predominantly people of non-European origin, are at best second-class British subjects since they have no right of abode in the UK. Moreover, whereas under the previous legislation those admitted with employment vouchers had the right to settle, under the new Act they had no right to stay on. They became subject to control by annual work permits and the constant threat of non-renewal. However, it was conceded that after four renewals they could apply for this condition to be removed. The effect of the Act was to put this category of UK citizens on the same footing as aliens and on less favourable terms than Irish and EEC nationals who were not subject to immigration controls.

It was for these reasons that the then Home Secretary was accused of racial discrimination in the House of Commons debate on the Immigration Bill in March 1971. He replied that he saw no reason why a country should not accord those who have a family connexion with it a particular and special status. Nevertheless, the effect of the Act was to make a *de facto* distinction between white and non-white citizens of the UK and Colonies.

The concept of patriality as defined by the 1971 Immigration Act was reinforced by the British Nationality Act 1981 which established patriality as the future criterion for British Citizenship and thus ensured that the vast majority of people who would be entitled to this status would be white. The Bill, which was introduced in the Commons in January 1981, proved to be highly controversial, and was subjected to an unprecedented degree of criticism, for a measure of this kind. There was strong opposition to various provisions in the Bill, both in the Lords and the Commons. Outside Parliament opposition came from the churches, immigrant organizations, the Commission for Racial Equality and the Law Society. As a result, the Bill was considerably amended in its passage through Parliament, but its more objectionable and divisive features remained unchanged.

Under the new Act citizenship of the UK and Colonies is replaced by three types of citizenship: British Citizenship, Citizenship of the British Dependent Territories and British Overseas Citizens.

British Citizenship will be accorded only to those people who were, or whose parents were, born, adopted, naturalized or registered in the United Kingdom – that is, those who are patrial under the 1971 Immigration Act. Citizenship of the British Dependent Territories will be acquired by those Citizens of the UK and Colonies who have that citizenship by reason of their own, or their parents' or their grandparents', birth, naturalization or registration in an existing dependency. All other existing citizens of the UK and Colonies who cannot claim either of these statuses will acquire British Overseas Citizenship.

Only British Citizenship will carry with it the right of entry and abode in the United Kingdom. Citizens of the British Dependent Territories will have a right of entry to the country in which their citizenship was acquired but British Overseas Citizens will have no right of entry anywhere and become virtually stateless. They will, however, be able to apply for a passport which will describe them as British Overseas Citizens and be entitled to 'consular protection'. Those living in Britain will acquire British Citizenship once they have completed five years residence and are free of conditions of stay.

The unsatisfactory position of those East African Asians who opted for British citizenship at the time of Uganda's and Kenya's independence and who have not yet received an entry voucher will continue. They can only acquire British Overseas Citizenship. Those who went temporarily from East Africa to India to await entry to the UK can expect to wait, on average, five years for an entry voucher. The voucher system will be continued, at the discretion of the Home Secretary, and once settled in this country they will be eligible to apply for British Citizenship after the completion of five years residence.

In a little more than three decades British law has moved from a position where citizens throughout the UK and Colonies enjoyed a common status as British nationals to one in which there are three unequal kinds of citizenship. The first tier of citizenship will be almost all white, the second tier almost all non-white and the third tier entirely non-white.

The Acts of 1962, 1965, 1971 and 1981 represent a progressive

abrogation by Britain of its responsibilities to peoples to whom it originally offered full citizenship. At no point has there been any attempt to
base immigration control on objective, non-racial criteria. Each step has
been accompanied by television programmes, radio broadcasts, newspaper
articles, parliamentary debates and public discussion of every kind. It is
the one topic which no political party can neglect since it is the one topic
on which the most indifferent voter has an opinion. The effect has been a
polarization of attitudes on either side of the colour line and a deterioration
of intergroup relations.

The white population has come to take it for granted that policies must
be instituted to prevent as many black people as possible from entering the
country. Not unreasonably, the conclusion is drawn that if those trying to
enter Britain pose some sort of threat to their quality of life, then so must
those who have already settled here. Inevitably, their perception of the
black community becomes problem-orientated, their sensibilities blunted,
and stereotypes about people from alien cultures serve as knowledge.

Black people, for their part, have come to accept that discrimination and
victimization rather than understanding and neighbourliness are the
dominant features of their relationships with the white majority. Their
children no longer expect to be accepted as British or treated with any
degree of equality. School leavers, deeply conscious of their blackness,
increasingly distance themselves from white society. They have little
incentive to adapt to a society which rejects them as people and despises
their culture. Recommendations for measures to reduce the gap between
them and the white-controlled society such as those contained in the
Scarman Report (Scarman 1981) are regarded with almost total cynicism.

The adoption of a law to promote racial equality only came when racial
disadvantage and discrimination were institutionalized, and there is little
doubt that the contradictions between the Race Relations Acts of 1965,
1968 and 1976 and the immigration and nationality laws has seriously
reduced their possible effectiveness. (Lester and Bindman, 1972 and
Bindman, 1980, provide a comprehensive commentary on the Race Relations Acts). The support for anti-discrimination legislation was not nearly
so fervent and vociferous as that for immigration restriction. Between
1952 and 1964 Fenner (now Lord) Brockway made 10 attempts to introduce anti-discrimination legislation.

The original Race Relations Act (1965) was so weak that it is difficult to
judge it as being any more than a declamatory document. The Act forbade
discrimination on the grounds of 'race, colour, ethnic or national origin' in
public places such as hotels, restaurants and places of entertainment. A
Race Relations Board was set up to investigate complaints but it had no
powers of enforcement except indirectly by reference to the Attorney
General who could, if he so wished, bring proceedings in the County
Court. Not a single case reached the County Court during the three years

this Act was in operation.

The 1968 Act extended the range of activities covered by the law to the critical areas of employment, housing and the provision of services. The Race Relations Board had the duty of investigating complaints of discrimination and of resolving disputes. When conciliation was unsuccessful it had the power to seek a settlement in court. The Act also established the Community Relations Commission, which had the duty of promoting harmonious community relations and of coordinating the work of locally based community relations councils.

It would be wrong to say that the 1968 Act was totally ineffective, but the evidence of its success is not impressive. Two reports, 'Racial Disadvantage in Employment' (Smith, 1974) and 'The Extent of Racial Discrimination' (Smith and McInlosh, 1974), indicate a decline in discrimination against black potential house purchasers between 1967 and 1974 and less discrimination against black job seekers with high qualifications. There was, nevertheless, a substantial number of incidences of discrimination, estimated in tens of thousands of cases, against unskilled Asian and West Indian workers when applying for jobs. In estimating the success of the legislation these figures must be set against, for example, the 150 employment complaints received by the Race Relations Board in 1973.

The Race Relations Board considered that the fundamental weakness of the Act was that it was a 'complaint-based system' which most victims of discrimination did not use because they were unaware of the procedure, thought no good would come of complaining, or because they feared that they would be victimized as troublemakers.

The drafting of the Race Relations Act 1976 took account of these criticisms by recognizing that a law which requires proof of deliberate acts of discrimination against individuals could have little effect on practices which were ostensibly of general application but discriminatory in effect. For example, an employer might require applicants to pass a test that had the effect of excluding black applicants but which was irrelevant to performing the tasks required by the job.

The Commission for Racial Equality (which replaced the Community Relations Commission under the Act) was empowered to initiate investigations where indirect discrimination was alleged or suspected and the right to issue 'non-discrimination notices' when it is satisfied that a contravention of the Act had occurred. If the discriminatory practice persists the Commission may seek a legal injunction.

The Commission was relieved of the duty of investigating individual cases of direct discrimination. Individual complainants now have direct access to the courts and Industrial Tribunals, although the Commission can give them assistance in preparing their cases. It must be admitted, however, that an unskilled black worker's prospects of success are not great if he chooses to challenge the practices of a multi-national company in the courts.

Since the purpose of the Act is to prevent discrimination by or against any person on the grounds of racial or ethnic origins, it follows that to favour a racial group would be unlawful. The Act, however, breaks new ground by permitting a limited range of 'positive action'.

Training bodies, employers, trade unions and professional organizations may provide special training facilities for particular racial groups to encourage them to take advantage of employment opportunities in areas of work where they are significantly under-represented. But there can be no favourable discrimination when the trainees come to apply for jobs.

The Act also provides for particular racial groups to have access to welfare or educational facilities to meet their special needs, for example, language classes for immigrants or birth control advice given by Indian women to Indian women.

The Race Relations Act 1976 represents a more determined attempt than its predecessors to control racial discrimination but its contribution to racial justice appears to be decidedly limited, whether this is judged by the number of successfully contested individual cases, the non-discriminatory notices issued by the Commission for Racial Equality or the adoption of special opportunities programmes by employers. Bindman (1980) reports, for example, that by the end of 1979, after the Act had been in operation for more than two years, the number of successfully contested individual cases alleging discrimination was 20. The Commission had started some 40 investigations into unlawful discriminatory practices and served six non-discrimination notices, all to very small organizations. In addition, the Commission had made strenuous efforts to encourage the type of positive action permitted under the Act, and had issued detailed guidance about it. There is, as yet, little widespread evidence of training schemes based on racial under-representation. Only a handful of schemes have been introduced by private employers and a few local authorities. There is little evidence of such schemes being initiated by Government.

It is, of course, quite fanciful to believe that any law against either direct or indirect discrimination can bring about equality of respect in the absence of social programmes designed to improve the housing, education and job prospects of the minority groups. As Lester and Bindman (1972) have pointed out, although the legal system may treat individuals as equals, it cannot change the inequalities within their relationships. Nor can the fact that the Race Relations Laws have failed to make much impression on discrimination be divorced from the effects of the Immigration and Nationality Laws. If the official view of black people is a negative one this will inevitably encourage distrust and the perpetuation of discriminatory practices.

Positive action

The White Paper 'Racial Discrimination' (1975) which preceded the Race Relations Act 1976 recognized that black communities suffered from both economic deprivation and racial discrimination and that the two were inter-connected:

> If, for example, job opportunities, educational facilities, housing and environmental conditions are all poor the next generation will grow up less well equipped to deal with the difficulties facing them. The wheel then comes full circle, as the second generation find themselves trapped in poor jobs and poor housing. If, at each stage of this process an element of racial discrimination enters in then an entire group of people are launched on a vicious downward spiral of deprivation. They may share each of the disadvantages with some other deprived group in society; but few other groups in society display all their accumulated disadvantages. (p. 3)

There is, however, little evidence that the remediable economic and social disadvantages of the ethnic minorities have been attacked with very much vigour or conviction.

Two strategies have been adopted. Under Section 11 of the Local Government Act 1966, local authorities may claim a grant towards the employment of extra staff if more than 2 per cent of the schoolchildren in their area have parents born in the New Commonwealth and arrived in the UK in the preceding 10 years. Secondly, under Urban Programme, instituted to arrest the economic decline of some inner-city areas, local authorities could apply for additional funds to improve the industrial, environmental and recreational provisions in their areas. The Urban Programme is not intended to deal specifically with the disadvantages of the black community. It was assumed that they would benefit equally with others in the area from the improved conditions made possible by the additional grants.

There is little indication that either strategy has been particularly successful in reducing racial disadvantage. Indeed, many local authorities have by-passed the issue by making declarations that their policies do not distinguish between racial groups.

In their report on urban deprivation (HMSO, 1977), the Commission for Racial Equality complained that it was not possible to examine closely the extent to which the needs of minorities were catered for, since so few records are kept which monitor the situation of ethnic minorities or their use of public services.

Money available under Section 11 is the only finance earmarked exclusively for combating racial disadvantage, but the operation of these provisions was found to be far from satisfactory. The fact that the Department of Education and Science ceased to record children by ethnic origin in 1972 has meant that grants have been paid on out-of-date information. Secondly, the take-up rate has been very uneven but, in any case, the 10 year rule means that some areas with substantial black populations of long settlement are no longer eligible. Thirdly, no requirement is placed on local authorities to ensure that staff appointments made under Section 11 are related to any appraisal of the need for special provision for minority groups or any programme to meet that need.

In 1978 the Labour Government produced proposals for the replacement of Section 11 by provisions more appropriate to current needs. Section 11 has not been reformed and Lord Scarman in his report *The Brixton Disorders 10–12 April 1981* (Scarman, 1981) took the view that reform 'must not be long delayed' (paragraph 6.34).

In the preceding paragraphs of his report Lord Scarman discusses three areas of deprivation which have a particularly severe impact on ethnic minorities: housing, education and employment. He considers that there is ample evidence of failure by both local and central government to provide a sufficiently well-coordinated and directed programme for combating the problem of racial disadvantage. In his judgement, if the balance is to be redressed, 'positive action' is required. Furthermore, he makes it clear that by 'positive action' he means neither a vague policy of universalism nor one of racial privilege. What he is advocating is that there should be a more just distribution of resources according to need, while recognizing that the major cause of the minorities' deprivation is racial discrimination. This principle, he points out, has already been recognized by the Race Relations Act 1976.

In other words, what is required is not changes in the law against discrimination but for a strengthening of the legal and economic powers of local authorities to induce them to apply more effective and carefully monitored policies for equal opportunity. But this will not come about unless central government is prepared to make more resources available and, more importantly, to demonstrate, more convincingly than hitherto, a commitment to racial equality.

Conclusions

We began with the proposition that although human beings are manifestly unequal in their skills and accomplishments they are equal in a number of fundamental characteristics which give rise to certain moral claims as to how they should be treated. The objection that some people can be regarded as inferior or superior to others by virtue of distinguishing physiological characteristics such as pigmentation was shown to be invalid and lacking any scientific justification. Consistent variations in the achievements and accomplishments of individuals within a society which coincide with ethnic boundaries can more plausibly be related to the social and political arrangements of that society than to differences in biological endowment.

If, therefore, all individuals are to have an equal opportunity for self-actualization, then there must be equality of access to the means of self-actualization. Equality of opportunity was seen to be an empty aspiration unless some attempt is made to remove remediable environmental impediments.

Despite the fact that there is good evidence that ethnic minorities suffer from a degree of multiple deprivation which is not found to the same extent amongst the white majority, successive governments continued to pursue the traditional policy of universalism. That is, a policy which sought to cater for equal need irrespective of ethnic or cultural considerations. But such a policy in a multi-ethnic society is unlikely to succeed unless there exists an equality of respect for the different ethnic groups within that society.

Equality of respect has been repeatedly denied by a series of immigration and nationality laws which categorized the ethnic minorities as unwanted, undesirable and non-patrial. Racial disadvantage for most of Britain's black community had as its starting point racially discriminatory immigration controls. The policy of rejection has not only subjected them to racial prejudice and insecurity, but curtailed their opportunities for jobs, housing and education. By contrast, the anti-discrimination legislation has been weak, limited in scope and difficult to enforce, while the accompanying programmes to combat racial disadvantage have been haphazard, unco-ordinated and largely ineffectual.

The two most enduring features of Britain's race relations policy over nearly three decades have been complacency and inconsistency. It was complacent to believe that thousands of New Commonwealth people could be happily settled in Britain without preparation for their arrival or any change in the existing services to meet their needs. It was, if anything, more complacent given the nature and extent of discrimination, to imagine that the black people would benefit in proportion to their needs and numbers from poorly monitored schemes aimed at the general elimination of social and economic disadvantage. It is an inconsistent policy which passes a succession of laws which are racially discriminatory and interleaves this succession with other laws which aim to promote racial equality.

In 1976 David Smith concluded his survey, *The Facts of Racial Disadvantage* with the warning:

> The first signs of more profound disillusionment, which might eventually form the basis for a new political force, are to be found among West Indian teenagers, an alarming proportion of whom are unemployed and homeless. The seriousness of these feelings, and the acuteness of the conditions from which they spring, should not be underestimated . . . . If the children (of Asians and West Indians) find they are unable to realize their parents' ambitions for them . . . if they find the educational system has passed them by, that they cannot get suitable jobs, and that they are not accepted by white teenagers, there will be the

profound frustration, bitterness and disorientation that is already seen in young West Indians (pp. 187–8).

In 1981 there were riots in Bristol, Brixton, Southall, Toxteth and Manchester.

Britain is irreversibly a multi-racial, multi-cultural country, but an unhappy and polarized one in which attitudes on both sides of the colour line are becoming more hostile and intransigent.

Nevertheless, now that the combined effects of the immigration and nationality laws have made it practically impossible for British people who are not white to settle here, there can be little political advantage left in the immigration issue for any of the main political parties. Relieved of the need to compete to be the most acceptable face of racist immigration control, one might hope that they could now at least address themselves to the construction of social and educational policies for reducing discrimination and disadvantage.

If some form of social justice and equality of respect is to be achieved we must change attitudes. But we also need to change the social, economic and political conditions which inform and reinforce those attitudes. There must be a two-way process if the cumulative progression from intergroup conflict to prejudice and prejudice to renewed conflict is to be arrested. Given the history of the present intergroup position, this would be an immensely difficult undertaking even if the determination and commitment, which is not much in evidence, were there.

If, however, we wish to begin to reduce the saliency of race in our social life then there is no more promising place to start than in the schools. Even the very young children in our primary schools, we found, had learned to make ethnic and racial distinctions and myopically perceived each other through adult stereotypes. Unless teachers can give children an alternative view of the intergroup relationships, by helping all children to understand those with whom they share their lives and enabling them to respond to the diversity of human groups without fear or hostility, then it is difficult to see a future for our society without an increasing polarization between blacks and whites and escalating intergroup tension.

4 Social categorization and social identity

William James, the great American psychologist, described the infants' universe as 'one big, blooming, buzzing confusion' (James, 1905). We now know that babies are a great deal more clever and better prepared for the world in which they find themselves than James, at the turn of the century, believed. Nevertheless, his apt description captures the essence of the objective situation which faces the human organism. It is, moreover, as James went on to write, a confusion which is 'potentially resolvable and demanding to be resolved'.

Strictly speaking, no stimulus situation repeats itself. No two faces, apples, chairs, dogs, or what you will, are precisely alike. Each is a unique combination of colour, size, shape and other attributes. Moreover, the objects we respond to as if they were identical from one point of time to the next, present us with changing sensory patterns as we shift from one point of vantage to another. A tilted circular plate, for example, presents an elliptical retinal image, yet we continue to regard it as a circular plate. Again, a person walking away from us presents a diminishing retinal image but we do not perceive a shrinking person. Even the consistency we regard as the self is a matter of some equivocation as the bar-room poet quoted by Bruner *et al.* (1956) realized when he wrote 'I aint what I've been. I aint what I'm going to be. I am what I am.' But if we cannot step into the same river twice, why are we not overwhelmed by the uniqueness of all things? Since learning requires that the present is perceived to have something to do with past, how do we come to make sense of our environment and act appropriately? The answer, of course, lies in our ability to group discriminably different objects, persons and events together and treat them *as if* they were equivalent for some purpose.

Without this ability we would be in a position analogous to that of the unfortunate Funes in the Jorge Luis Borges (1970) short story 'Funes the Memorious'. Funes was cursed with perfect recall so that he was unable to forget any detail of his sensory impressions.

> Not only was it difficult for him to comprehend that the generic symbol 'dog' embraces so many unlike individuals of diverse size and form; it bothered him that the dog at three (seen from the side) should have the same name as the

dog at three-fifteen (seen from the front). His own face in the mirror, his own hands, surprised him every time he saw them.

. . . with no effort he had learned English, French, Portuguese and Latin. I suspect, however, that he was not very capable of thought. To think is to forget differences, generalize, make abstractions. In the teeming world of Funes, there were only details, almost immediate in their presence. (pp. 93–4)

Categorization at the simplest level consists of abstracting some prominent perceptual feature and subordinating all other characteristics to it as, for example, when a small child refers to all four-legged, furry objects as 'doggy.' More complex forms of categorization are not amenable to perceptual immediacy and a classification can only be achieved after a fairly elaborate search procedure. Is this an acid or an alkali? Is this material fissionable or non-fissionable? Is this an ally or an antagonist? In other words, constructing equivalence categories to systematize the environment and fitting the environment into our existing category systems is a continuous process which lies at the root of our cognitive development, from our earliest attempts to manage the immediate environment to our most sophisticated attempts to formulate laws regarding the ordering of natural and social phenomena.

Assigning people to social categories is, of course, a vastly more complicated process than classifying objects. For the people with whom we participate in our interpersonal relationships are unique individuals who have purposes, motives and intentions, which are not only difficult to discern and understand, but which change as conditions change. But we must continue to try to understand them, for their purposes affect our purposes and our conception of ourselves is to a large extent dependent on the significance we have for others. Typically, we resolve the problem of weighing and contrasting the innumerable shifting cues by creating social constancies. We attribute consistent and repeatable characteristics to others, either as individuals or as exemplars of social groups and respond to them according to their role, function, status or group membership.

It is clear from the early study of Hartley, Rosenbaum and Schwartz (1948) that where ethnic, national and religious differences are in evidence that children will use them to form person categories long before they have mastered the adult rules of inclusion and exclusion. These investigators found that with increasing age (three to ten) progressively more children described both themselves and others in ethnic terms but up to the age of eight most of them were having difficulty with multiple group membership, especially those involving religious and ethnic attributes. For some children, for example, it appeared to be possible to be both Jewish and Catholic but not Jewish and American. One five-year-old solved his problem by deciding that he was a Jew when he was awake but an American when he was asleep.

Similarly, children are known to use social differences in their efforts to simplify and order the world around them. Using a pictorial jigsaw puzzle technique Jahoda (1959) found that children between six and ten, from each of four socioeconomic groups, were able to make increasingly fine and accurate social distinctions. By the age of ten, it appears, very few children are unaware of the principal attributes of the social divisions in society and most of them are able to verbalize the cues on which their judgements are based. What was particularly striking about many of the children's responses was the tendency to go beyond the pictorial evidence and to sharpen their distinctions between the working-class and middle-class people by such epithets as: 'messy', 'dirty', 'not well mannered'. For example:

'This lady (working-class) looks quite lazy.'
(lower middle-class girl age nine).
'You wouldn't like to shake hands with a workman because their hands are dirty.'
(upper-middle-class girl age eight)

There was no indication in the pictures that the man's hands were dirty or that the woman might be lazy.

Clearly a number of social influences had been at work to produce the group perspectives of these children.

There are, in fact, important differences in the consequences which can follow from gathering people together into classes of equivalence and the generalizations we make about the physical environment in order to facilitate our daily adjustments. We shall return to these later, but first it is necessary to outline the essential continuity in the cognitive functions served by both types of categorizing.

The achievements of categorization

The underlying continuity between the categorization of objects and the categorization of persons becomes clear when we take what Bruner, Goodnow and Austin (1956) call the 'achievements of categorizing' and apply them to some social examples.

The first achievement of categorizing will already have become obvious from our previous discussion. By categorizing discriminably different people, objects or events as equivalent, we reduce the complexity of the constant flow of information we receive from the environment. In the course of a day, for instance, we encounter literally thousands of colours, but most of us reduce these to a dozen or so by abstracting a limited number of combinations of hue, brightness and saturation and generalizing to the nearest equivalent in our colour code. In much the same way, a handful of real or imagined physical, ethnic, social or national attributes are used to transmute the multiplicity of overlapping human groups into a few readily distinguishable ones. This process of assigning a limited range of characteristics to individuals on the basis of their ethnic or national group membership can be seen at work in Katz and Braly's (1933) classic study of stereotypes. Jews were generally believed to be shrewd, mercenary and industrious, Turks religious, treacherous and cruel, and Negroes lazy, happy-go-lucky and superstitious. Collectively, an individual's stereotypes may constitute his or her view of the social world. It will not be a complete or very accurate view of the world. It is for the individual, however, a coherent ordering of an otherwise bewildering variety of data and one which keeps the world a familiar and predictable place.

The second achievement of categorization is closely related to the first. By simplifying our social world in this way we provide ourselves with the means of rapid identification; it's red, it's round, it's edible, it's dangerous. Without our schemata of categories we should be constantly in a state of indecision. In a revealing experiment in South Africa, Pettigrew and his co-workers (1958) presented their subjects, by means of a stereoscope, with two different photographs simultaneously, one to each eye. The full-face photographs were of members of the main population groupings, Bantu, Cape Coloured, Indians and Europeans, and pairs of photographs were arranged to include every possible combination. The subjects' task was to identify the racial membership of the composite face presented by the stereoscope. The experimenter's object was to ascertain how the subject would resolve the binocular conflict created by the separate stimulus to each eye. From the point of view of the present discussion, the most interesting results were obtained from the Afrikaner subjects. Whereas other groups tended to see, say, a European/Bantu pair as Cape Coloured or Indian, the Afrikaners had a pronounced tendency to perceive the mixed-race pairs of faces as 'African' or, less frequently, as 'European'. Relatively little use was made of the 'Cape Coloured' or 'Indian' categories, and any ambiguous pairs were designated 'African'.

Seemingly, if a person's principal concern is maintaining white supremacy, it is functionally useful to reduce the range of ethnic and racial differences to black and white, since in this way anyone outside the category 'white', who could pose a threat to the white self-image and life style, is more rapidly identified.

Perceptible differences such as pigmentation, age, gender or style of dress, are of primary importance for the rapid identification of another's membership group, but other less easily discernible cues will be used to reduce uncertainty when visible cues are ambiguous or unavailable. People categorize what is of importance to them and they become remarkably adept at learning what goes with what in order to make their category ascriptions. It is said, for example, that in Belfast, one speaker can detect whether another speaker is a Catholic or Protestant after 10 minutes conversation. Be that as it may, there is certainly good evidence that people frequently rely on verbal cues both to determine the social group membership of others and to 'detect' their unobservable attributes.

Asch (1946), in his well known experiment, gave people lists of personality traits and asked them to write a character sketch of the person. He found that on the basis of no more than a few verbal cues such as 'energetic, talkative, cold, inquisitive' that they felt quite able to make inferences about other aspects of the imaginary person's personality and even describe what he or she might look like. If, however, the word 'warm' was substituted for 'cold' in an otherwise identical list of personality traits, a markedly different character sketch was produced.

Veness and Brierly (1963) obtained similar contrasting personality descriptions in response to two tape-recordings in which the same speaker merely varied the tonal qualities of his voice. Again, Fielding and Evered (1980) in an experimental study of the diagnostic processes of medical practitioners, found that the patient's speech style not only influenced the doctor's perception of the patient's social status but also the diagnostic category to which the patient was allocated. Nevertheless, people strive for maximum clarity and distinctiveness in their social classifications so that visual cues, when available, tend to dominate all others in early encounters. It is, perhaps, worth remembering that the origin of coats of arms was to distinguish friend from foe on the battlefield.

We feel that we know something about a person who wears a policeman's uniform, a CND badge, has a particular arrangement of stripes on his tie, or has a black skin. But as Gergen (1967) observes, unlike a uniform, a badge or a tie, skin colour cannot be donned and doffed as the situation may demand. A black person is not only disadvantaged because of the liabilities which may accrue to his pigmentation, he is disadvantaged 'because he must always present to others information about his racial background. In essence he is disadvantaged with regard to information control in the situation' (p. 402). As a result of this uncontrolled presentation of information, he can never be certain at the outset of his relationships with persons of another racial group whether they are responding to him as an individual or to his skin colour. 'He cannot be certain, in effect, whether a warm smile or a cold remark is a reaction to his racial category or to his more individual personage' (p. 402).

Simplification and identification prepare the way for the third achievement of our category system, which is to provide signals for appropriate action. To be as sure as possible, as soon as possible, is often vitally important for our survival. We need prior warning that a substance is poisonous, an animal dangerous or a man dishonest, so that we can be prepared to take the necessary actions. Learning to notice the subtle differences which distinguish the out-group from the members of one's own group is not an end in itself but a precursor of conduct. Allport and Kramer (1946), for example, presented 200 of their Harvard students with a series of photographs and asked them to classify each face as Jewish or non-Jewish, having previously assessed the students' attitudes towards Jews. It was found that the students with high prejudice scores not only found more Jewish faces among the photographs, but were more often correct in their identification than the non-prejudiced students. For people who are not anti-semitic, it is of little importance whether another is Jewish or not. But for those who in some way feel threatened by Jews, learning the stigmata of the hated group so that they can be rapidly identified is an important preliminary to evasive or discriminating action.

An earlier experiment by Seeleman (1940) provides a useful complement to that of Allport and Kramer's. She found that people with an anti-black bias were unable to recognize the faces of as many individual black people, whose photographs they had previously seen, as accurately as they recognized the individual faces of white people.

The twin processes of exaggerating differences between categories and minimizing the differences within categories demonstrated in these two experiments were later brought together in an investigation by Tajfel and Wilkes (1963). They presented three groups of students with a series of eight lines which progressively differed in length from each other by a constant ratio of 5 per cent. The lines were shown in a random order and the students were asked to estimate the length of each line in turn. For one group, each of the four shorter lines had a large A above it and each of the four longer lines was labelled B. That is to say, this group was presented with an easily detectable classification scheme in which labels had a predictable and reliable relationship with the length of lines to be judged. For the second group, four of the lines were again labelled A and four of them B, but the labelling bore no relationship with the lengths of the lines. For the third group, the conditions of presentation were identical to those for the other two groups except that the lines were shown without any letters. Although the students were not asked to classify the lines but to estimate their length, the results from the first group demonstrated that they employed the readily available cues, A and B, to reduce the lines to two categories. Compared with the results from the two control groups, the first group's estimates showed a significant exaggeration of the difference between the shorter and longer lines so that the lines were in effect grouped into two distinct classes. There was also evidence that the lines within each class were judged as more similar to one another than was the case in either of the control groups.

These findings, Tajfel considers, have wide implications for the biases found in judgements of individuals belonging to various social groups. If the length of the lines is assumed to represent some personal attribute such as 'intelligence', 'sociability' or 'dishonesty' and the labels 'A' and 'B' are taken to represent social groups – Jews, Arabs, Protestants, Catholics, or what you will – with which these attributes are habitually associated, then we have all the features of a full-blown stereotype (Tajfel, 1969, 1981). The social groups will be seen as more different than they actually are and the individuals within the groups will present a relatively undifferentiated uniformity. Stereotypes are judgements concerning a class or category of people we 'know' *about*, as distinct from people we know individually (Kelvin, 1969). If for a moment we reflect on the sort of search behaviour we exhibit at a party, or any heterogeneous social gathering, we will quickly realize that as long as we lack specific knowledge about individuals we ascribe to them the characteristics of their assumed group membership be it professor, politician or policeman. If the feedback from our probes is not to our liking, the *ad hoc* engagement may be broken off and all further learning precluded. This is a point to which we shall return later.

It is important to note that in the Tajfel and Wilkes experiment the exaggerating effects of labelling were readily demonstrated with simple, neutral stimuli which were of minimal significance to the students taking part. If we contrast this with the emotionally toned labels we use to resolve the ambiguities of our social lives, it is hardly surprising to find that the mere process of labelling can bias our perception of others. Allport (1954) called the words we use to form clusters of people, 'nouns which cut slices' (p. 174) by which he meant emotionally ingrained identifiers which take away people's individuality.

'Ethnic labels', Allport wrote, 'are often of this type particularly if they refer to some highly visible feature, e.g. Negro, Oriental. They resemble labels that point to some outstanding incapacity – feeble-minded, cripple, blind man . . . These symbols act like shrieking sirens, deafening us to all finer discriminations that we might otherwise perceive' (p. 175).

As Allport recognized, this is even more true of terms such as nigger, wog, coon, papist, yid, and the like, which are used, not merely to characterize group membership, but with the intent to disparage.

But even proper names may act as 'nouns which cut slices' if they arouse ethnic associations, as a study by Razran (1950) demonstrated. He presented his subjects with a series of photographs of girls' faces which had been judged to be 'ethnically non-specific'. The subjects were asked to rate each photograph for such characteristics as likeability, beauty, intelligence and character. Some two months later the subjects were again presented with the photographs mixed in with a few new ones. This time, however, the girls were given names, some of which were common Italian, Jewish or Irish names, D'Angelo, Rabinowitz or O'Shaughnessy, for example. Others were plainly white-Anglo-Saxon-protestant names such as Adams and Clark. The names were randomly assigned to the faces and again the subjects were asked to rate the photographs on the same characteristics as before. The ratings were found to shift in accordance with the then current stereotype of the ethnic group to which the girls were presumed to belong. The 'Jewish' ones, for example, went down on likeability, beauty and character and up in ambition and intelligence. The shift downwards on these traits was less for the 'Italian' and 'Irish' girls but they were also judged to be more ambitious than previously.

It is not necessary, of course, for all categorizations in terms of stereotypes to be derogatory. It may be thought that all Germans are industrious, that all French people are logical or that all West Indians have a natural sense of rhythm. Such simplifying generalizations may, nevertheless, regulate our transactions with German, French and West Indian people and rob them of their individuality.

Categorizing people

So far we have been concerned to emphasize the continuity in the general cognitive processes which underlie the categorization of both our physical and social environment. As Allport (1954) observed: 'We cannot possibly avoid this process. Orderly living depends on it' (p. 19). There are, however, a number of lines of evidence which indicate that it would be a mistake to consider that an understanding of how social categories persist and function can be derived entirely from generalizations about the categorization of objects.

The differences between the two types of classification are not merely due to the fact that people are more complicated and ambiguous than objects, but that our social classifications are usually accompanied by some affect or emotion. People are seen as 'good' or 'bad', 'liked' or 'disliked', 'friendly' or 'hostile' and as having purposes and intentions which are of consequence to ourselves. As a result, although we usually classify objects by some value-free criteria, we begin polarizing people along some simple egocentric dimension according to how we feel about them or how we know, or anticipate, their actions will be directed towards helping or harming us.

This distinction between people and objects in terms of value-laden and value-free systems of classification is, of course, not absolute; it is a more-or-less division. A child may dislike eating greens as much as he dislikes Uncle Charlie, and for certain purposes we may classify people by purely objective criteria – taller than, heavier than and so on. Nevertheless, it remains true that value differentials are used as the basis of distinction, or are superimposed on other criteria more readily in the case of social classifications than in judgements where people or groups of people are not involved.

Differentiations in terms of values not only make for more clear-cut distinctions between categories, but render them relatively impervious to contradictory evidence. Tajfel (1981) describes two important functional differences between the judgemental processes which apply to neutral categories and those employed in the self-maintaining classifications based on values.

The first concerns the kind of errors which can be made in the assignment of items to particular categories. Two types of error are possible; over-inclusion and under-inclusion. The first consists of including in a category an item which, on specified criteria, does not belong to it; the second results in excluding an item which does. Examples of both kinds are not difficult to find. The search for non-Aryans in Nazi Germany provides a good example of the first process and the vetting of applicants for membership of an exclusive club or society, an example of the second.

Individuals, of course, are likely to commit errors of over-inclusion or under-inclusion in any situation where there are ambiguous items to be classified but there is good experimental evidence to support Tajfel's contention that the greater the difference in value between social categories, the more likely it is that errors of assignment into a negatively valued category will tend towards over-inclusion and errors of assignment into a positively valued category will be in the direction of under-inclusion.

A good example is to be found in the studies of Allport and Kramer (1946) and Scodel and Austrin (1957). In both cases, those who devalued Jews, the anti-semites, found more Jewish faces in series of photographs than the non-anti-semites.

Similar supporting evidence is provided by the Afrikaner subjects in the experiment of Pettigrew, Allport and Barnett (1958) cited in the previous section. Compared with the other subjects, the Afrikaners were very cautious in their use of the 'European' category in identifying the composite photographs and over-consigned ambiguous items to the 'African' category.

The second factor which helps to ensure the maintenance of social categories determined by value-laden criteria, concerns their resistance to contradictory information. In the case of judgements applying to the physical world, erroneous inferences from defining attributes to categorical identity are usually maladaptive, unrewarding or even dangerous. Errors such as mistaking toadstools for mushrooms, a fake for a Whistler, or thin ice for thick ice have obvious consequences which lead to the elimination of error. Where, however, there is an emotional investment in a mode of categorization, change does not occur so readily. Indeed, the inflexibility of another's value judgement is often taken as sufficient grounds for accusing them of stereotypical thinking.

There are several reasons why this should be so. First, the perception of others depends upon inferences from the cues that are noticed, not on all the available distinguishable cues. People more readily pick up the cues which are relevant to their values and expectations and filter out those which are not. It has been shown, for example, that people with an anti-black bias will misperceive pictures involving interactions between black and white people (Allport and Postman, 1947), and that interviewers may anticipate their respondents' answers and ignore those which are dissonant with their expectations (Kahn and Cannell, 1957). Similarly, Rosenhan's (1973) pseudo-patients found that it was impossible to be categorized as sane in a psychiatric hospital.

Secondly, in the case of social categories ther will be a consensual validation of the erroneous judgements since they will be shared by large numbers of other people within the perceiver's membership groups. Little supporting information is required to confirm the inferiority of a minority group in a discriminatory social system, but a vast amount of widely diffused positive information would be necessary for a re-evaluation of its attributes.

Thirdly, mistaken social judgements are rarely followed by the kind of personal penalties which are so often contingent on inaccurate judgements about the physical world. On the contrary, the preservation of these judgements is self-rewarding, particularly when the biased judgements are made in a social context which is strongly supportive of hostile attitudes towards the particular group.

As Hartman and Husband (1974) observe, as long as it appears normal for blacks to be badly housed, employed in menial work and socially disadvantaged, it will be accepted as normal for whites to expect preferment over blacks. Any acknowledgement of error would not only imply a revision of the value system but the privileged life-style it justifies.

A further factor which contributes to the rigidity of value-laden social categories is the common, but often implicit, expectation that other people's attitudes, beliefs and habits should be like our own.

Sumner, the American sociologist, in his book *Folkways* (1906) coined the term 'ethnocentrism' for what he regarded to be the universal tendency to regard one's own group 'as the centre of everything'. Put crudely, it is the tendency to believe that all right-minded people think as we do. We like people who are like us. We believe, not unreasonably, that it is less probable that we shall have rewarding experiences with people with whom we think we have little in common and that it is less likely that we shall receive approbation from people who do not share our views and opinions.

Prejudice arises when individuals, conscious of some difference between themselves, the in-group, and others, the out-group, begin to believe: 'they don't think like we do'; 'they don't feel about things the way we do'; 'they don't want what we want' (Kelvin, 1969). These ethnocentric attitudes tend to be self-perpetuating since they discourage interaction between the members of the respective groups. The less contact there is between groups, the fewer the opportunities for mutual learning and the more probable it is that images will develop which simultaneously boost the in-group's self-esteem and reduce the desire for social exchanges. Intergroup feuds have been nourished and perpetuated universally on variations of such accusations as: 'We are loyal, they are clannish'. 'We have self-respect, they are self-centred'. 'We are brave, they are aggressive'.

However, where information is not tightly controlled and where there are no physical or legal barriers to interaction, individuals must inevitably find themselves in the course of their occupational, educational or social transactions, in contact with exemplars of their social categories who conflict with their preconceptions. Sometimes affection sparks across the gap, but even when people have pleasant or rewarding exchanges with members of disliked groups, there are a number of mental devices which can be employed to obviate the necessity of revising their category system in order to accommodate contradictory evidence.

The most common of these is what Allport (1954) called the 'refencing device'. When an individual cannot be fitted satisfactorily into a category for which value differentials serve as the main criteria an exception can be acknowledged. 'Of course, there are some very nice black people' or 'Some of my best friends are Jews'. Once the deviant has been admitted the category is then hastily closed or 'refenced'. By disarmingly excluding a few exceptional cases the negative criteria are kept intact for all other cases. The contrary evidence is not allowed to modify the generalization, rather it is perfunctorily acknowledged only to exclude it from further consideration.

The second device employs a situational explanation and is the complement of the first. If two people find they are getting along pretty well in some necessary interaction, perhaps doing a job or at a social gathering, despite their different membership groups, it can either be attributed to the individual's intrinsic qualities in which case they can be classified as exceptional, or it can be attributed to the norms or demands of the situation. 'Of course, he was on his best behaviour in that company' or 'It's good for public relationships to have a drink with them from time to time, but you certainly couldn't invite them home.'

This sort of socially sanctioned inconsistency is recorded by Minard (1952) in his study of a small coal mining community in West Virginia. Black miners and white miners in their dangerous underground environment worked confidently together on terms of complete equality. Back on the surface, however, the traditional anti-black sentiments of the white southerners reasserted themselves, beginning with segregated locker rooms and baths at the pit head. At first sight it seems an odd sort of discrimination which operates above ground but becomes dormant below ground, but by encapsulating their black co-workers according to fixed roles, the white miners not only protected their simplifying schemata of categories but their society's value system.

Finally, there is the device of incorporating evidence supporting the positive attributes of the despised group into the criteria of a category in order to validate a negative evaluation. Billig (1978) for example, cites several instances in the publications of the National Front where the impressive achievements of Jews have been used to underline the Front's warning of the Jews' capabilities and intentions to take over the world.

People with less emotional commitment to intergroup hatred than members of the National Front would require a little more subtlety for self-deception to be successful. Nevertheless, most people's value systems are too deeply ingrained in their way of life and receive too much support from the people around them for the systems to be easily upset by contradictory evidence which is unaccompanied by some persuasive change in the social context.

To sum up, the principal function of categorizing is to reduce the complexity of the environment. By constructing categories to fit the environment and simplifying the environment to fit our categories, we provide ourselves with the means of rapid identification and a guide to action. In our attempts to contrive to live in a stable and familiar world, we select and over-generalize the cues by which we create categories. People and objects are allocated to classes of equivalence on a fraction of their attributes. Conversely the assumed class membership of a particular item is used to ascribe to it the characteristics of the class as a whole. Inevitably, this has the effect of emphasizing the similarities of items within a category and exaggerating the differences between categories.

As long as the system of categorization remains relatively value-free it will serve as a useful, if over-simple, classifying device which is amenable to change and sensitive to error. The ordering of individuals into social groups, however, tends to be in terms of value-laden criteria which emphasize the distinctiveness between the favoured and unfavoured groups along the selected dimensions. By selecting and accentuating information which is consonant with our preconceptions and filtering out, or suitably reprocessing that which is not, we endeavour both to preserve our schemata of social categories and the values which determine it.

Where the division into groups is based on values which are widely shared, such as those derived from cultural, economic and political self-interest, the category system will be particularly resistant to disconfirming evidence which would require its revision since the correctness of the individuals' perception of the out-group will be repeatedly confirmed. Moreover, satisfying social interactions will be facilitated by a consciousness of a common group affiliation and a shared interpretation of the social world.

Racial awareness and social identity

So far we have been concerned with categorizing as a means of simplifying and managing the environment. We now move to the principal focus of our investigations which explored some of the factors associated with the development of racial awareness in children and their value distinctions between their own and other groups. At an operational level, we were occupied with the intergroup choices and beliefs of white, West Indian and Asian children interacting in a multi-cultural environment. The perspective and implications of the study are, however, broader than this, in so far that the children were not responding to each other in situations of their own making. The perceptions, feelings and beliefs which informed their choices were reflections of their community's intergroup interpretational system.

In every society there is a range of groups coexisting in various states of cooperation, competition or hostility. Each society selects certain attributes for identifying categories of individuals and ignores others. Some attributes may involve matters of achievement such as membership of a church, occupation, a club or a professional association but others will involve unalterable characteristics like gender, pigmentation, ethnicity or national origin.

Children enter a society which is a going concern and the learning and utilization of its category system and the differential practices and forms of conduct related to it are the principal means by which they are initiated into their society. We know that very early in life children begin to notice differences in the objects and people around them and that this evokes some sort of categorization process, but it does not follow of necessity that those who are not visibly similar to ourselves have to be negatively evaluated. 'If', writes Gergen (1967), 'persons were aware that pigmentation was all that differentiated them from other racial groups, the climate for generating positive relations would be vastly improved' (p. 395).

Gergen goes on to discuss the rich semantic values associated with 'black' and 'white' which may lead to an emotional response to pigmentation differences at a very early age, but the quasi-racial differences which stake out the boundaries between blacks and whites in Britain are not simply products of hidden emotional structures laid down in early childhood. As Figueroa (1981) has argued:

> What matters is not just the actual differences (in appearance, for instance) but the way these are related to and invested with meaning and importance through interaction. What is significant are the patterns of relations that are established, along what lines they are drawn and the myths and assumptions that go along with and inform this. 'Race' refers both to the network of largely unspoken, taken-for-granted assumptions and the actual constellation of relationships. (p. 3)

This network of assumptions and interactions becomes a lived-in frame of reference for children growing up in a multi-racial society and it is within this framework that they become affectively orientated to their own and other groups. Children's social evaluations begin well before they have any true understanding of the social categories to which they apply. The results of many studies suggest that children's intergroup preferences are influenced by a rudimentary sense of the social position of groups in their community (see Pushkin and Veness, 1973 for a review). For example, in a study of nursery school children in Virginia, Morland (1958) found that most of the white children questioned and a majority of the black children, wish to have white playmates. Similarly, Vaughan (1964) in New Zealand, found a general tendency for both white and Maori children to favour whites.

In a London study in the early 1960s Pushkin (1967/1983) presented 172 white children, aged between three and seven, with a dolls' tea-party. Each child was asked to select from an array of black and white dolls which he would invite to the party. 33 per cent of the three-year-olds and 82 per cent of the six-year-olds were rated as having a rejecting attitude towards the black dolls. A test which involved choosing a companion for a white doll on a see-saw evoked the same marked preference for white dolls.

In each of these studies of ethnic preference, the children's choices were made easier by visual cues which enable them to locate the dolls or pictures in a social category, but the same sensitivity to social influences has been demonstrated in children's negative evaluations of out-groups where no clear or consistent physical differences exist.

As part of a large-scale international study of children's national attitudes, Tajfel and his co-workers (1970) presented primary school children with 20 photographs of young men and asked them to sort the photographs into four boxes labelled respectively: 'I like him very much,' 'I like him a little,' 'I dislike him a little,' 'I dislike him very much'. Some weeks later the children were again given the photographs but this time they were asked to sort them into two boxes according to whether they thought the young man was 'English' or 'not English'. There was a high degree of concordance in the assignment of a photograph to the category 'English' on the one hand and the degree of liking on the other. The same photographs were presented to children in several other countries where much the same correlation was obtained between degree of liking and own nationality.

The ready acquisition by children of the value differentials between their own and other groups testifies to their growing awareness to the socially sanctioned modes of categorization which exist in their society. Indeed, as long ago as the 1930s Horowitz (1936), finding that children in the northern States of America were as prejudiced towards black people as those in the southern States, concluded that negative attitudes were not determined by contact with black people but by contact with attitudes towards black people – principally those of the parents.

In other studies, neighbourhoods, schools and the mass media have all been implicated in this transmission process.

Pushkin (1967, 1983), for example, found a closer relationship between the type of area in which children lived and their hostile attitudes, than between the children's attitudes and those of their parents. Children in an area pervaded by racial tension tended to develop hostility towards black people regardless of their mother's attitudes, whereas children living in a district in which harmonious intergroup relationships prevailed, were closer in their attitudes to children living in a no-contact area. Hartman and Husband (1974) found that high concentrations of black people gave rise to greater hostility but this in its turn was determined 'by whether the city or conurbation as a whole, as opposed to the immediate neighbourhood, was an immigrant area or not' (p. 91).

Husband (1975, 1977, 1979) has also provided several invaluable analyses of how television and the press have presented the 'immigrant problem' and buttressed the white Britons' perception of themselves as a superior group threatened by an inferior out-group.

The ethnocentric nature of many school texts and the omission of black figures from reading books and children's fiction, or their stereotyped or derogatory portrayal has been the subject of several articles (Hatch, 1962; Glendenning, 1971; Laishley, 1975; Dixon, 1977). Practically any school subject can be taught in a way which gives the child a fraudulent view of the world. History can be taught in such a way as to induce a belief in the superiority of one's own society and culture. Geography can be used to induce a subtle contempt of other communities and their way of life. Literature can be selected and presented in a manner which gives children a myopic view of human diversity. Perhaps more significantly, some teachers, by persistently indicating their low expectations of some children, may insinuate into their minds diminished concepts of themselves. If such beliefs are consistently manifested by large numbers of educators with regard to a group distinguishable by, say, its language, colour or religion, then the entire group may come to lack confidence in the educational enterprise and reject its offerings (Davey, 1973; Stone, 1981).

Children's intergroup perspectives are, therefore, fashioned in many social contexts, family, peer groups, schools, neighbourhood, to name but a few. Many of the influences to which he or she is subjected, by virtue of multigroup membership, may be criss-crossing and even contradictory. It is plainly inadequate to say that children acquire their intergroup attitudes as part of the general process of socialization and leave it at that. The mere exposure to the attitudes and value judgements of others is not in itself a sufficient condition for their acquisition. There is no generalized tendency to imitate our parents, for instance, otherwise parenting would be an easier job than it often is. Assimilation and learning are selective. There must be some motive and some reinforcement or pay-off.

It is at this point that Tajfel's (1974, 1978) theory of intergroup relations becomes pertinent. As in the work of Berger (1966), it is postulated that the individual realizes and recognizes his identity in socially defined terms. Ordering the social environment into groupings of persons in a manner which is meaningful to the individual is one of the principal means by which this social identity is achieved. Social identity is defined as people's consciousness of their membership of various social groups and the value they attach to that membership. However, 'the characteristics of one's group as a whole (such as its status, its richness or poverty, its skin colour or its ability to reach its aims) achieve most of its significance in relation to perceived differences from other groups and the value connotation of these differences' (1978, p. 66). Tajfel, therefore, argues that a social group will only be capable of sustaining a positive social identity for its members if it manages to maintain a positively valued distinctiveness. Group members are thus motivated to perceive themselves as superior, or make themselves so, in any social comparison process, in order to maintain a satisfactory social identity.

In other words, central to the motives of children coming to share the attitudes and values of those around them is the fundamental need to establish their social identity. Very early in our development the questions are asked: Who am I? Am I the person they say I am? Am I the person I want to be?

However, children cannot perceive themselves apart from the reactions of others. They cannot evaluate themselves apart from the values by which individuals in their position are judged. Their social identity cannot be achieved outside the context of their own group and its position relative to other groups in their environment. To understand how their group membership defines their place in the order of things they must comprehend the significance of their own group along socially defined value dimensions in relationship to other groups. Inevitably, therefore, children acquire their biases towards other groups at the same time and by the same process as they acquire favourable and positive attitudes towards their own. They begin to notice the responses of people 'like us' towards people 'not like us'. They learn to describe them in favourable or unfavourable terms. They acquire the linguistic tags which are applied to them and the behaviour it is appropriate to adopt towards them. In this way, children not only extend their mastery over the social environment but learn to define themselves.

Tajfel's theory of intergroup relations is a general one and its explanatory usefulness is not restricted to inter-ethnic contexts. Nevertheless, if an important part of our self-image is dependent on social categorization and social comparisons, it is obvious that in a culture such as our own which is suffused with racial imagery and values (Husband, 1975, 1977) that children will employ ethnic distinctions in their efforts to establish a positive social identity. The socially constructed category of 'race' based on colour, offers itself to the child as a ready-made tool for reducing the complexity of the environment.

The principal object of the study reported in the succeeding chapters was to investigate the extent to which ethnic criteria were employed by white, West Indian and Asian children in constructing their social identities via the processes of social comparison and social differences. In particular, we were concerned to understand the implications of those value-laden comparisons on the realization of a satisfactory social identity by the minority group children.

5 The plan of the study

In coming to terms with the way in which people are categorized in their society, children are faced with three interrelated learning tasks. First, they must be able to perceive the differences between the major groups in their community and identify the one to which they belong. That is to say, they are required to make a 'like me', 'not like me' classification. Secondly, they must learn the cues, or social markers, by which people are classified as members or non-members of groups. Thirdly, they must learn the socially sanctioned behavioural and attitudinal responses towards people classified in a particular way.

In designing a study to investigate the acquisition of ethnic awareness in primary school children, we began, therefore, by devising a number of simple techniques which would enable us to sample the children's responses in each of these three areas. Thus, there are two measures of the perception of differences (the identification and preference tests, Chapter 7), two measures of cue saliency (the sorting and puzzle tests, Chapter 8), and three measures of associated affect, or liking and disliking (the paired comparisons, limited choice and stereotypes tests, Chapter 9). Basically we were seeking the answers to three questions:

How do children categorize themselves and others?
What kinds of cues do they use?
What are their feelings and attitudes towards others perceived to belong to groups other than their own?

An assessment was also made of the children's abilities to group ethnically neutral objects into classes of equivalence (Chapter 6) and a sociometric study was made of the children's friendship patterns (Chapter 10). Finally, since the parental influence was likely to be an important determinant of early beliefs and attitudes, all the parents who had given their consent for their children to take part in the study were visited at home by experienced own-race (and, for the Asian parents, own-language) interviewers (Chapter 11).

Materials and procedure

For the children's tests, with the exception of concept formation, stereotypes and sociometrics, professionally produced full-length photographs of primary school children and adults from the three ethnic groups were used. The photographed children were identically dressed, the boys in jeans and sweaters and the girls in jumpers and skirts. All were approximately in the middle of the primary school age range. Black and white half-plate prints were chosen in preference to coloured photographs, since skin shade could be a critical factor for West Indian children, and it was thought that good quality monochrome would allow them to freely project their preferred skin shade.

For the concept test 42 small coloured pictures of everyday objects were used, based on those employed by Davey (1968) on the Tristan da Cunhan investigation.

The stereotype test consisted of four wooden posting boxes, identified by photographs of man and woman couples for each ethnic group, and a box marked 'Nobody'. The children were presented with messages printed on small cards which they posted as they thought appropriate.

A full description of the tests and their administration is given in the appropriate chapters which follow and Appendix I.

The children were seen individually in a quiet room in their school on two occasions, separated by some four to six weeks. An atmosphere of informality was aimed at, and, in order to maintain interest, a procedure was devised whereby the sessions were kept short (between 30 and 40 minutes), and the child was asked to participate in a number of different activities during each session.

Race of the tester

The children's tests were administered by white investigators, two male and two female, each investigator testing roughly equal numbers of boys and girls.

There has been a considerable amount of debate in this area of research regarding the possibility of white investigators unintentionally influencing black children's responses towards greater favourability to whites. The evidence on this issue is ambiguous. Sattler (1970), in a general review of racial experimenter effects, concluded that there was evidence that the experimenter's race could affect the attitude and preference responses of kindergarten children and adolescents. 'Middle-year' children appeared to be unaffected. Subsequently, Jahoda *et al.* (1972) produced a significant shift in re-test response of *both* Scottish and Pakistani children after the introduction of a female Indian tester. Against this must be set the findings of the many investigators who have controlled for this type of experimenter effect and failed to establish the tester's race as a significant variable: e.g. Morland (1962, 1963, 1966); Hraba and Grant (1970); Banks and Romf (1973); Bunton and Weissbach (1974); Bagley and Coard (1975); Moore (1976) and Teplin (1977).

Some investigators have used own-race testers for each group of subjects but, as Milner (1973) observes, this is really no solution at all since it is equally plausible that own race testers may unwittingly induce a bias towards a more favourable in-group response. Moreover, at least two investigations (Epstein *et al.*, 1976; Thomas, 1978) have found that significantly more black children expressed a preference for their own group when interviewed by a white person, than those interviewed by a black person. As Thomas points out, such results appear to contradict the view that a white tester necessarily inhibits the responses of black pupils.

The weight of the evidence gives little support for the contention that the phenomenon of out-group preference is an artefact evinced by white testers. Nevertheless, as Jahoda *et al.* (1972) observe, there must always be an element of uncertainty in investigations of this kind. We change more than pigmentation when we change experimenters. Any of the experimenters characteristics – ethnicity, age, sex, attractiveness, etc. – may interact with those of the child and lead him or her to give what appears to be the situationally appropriate responses. As pointed out elsewhere (Davey, 1976), our attitudes are positively related to beliefs about ourselves, and ourselves in relationship to significant parts of the environment, but each presentation of ourselves in different situations is equally valid.

In the light of these considerations and the fact that the primary focus of our investigation was on the response of minority group children to growing up in a predominantly white society (even in the eight schools composed of 50 per cent or more minority group children, there was a total of only six non-white teachers) white testers were considered to be the most appropriate.

The children

Equal numbers of children at ages seven, eight, nine and ten + were drawn from 16 primary schools, eight in London and eight in industrial Yorkshire. Of these, 256 children were white, 128 were of West Indian parentage and 128 were of Asian parentage.

A factorial design was adopted which has the advantage of sampling a wide range of possible relationships which can be used repeatedly in different combinations. Thus in each region, north and south, two of the schools had 50 per cent, or more, Asian children; two had 50 per cent, or more, West Indian children; two had 20 per cent, or less, Asian children and two had 20 per cent, or less, West Indian children. In each school, a white child was paired by age and sex with an Asian or a West Indian child so that each school unit was composed of:

2 races $\times$ 2 sexes $\times$ 4 ages $\times$ 2 children = 32.

The main sample, therefore, consisted of:

2 regions $\times$ 2 densities $\times$ 4 schools $\times$ 32 children = 512.

In addition, there was a small 'no contact' white sub-sample which was taken from two schools in North Yorkshire where there were no minority group children. The 'no contact' sample is used only as a control group when examining the effects on white children of different concentrations of Asian and West Indian children in the schools. Apart from the fact that it was composed only of white children, it was constructed in exactly the same way as the main sample. That is:

1 region $\times$ 2 schools $\times$ 4 ages $\times$ 2 sexes $\times$ 2 children = 32.

Therefore, the total sample was

512 + 32 = 544.

After excluding any children whose parents were known to be of different ethnic groups, the selection, within the constraints of age and sex, was made randomly from the school registers. Letters were then sent to parents via the Head Teachers, briefly explaining the study and requesting their consent for their children to take part. The letters, which were accompanied by a Gujerati, Punjabi or Urdu translation for Asian parents, also asked the parents to indicate their willingness to be interviewed at a later date.

Very few parents indeed refused to take part or to allow their children to participate, but due to families moving out of the district or emigrating between the school testing programme and making contact with the parents, there was a small parent sample loss of 4 per cent. In all, 523 parents were interviewed.

In addition, one southern low-density Asian school did not complete the preference test, reducing the sample size for this test to 480 children. Otherwise, missing data due to absenteeism or removals was less than 3 per cent amongst the children. Reduced totals, where employed, are clearly indicated in the text and the tables which follow.

The children's parents

Before considering the following brief descriptive profile of the children's parents, it is perhaps worth emphasizing the obvious. The sample is not a representative one since the only necessary criterion for an individual to be interviewed is that he or she should be a parent of one of the children taking part in the project. It follows, therefore, that it is not possible to draw inferences from these data for any particular ethnic population as a whole.

58 per cent of the fathers of the white children were in non-manual or skilled occupations compared with 45 per cent of the Asian fathers and 33 per cent of the West Indians (see Table 11.1, p. 147). In all the groups the proportion of fathers in semi-skilled or unskilled work was higher in the north than in the south. Unemployment was also more in evidence in the north; the highest incidence being among the northern Asian fathers.

The proportion of mothers going out to work varied between the ethnic groups; 79 per cent of West Indian mothers did so, 61 per cent of whites, and 38 per cent of Asians. While there were no regional differences among the white and West Indian groups, there was a marked difference among Asian mothers; 70 per cent worked in the south, less than 5 per cent did so in the north. More than two-thirds of the white mothers in employment worked only part-time but 70 per cent of the working mothers in the two minority groups had full-time jobs.

42 children (8 per cent) came from single-parent households. In all but two cases, the single parent was the mother and these, with the exception of a single Asian family, were evenly divided between whites and West Indians.

There are considerable differences in family size both between and within the ethnic groups: 46 per cent of whites had one or two children, compared with 21 per cent of West Indians and 26 per cent of Asians. Only 9 per cent of white families had five children or more, contrasting with 32 per cent of West Indians and 40 per cent of Asians. The Asian figure, however, conceals a strong regional difference: 61 per cent of those in the north have large families compared with 17 per cent in the south.

It is evident that the Asian family pattern in the south (in respect of parental occupation, working mothers and family size) corresponds more closely to that of the whites than to that of the Asians in the north. No questions were asked about a person's religion, nor, for obvious reasons, about length of residence, but our distinct impression was that northern Asian families were more likely to be of more recent settlement, Muslim and from rural areas.

The areas served by the schools

The eight London primary schools, which the children in the southern segment of our sample attended, were located in two geographically separated boroughs. The two areas not only differed from each other in their demographic characteristics but, like many London boroughs, contained a heterogeneity of neighbourhoods within themselves.

The four schools from which our southern white/West Indian sample was drawn were located in a borough with one of the highest incidences of immigrant settlement in the country. The main immigrant group comes from the West Indies but there are also a few settlers from the Indian sub-continent and West Africa. There are also small communities of Poles, Czechs, Cypriots and Japanese.

Webber and Craig's (1978) *Socio-economic Classification of Local Authority Areas* shows the population of this borough to be younger than the national average with a high proportion of it under 45. Most of the immigrants are young with growing families and more than 25 per cent of the school population are children whose parents were born in the New Commonwealth or Pakistan (Department of Education and Science, 1973). The children are not, of course, distributed evenly throughout the various neighbourhoods of the borough, so that whereas the proportion of children of West Indian parentage is above 80 per cent in some schools, it is below 20 per cent in others.

The borough is beset with all the housing problems of an inner-city area. A high proportion of the housing stock is dilapidated and lacking the basic amenities of running hot water and inside sanitation. There is serious over-crowding in some parts of the area and a higher proportion of people than the national average live in shared dwellings and privately rented accommodation (Webber and Craig, 1978). There are, however, contrasts between different sections of the borough. Two of the schools in our sample were housed in late nineteenth-century buildings surrounded by decaying terraced houses, mainly multi-occupied by West Indian families, ageing blocks of local authority flats, boarded-up buildings and partly demolished streets. The other two schools were housed in modern post-war buildings in a more prosperous residential area. One next door to a swimming pool and sports centre with plenty of outdoor space, the other was set with its generous playing fields on the edge of an estate of expensive detached houses.

There is little skilled work available in the area, but there is a higher than average number of working women who are largely employed as unskilled or semi-skilled workers in the service industries which predominate in London.

The London area from which the southern white/Asian part of the sample was drawn, is to the west of the capital. The largest immigrant group comes from the Indian sub-continent, but some Caribbean, Spanish and Chinese families were also settled in the area. As far as can be estimated from the DES (1973) Statistics[1], between 16 and 20 per cent of the school population are children of New Commonwealth and Pakistan parents. Again, the distribution between schools varies but none of the schools have percentages as high as in the other London borough.

The family structure, too, would seem to differ from the other borough. The birth rate appears to be lower than the national average; there is a higher proportion of married couples and there are fewer one-parent families (Webber and Craig, 1978).

The housing stock, on the whole, is of more recent origin and in better condition than in the borough first described. There is a large number of between-the-wars, semi-detached houses, with a high proportion of owner-occupiers, but there is also a substantial number of shared dwellings.

Three of the schools had been built immediately before the war and the fourth in 1951. All were in a good state of repair, with ample playing space. Two were sited in residential areas composed mainly of between-the-wars, semi-detached houses, while the other two were in areas with a more mixed pattern of privately owned and local authority housing near a large industrial estate.

At the time of the investigation, unemployment was below the national average. A higher proportion of married women were working than in the other London borough but the pattern of employment differed. More people

---

1. The DES discontinued the collection of statistics on the 'immigrant' school population in 1972.

in this area were engaged in professional and white-collar occupations and fewer were working in unskilled and semi-skilled jobs.

All of the eight northern schools in the main sample were located in a single, large metropolitan district where the incidence of post-war immigrant settlement has been one of the highest outside of the Greater London area. The two principal groups of settlers have been people from the West Indies and the sub-continent but the district also has a scattered Irish-born population and small communities of Chinese, Italians and people from Eastern Europe. The West Indian families form the most concentrated group, having settled almost exclusively in one of the old boroughs. The Indian families have settled in two major zones, but the Pakistani residents are somewhat scattered around three core areas of settlement. The estimated proportion of children in the schools from the New Commonwealth and Pakistan is around 13 per cent.

The housing is ageing and a high proportion of it is composed of nineteenth-century terrace dwellings, but there is also a substantial amount of council housing. In some areas, with little council property, there are high levels of overcrowding and an absence of standard amenities such as a fixed bath and inside sanitation. In general, social conditions tend to improve as one moves outwards from the urban and industrial centres.

Five of the eight sample schools were housed in Victorian buildings with no playing fields and a limited amount of playing space. One school still retained a terraced yard, originally designed so that the teacher could see the children in the back row when they were doing their morning drill. All of these schools were in mainly working-class residential neighbourhoods with a mixture of local authority housing and older terraced houses, many of which were owner-occupied. The remaining three schools were of a modern design with considerably better amenities. One was in a quiet cul-de-sac in a residential area where owner-occupied semi-detached houses predominated; another was on a modern, attractive council estate; and the third was flanked by a council estate on one side and Victorian terrace houses on the other.

In the metropolitan borough as a whole, skilled workers formed the largest category of employed persons but in the areas in which the sample schools were situated, semi-skilled and unskilled workers predominated. Unemployment was also relatively higher in these districts than in the rest of the borough. Nevertheless, there were more married women in work than in the southern portion of the sample, but only a tiny percentage of Asian mothers were in employment.

The two 'no contact' schools were located in North Yorkshire. The larger of the two serves an estate which was originally built during the second decade of this century for employees at a local factory. The village is still administered by a Trust set up by the manufacturer, but the houses are now let to non-employees. The estate presents a semi-rural appearance with established trees and grassed open spaces. The houses themselves are all extremely well maintained with terraced, semi-detached and detached houses in juxtaposition with one another. The intention was that different grades of employees would live in an integrated community. There are no New Commonwealth or Pakistani settlements in or near the estate but from time to time an overseas family will rent a house. Quite often these are the families of professional workers who are employed at the hospital some three miles away.

The second 'no contact' school serves a large village about 15 miles to the north of the estate school. It is the smallest school in the sample with a roll of 120 children. As is common in many rural settlements, detached dwellings predominate with most of the rented property being owned by local farmers. There is, in addition, a small estate of local authority housing on the edge of the village. Most of the families are engaged in some form of agricultural work but there is a small group of commuters. The village has no railway station and only an occasional bus to the town, so that most of the commuters are in professional or managerial occupations. At the time of the study there were no families from overseas living in the village.

Schools and teachers

The schools varied quite considerably in size. Apart from the village school of 120 children, just mentioned, the range ran from rolls of around 300 children to the largest school with 840 children. The majority of the school rolls were between 350–450 children.

In general, staff-pupil ratios were rather better in London than in the northern schools. The average for London was 1:24 compared with 1:30 in the north. Six out of the 16 main sample schools, two in the south and four in the north, had been designated 'schools under stress', which meant that the teachers received an additional allowance to their normal pay and, in some cases, that the schools were more generously staffed. This arrangement had led to a certain amount of resentment amongst some of the northern head teachers, who felt that their schools were in as much, or more, need of special consideration as those which had been designated as 'schools under stress'.

Despite the difficulties under which many of the schools were functioning, most of them appeared able to retain their staff. The consensus amongst the head teachers was that the staff turnover position had improved considerably during the previous two years. All but two of them considered their turnover rate to be 'manageable', 'average' or 'low'. The remaining two schools, one in the north and one in the south, both with a high concentration of children of West Indian parentage, had high turnover rates. The northern school had lost more than a quarter of its staff in the previous year so that a teacher with three years' service in that school was the second-longest serving member.

The same two schools also had the highest number of teachers in their probationary year, four in each case. Otherwise, there were comparatively few inexperienced teachers in the sample schools. Overall, there were 11 in the 'high density' schools and seven in the 'low density' schools; seven schools had no probationers at all.

In 13 of the schools with minority group children, none of the staff had been on in-service courses for teachers in multi-cultural schools, although in both regions, courses had been available. However, in one of the northern schools, several members of staff were about to attend a course arranged by a member of the local authority's advisory staff. At one London school, a teacher had been seconded for a one-year course at the Institute of Education and was holding regular briefing meetings with her colleagues back at the school.

Although there were more minority group teachers in the eight schools with a high percentage of minority group pupils, the total number was very small indeed. There were three minority group teachers in the 'low density' schools and six in the 'high density' schools, but nine schools, including four where the proportion of minority children was above 50 per cent, had no minority group teachers at all. Moreover, the opportunities for minority group children to work in their own language or to study their own language as part of the school curriculum were even less than these figures suggest, since two of the minority group teachers were in schools where there were no children of the same linguistic community as themselves.

We also asked the teachers in each school what provision was made for children who needed help with English as a foreign language. It quickly became apparent that EFL teaching and remedial teaching were regarded as much the same thing. All the schools had some remedial provision and some had parents coming into the school to help with 'slow readers'. One southern school had a voluntary remedial group run by a parent after school. Only three schools, one in the south and two in the north, had planned EFL tuition but in the case of one of the northern schools the classes also catered for children from several nearby schools. Children of both Asian and Caribbean origin were included in this arrangement.

None of the schools admitted to rigid streaming as their organizational policy. All of them subscribed, to a greater or lesser extent, to the ideal of mixed-ability teaching but less than half of them could be truly described as mixed-ability schools. Some set for English and mathematics, others where eleven-plus selection was still in existence overtly streamed in their third and fourth years. One school which had a strong music tradition and which did pursue mixed-ability teaching in a committed way, had the school orchestra taught as a separate self-contained class in the fourth year with the idea of compensating for time spent in rehearsals. We noted, however, that many teachers contrived to create what Barker Lunn (1970) called a 'streamed atmosphere' within their non-streamed classes. In some classes there were 'top tables' and 'bottom tables'; in others the 'brightest and best' sat in the rows to the right of the teacher with the 'not so bright' on the left. In one class, where the head teacher had a habit of popping in to give extra tuition to the 'brightest group', a 'head-teacher's table' had been created.

We also looked for ways in which the schools might be adapting to accommodate the different cultural traditions of the minority group pupils. Displays of children's work in the school vestibule, the posters and pictures on the wall and the general decor of the school entrance, are of primary importance in giving the visitor an impression of the school. Despite the unpromising buildings in which many staffs were working, most had contrived to give the main entrance a colourful, lively and inviting appearance. Nevertheless, very few of the entrance displays gave the visitor any indication of the school's multi-cultural character. One northern school, however, was outstanding in this respect. The vestibule display was dominated by a large colourful picture of an Indian wedding, the joint work of several children. The walls of the corridors were covered with pictures painted by children from different cultural groups and one felt that both staff and children were eager for the visitor to know about what was going on in their school.

How to give the morning assembly in a multi-ethnic school both a unifying and religious function is a matter of continuous debate. In six of the schools, all in the north, the assemblies could neither be described as multi-religious or even ecumenical, but the remaining schools were, in various ways, trying to achieve a multi-cultural emphasis. One head teacher appeared to have a pantheistic approach and said he confined himself to 'the wonders of nature and the universe'. Another alternated his readings from the Bible and the Koran, while a third gave a series of assemblies on the world's religions. One London school with a high percentage of West Indian children had all its assemblies accompanied by the school's steel band or a calypso group.

The extent to which multi-cultural thinking had entered into the planning of the curriculum and individual lessons varied considerably from school to school. At one London school the teachers had been so concerned about the content of the standard history and geography books that they had abandoned them and spent a great deal of time constructing their own teaching material. At another London school the teachers had built up a very impressive collection of Caribbean folk tales and modern story books. In contrast, the literary diet for one remedial group in the north, composed largely of Asian children, consisted almost exclusively of Greek myths.

Some teachers plainly regarded the 'curious' ways of minority group children as a 'nuisance'. Occasionally there were expressions of overt racialism in the staff-room, as when one fourth year teacher spoke of looking forward to getting rid of 'the West Indian rubbish' in his class. In another school, a very formal teacher who appeared to require her children to work in absolute silence, could not be restrained, when a researcher entered the class-room, from giving a loud-voiced monologue on her opinion of West Indian children. She was near retirement and looked back nostalgically to the days when she taught an 11-plus class. She considered West Indian children to be lazy and disruptive but that, she thought, was because: 'we only get the dregs over here, not the cream; that's why they come.'

This kind of incident was happily balanced by the many teachers who were patently sensitive to the needs of minority group children and were alert to the necessity of working towards harmonious intergroup relationships and of checking any signs of discrimination and intergroup hostility as soon as they occurred. 'We never turn a blind eye', said one London head teacher. 'Every instance of overt discrimination, whether verbal or physical, is immediately investigated'. Nevertheless, there did seem to be a certain amount of ethnocentricism on the part of some teachers which was often expressed as; 'the PE and games problem with Asian girls' or 'the trouser problem with Muslim girls' or 'the food problem'.

For the most part, matters of dress were sensibly handled in the schools and were not a contentious issue for either minority or white children. Seven schools had no uniform at all and in the other schools the wearing of school uniform was a matter of parental choice. We did, however, observe two interesting anomalies, both in northern schools with a high percentage of Asian children.

In one school, which had no school uniform, the head teacher insisted that all the boys should wear short trousers, but he allowed the Muslim girls to wear their long trousers. This excited a certain amount of criticism from white parents. In another school, the head teacher had banned trousers for all females, this included both staff and Muslim girls. The result was that the Muslim girls took their trousers off on reaching school and put them on again to go home. Surprisingly enough, the head teacher was on excellent terms with the Asian parents and did a great deal of work on behalf of the local Asian community in his spare time. There seemed to be an agreement that while the mosque ruled outside the school, his authority began at the school gates.

With regard to the so-called 'food problem', nine of the schools with minority group children provided an alternative vegetarian meal at dinner time, but three of the schools attended by Asian children made no special concession to their dietary requirements. Many of the children went home at mid-day, but those that remained had to content themselves with the vegetable portion of the standard school dinner.

Finally, we asked the schools to tell us about the arrangements they made for maintaining home and school relationships. All of the schools appeared to recognize these to be an important part of their work but saw themselves as having differing degrees of success.

Nine of the schools had active parent-teacher associations and in one London school the father of one of the Asian children had just been elected as president. Many of the schools felt that invitations to formal events and meetings were not enough even though they were well attended and there was the usual complaint about 'those you most want to see don't come'. All the schools purported to have an informal open-door policy but it was difficult to judge how welcomed some of the parents felt themselves to be in the schools. In about a third of the schools, parents were about the school throughout the school day. In others it seemed to be a case of after-school appointments only. All the head teachers regarded themselves as 'approachable' or 'always will-ing to listen', but the infrequency of visits in some schools made one wonder if they had succeeded in conveying this image to the parents.

The limitations of the study

The main focus of this study, the acquisition of ethnic awareness by young children and how this process may be influenced by age, sex, ethnicity, region and the ethnic composition of their schools, determined how the participa-ting schools would be chosen. The north–south and high–low density dimensions segmented the schools into four groups, but it is obvious that within these groupings there is a considerable degree of variation both within and between schools. Every research project must have its boundaries and decisions have to be taken as to what potential influences are to be excluded from consideration.

It would only have been possible, for example, to have taken account in a systematic way, of the differences in amenities, organization and staffs of schools, if we had designed a more circumscribed but considerably more complex type of study. It is unlikely that the variations we have described are such as to invalidate the various comparisons that have been made between children in different ethnic groups, although, as we shall see, they could be the source of some minor unexplained differences.

The presentation of the results

The findings which are discussed in the following chapters are based on a detailed and often complex statistical analyses. Statistics, however, are not an end in themselves; they are merely one possible means of improving our understanding of social phenomena and of increasing our confidence in our deductions. Nevertheless, statistical computation is not an irrelevancy or an option for the quantitative social researcher. While it is true that no amount of sophisticated statistical manipulation can compensate for ill-considered and ineptly gathered data, it is equally true that sound information may be lost by the failure to undertake an appropriate form of statistical analysis.

We have, therefore, tried to strike a balance between the obligation to substantiate and validate our findings, as far as we are able, and to provide a readily accessible account of our study for teachers, social workers, parents and others who are interested in young children growing up in a multi-cultural society.

For research workers and other technically inclined readers, we have included in appendices the details of the methods we have employed and the rationale for the various statistical techniques we used. In addition, an exhaustive account of the results of our analysis is available from the British Library Lending Division (Davey and Pushkin, 1980); and the raw data from the parental sample, together with all the documents relating to it, have been deposited with the SSRC Data Archive at the University of Essex (Davey, 1980).

We have kept the text itself uncluttered with statistics, but we have followed the conventional practice of referring to any result which has less than one chance in 20 of being in error as 'significant' or 'reliable' (although most of the results have a higher confidence level than this).

In general, the term 'statistically significant' indicates that a difference or an association is likely to be repeated in a wider population and is not merely a chance artefact of the particular sample of people under consideration. But a statistically significant result may not be particularly interesting or noteworthy. Conversely, a non-significant result may be suggestive or illuminating. It is only when the results of significance tests are interpreted in the context of an explanatory theory that they acquire significance within the everyday meaning of the term.

Consequently, not every statistically significant result that was found in the course of the study is commented on in the text. Nor, for that matter, have all our statistical tables and test results been included. To do so would have risked obscuring the most interesting results and added more than a 100 pages of figures to the book. What have been included are those tables which are essential for the understanding of the text and those data, whether statistically significant or not, which have a genuine explanatory value in the context of the relevant theory. Where, however, there are good reasons, on *a priori* theoretical grounds and on evidence from related tests, for believing that a relationship, or a difference, is of importance, despite failing to reach the conventional level of statistical confidence, it will be described as a 'trend'.

6 The children's grouping strategies

In Chapter 4 it was proposed that the ability to group together discriminably different objects, people or events and to treat them as equivalent for some purpose, was fundamental to both our cognitive and social development. We went on to argue that, although there was a continuity between the categorization of objects and the categorization of people, a distinction should be drawn between the two types of classification in that we more readily employ emotive, value-laden criteria when we attempt to establish generalizations about people.

Our principal operational approach to ethnic awareness was to investigate, with the aid of a number of simple discrimination and classification tasks, how the prevalent value system of a multi-ethnic society might influence the way in which children categorize themselves and others. We therefore decided that a task which allowed the children to demonstrate their grouping strategies with ethnically neutral material not only offered practical advantages, but would also produce results of considerable intrinsic interest. An object discrimination task, it was thought, would give us the opportunity to establish friendly and cooperative relations with the children and familiarize them with the kinds of tests and instructions which were to follow. It would also enable us to determine that all the children had attained sufficient competence in their grouping skills to be able to cope with the main experimental tasks. Additionally, it would be possible to compare the children's object grouping procedures with their affective responses to discriminably different groups of people and to compare grouping strategies both within and between the three ethnic groups.

The essence of the classical approach to concept attainment, or learning to categorize, is that the subject should respond in some consistent manner to recurring features built into the experimental material and thus indicate that he or she either possess, or has learned, the category which the experimenter has in mind. For example, Vygotsky (1962) presented his subjects with an array of blocks, varying in shape, size and colour, which were to be classified according to various combinations of attributes – large and heavy, small and light, and so on. Each block had a nonsense syllable concealed on its underside and the criterion of correct grouping was that all the blocks in a group were designated by the same nonsense syllable.

The subject, on completing his groupings was required to verbalize the attributes of the groups. The experimenter then supplies confirmation or otherwise by lifting the blocks and showing the subject the nonsense syllables. Using this technique, Vygotsky went on to provide a descriptive analysis of what he regarded as the various stages on the way to the attainment of a 'true concept'.

Vygotsky undoubtedly developed an illuminating technique for studying the strategies employed in categorizing but, for our purposes, it suffers from the disadvantage that both the concepts to be attained and their criterial attributes are predetermined by the experimenter. It cannot be assumed that the maladaptive responses pinpointed by Vygotsky will necessarily characterize the various steps towards the attainment of 'true concepts', when children are able to impose order on diversity by sorting into classes which are meaningful to themselves.

The obligation to reduce the complexity of the environment by constructing equivalence categories is a universal one but, as Bruner, Goodnow and Austin (1956) have observed, since the categories into which people sort their world are inventions not discoveries, they inevitably reflect the culture in which they arise. It follows, therefore, that any investigation which crosses cultural boundaries, such as our own, requires a method which will both allow the participants to demonstrate their habitual modes of categorizing and give the investigator some insight into how the categories are attained.

The method evolved by Bruner and his co-workers at Harvard (Bruner, Olver and Greenfield, 1966) provides such an approach. The method owes a great deal to the broad framework provided by Vygotsky, but departs from it significantly by neither prescribing the 'correct' attributes to be abstracted nor the categories to be constructed. In the present study we have adopted the Olver-Rigney variant of the technique as used by Davey (1968) in a study of the Tristan da Cunhan children, but with some modifications to the pictorial array and the mode of analysis.

The material and procedure

The children were individually presented with an array of 42 coloured pictures of everyday objects. The pictures were always set out in the same positions in six columns of seven. The children were first asked to name each picture to ensure that they looked at and recognized every card. Then the experimenter says: 'Look at them all again. Choose the cards which belong together. Anyway you do it is fine but tell me why they go together. You can choose as many as you like.'

This was repeated five times. After each trial the cards were replaced in their original positions and the child's explanation was recorded verbatim so that each grouping can be analysed by strategy and attributes.

The classification of groupings

Three principal types of grouping were distinguished: superordinates, complexes and themes. A description of each type and sub-type, together with an example extracted from the protocols, is given below. These take account of both the strategies employed and the features of the objects – colour, size, function, etc. – which the children used to form their groupings (Appendix III provides a more detailed account of the preparation of the raw data for statistical analysis).

1. Superordinates

The essential feature of all superordinates is that items are grouped on the basis of one or more attributes common to them all. This can be achieved in a number of ways:

a. *Linguistic superordinates* The child indicates that a common attribute has been perceived by using a class name. 'They are all tools (animals, fruit, etc.)'

b. *Functional superordinates* Items are equated in terms of some intrinsic property they possess in common e.g. flower and tree, 'They both grow', or in terms of what can be done with them or to them, e.g. coat, boots, gloves, 'You can wear a coat and boots and you wear gloves'.

c. *Perceptual superordinates* The items are grouped on the basis of some shared surface quality, such as shape, colour or by some detail of the object, e.g. clock and ten-penny piece, 'They are both round', car and bicycle, 'They both have wheels'.

2. Complexes

A group is formed by selecting a variety of attributes none of which is common to them all. This strategy may take a number of forms:

a. *Collections* Different attributes are specified for each item but the child fails to abstract any superordinating quality. e.g. hammer and saw, 'With a hammer you hit nails and a saw saws wood'.

b. *Chains* There is no common attribute but each item is linked to the one which precedes it, e.g. nail, screw, rabbit, 'The nail and the screw go together because they have both got little points and the rabbit is the same colour as the screw'.

c. *Key rings* The complex has a central nucleus but no link between the subordinate items is made explicit, e.g. house, dog, bicycle, doll, 'The dog can go in the house, the bike can go in the house and the little girl can go in the house'.

d. *Fiat* The child either itemizes differences or simply asserts that an unspecified relationship exists, e.g. apple, orange, 'Well that's orange and that's got green and red on it'; cow, barn, 'Because they go together'.

3. Themas

The items are not linked by a common bond but are held together by the child's imaginative account, e.g. dog, car, 'A car might run over a dog'; bicycle, doll, ten-penny piece, 'I get on my bike and I go and buy a doll at the corner shop with my money'.

The presentation of the results

Each child had five trials and structuring these by the five independent variables, age, race, sex, region and density, yielded 25 tables – clearly too many for even the most enthusiastic of readers. Therefore, in order to render the information manageable, the following plan has been adopted. The frequencies for a particular grouping strategy over all trials have been aggregated and recorded as percentages. Thus, on Table 6.1, the entry 35.6 per cent in the column headed 10-year-old, white children for linguistic superordinates means that of a total of 320 groupings (64 children $\times$ 5 trials), 114 were linguistic superordinates. The results for the four age groups gives the relevant proportion for an ethnic group considered as a whole, and this has been entered in the column marked 'All'.

As can be seen from Table 6.1, age brings a progressive independence from the surface qualities of objects as a basis for grouping in favour of an increasing reliance on their functional properties. Linguistic and functional superordinates increase significantly with age and perceptual superordinates decline. Whereas some 36 per cent of the seven-year-olds' groupings were formed by abstracting some common non-perceptual attribute, 62 per cent of the 10-year-olds' groupings were formed in this way. Conversely whereas 12 per cent of the seven-year-olds' equivalence groupings relied upon common perceptual attributes only 3 per cent of the 10-year-olds' groupings did so. By the age of seven most of the children were beginning to realize the limitations of confining themselves to the picturable and point-at-able features of objects for creating units of belonging, but it is notable that the perceptual-functional trend is accompanied by a quite extensive use of the thematic strategy. The thematic mode appears to be an intermediary step between the perceptual mode and the functional linguistic approach to groupings. The explanation could be that as the children's ability for finer discriminations develops they become increasingly aware of the unique specificity of things. But this growing capacity to discriminate is not necessarily complemented by either the vocabulary or the ability to generate the more sophisticated moves for achieving equivalence. One way out of the dilemma is to unite things according to the situational conjunctions that the children experience in their daily lives hence: bike, doll, money and shop. It is not an economical form of packaging since a thema is not less than the sum of its parts, but at least it serves to release the perceiver from the vivid individuality of things

Table 6.1: *Concept level by race and age*
(average per cent)

	Whites					West Indians					Asians					All				
	7^+	8^+	9^+	10^+	All	7^+	8^+	9^+	10^+	All	7^+	8^+	9^+	10^+	All	7^+	8^+	9^+	10^+	All
Linguistic superordinate	13.6	21.4	30.6	35.6	25.3	13.8	15.6	15.0	30.0	18.6	6.9	15.6	23.1	21.3	16.7	12.0	18.5	24.8	30.6	21.5
Functional superordinate	24.5	28.4	30.1	27.6	27.7	24.4	32.5	21.3	34.4	28.1	24.4	25.0	31.3	35.6	29.1	24.4	28.6	28.2	31.3	28.2
Perceptual superordinate	10.7	4.0	3.8	2.4	5.2	11.3	6.9	5.0	1.9	6.3	15.0	6.3	5.0	4.4	7.7	11.9	5.3	4.4	2.8	6.1
Complexes	5.3	4.8	5.0	3.9	4.8	3.8	0.6	10.0	5.0	4.8	6.3	6.9	6.3	8.1	6.9	5.2	4.3	6.6	5.2	5.3
Themas	43.4	39.0	29.0	28.2	34.9	41.9	37.5	45.6	23.1	37.0	37.5	43.1	34.4	26.9	35.5	41.5	39.6	34.5	26.6	35.5
Collections	1.2	1.5	0.4	1.8	1.2	3.1	3.8	1.9	5.6	3.6	1.9	2.5	0	3.1	1.9	1.9	2.3	0.7	3.1	2.0
Other	1.2	0.9	1.2	0.7	1.0	1.9	3.1	1.3	0	1.6	8.1	0.6	0	0.6	2.3	3.1	1.4	0.9	0.5	1.5
Totals	100	100	100	100	100	100	100	100	100	100	100	100	100	100	100	100	100	100	100	100
Subjects	64	64	64	64	256	32	32	32	32	128	32	32	32	32	128	128	128	128	128	512
Trials	5	5	5	5	5	5	5	5	5	5	5	5	5	5	5	5	5	5	5	5

until the superordinating strategy can be extended beyond mere perceptual inclusion.

The overall perceptual-functional age trend, with thematizing as a possible intermediary step, is repeated within each ethnic group but only for the white group, where the number of children is twice that in the other two, does it exceed the conventional level of statistical significance. Nevertheless, the repetition of the direction and strength of the trend within each group lends confidence to the reality of the phenomenon.

There were no significant overall differences between the sexes or within groups. There is, however, a suggestion in the data that Asian girls may be progressing somewhat more slowly towards competence with the more sophisticated grouping strategies than Asian boys. Whereas 50 per cent of the groupings made by Asian boys were linguistic or functional superordinates only 40 per cent of the girls' groupings were formed by these strategies. It may well be that this is a reflection of the differences in the socialization of boys and girls in Asian communities, but on the basis of the present data this can be no more than speculation.

It can be seen by inspection of Table 6.1 that, overall, there are no significant differences between the West Indian and Asian children in the sophistication of their grouping strategies. As judged by the frequency with which they employed the linguistic and functional strategies, they are equally competent in abstracting the similarity between groups of visually dissimilar objects. There is, however, a significant difference between both the minority groups and the white children in their use of linguistic superordinates. To some extent the minority children compensate for this apparent difference in superordinatory skill by their marginally greater use of functional superordinates. When the two categories, linguistic and functional, are combined the difference between the white and minority groups is less marked and drops below the conventional level of statistical significance.

Neither the geographical location nor the size of the concentration of minority group children in a school appreciably affects the trend away from classifications employing the surface aspects of objects towards those formed on the basis of their functional qualities. The children in the south made marginally more functional groupings than those in the north but none of the within-group comparisons were significant. Also, there is a tendency for children in the low-density schools to use the rules of linguistic and functional inclusion more frequently than those in schools with a high concentration of minority group children. For example, the proportions of functional groupings (with or without a class name) constructed by white children were 48, 58 and 61 per cent in high density, low density and 'no contact' schools respectively. However, neither the between-groups nor within-group comparisons proved to be significant. Given the consistency of this trend across ethnic boundaries, it is probably a reflection of the interlocking inequalities suffered by many children in inner-city areas. With age and ethnicity held constant all children in low-density districts appear to be advancing more rapidly towards the functional mode of analysis than those in high-density districts.

Ethnocentrism and cognitive strategies

It has been suggested by Ehrlich (1973) that, since our cognitive abilities mediate between the prevalent attitudes in the community and what is incorporated into our belief systems, *a priori* one would assume that there would be a discernible relationship between cognitive ability and ethnic prejudice. He goes on to postulate that the acquisition and retention of ethnic prejudice is inversely related to cognitive ability.

This hypothesis is not strongly supported by the present data. Across the three ethnic groups there is a weak but positive relationship between the use of the less sophisticated strategies and high ethnocentricity (as ascertained by our composite measure, the Own Race Preference Scale; see Appendix III). It could not be said with any degree of confidence that changes in cognitive style would be accompanied by changes in the degree of ethnocentricity. Cognitive ability is not among the causes of prejudice but merely one of its mechanisms, although the two may be linked by a third factor, such as, for example, mental rigidity (Frenkel-Brunswick, 1949; Rokeach, 1956) which could lead the individual to attempt to resolve social and physical ambiguities in a similar way.

Summary and discussion

Bruner and Olver (1963) postulate that any efficient grouping plan should exhibit two features. First, there should be a reduction of cognitive load. That is to say, the grouping should be less complex than the sum of all the distinguishable features of the elements in the collection. Secondly, the grouping rule should have the property of being a generalizing rule, so that fresh instances or previous groupings can be incorporated within the content of the established group.

Whereas the superordinating strategy serves the function of cognitive economy by repackaging instances into a single class on a fraction of the available attributes, it is clear that complexes and collections are not much less than the sum of their parts. Moreover, whilst the combinatorial rule of a superordinate can encompass previous groupings or new items, by logical addition – as in the series: men, primates, vertebrates, animals, organisms – the addition of a fresh item to, say, a chain requires no less effort than the original linking of the first two items.

Therefore, assuming all was going well with the process of chunking up the environment into manageable units of belonging, one would expect that collections, complexes and superordinates based on perceptible features of things would decrease with age and that functionally based superordinates would increase. This is the case with the present sample of children. It is notable that by the age of seven only 7 per cent of their groupings were complexes or collections, and that they had already moved away from the exclusive use of the surface qualities of objects to the exploration of the richer combinatorial possibilities of their functional properties. Across the age groups, this transition was accompanied by the intermediary step of thematizing which was used with decreasing frequency as the more extensive use of functional superordinates developed. We therefore felt confident that all the children had sufficient competence to be able to carry out the simple discrimination and classification tasks which were to be the principal instruments in our enquiry.

Although the same perceptible-functional age trend can be observed in all three ethnic groups, the white children, age for age, appeared more adept than the minority children in accurately pin-pointing in a word the organizational principle they had employed: 'They are all tools (food, clothes, transport, etc.)' The minority children were more likely to describe their operations in personal-enactive terms, for example, 'You can eat them, wear them, ride on them, etc.' That this is a difference in linguistic competence, rather than in abstracting and generalizing ability, would seem to be supported by the fact that there is no significant difference between the three groups of children in their use of the functional superordinating strategy.

As their experience widens, children become more dependent on language as a means of representing the recurrent regularities in their environment. In Bruner's (1964) words: 'To transcend the immediately perceptual, to get beyond what is vividly present to a more extended model of the environment, the child needs a system that permits him to deal with the non-present, with things that are remote in space, qualitative similarity, and time, from the present situation' (p. 13). The fact that the minority children appeared to be somewhat slower than their white counterparts in coupling the technology of language to their cognitive operations could have been due to a number of interrelated factors. It is obvious that Asian children can suffer some disadvantage by being taught in a language which does not encode reality in precisely the same way as their mother tongue. But the linguistic disadvantages of West Indian children, although less obvious, can be no less acute. A great many of these children will speak English in a way which is indistinguishable from that of the dialect of the region in which their school is located. At home, however, and amongst their peers, they are likely to speak the language which their parents brought with them from the Caribbean, probably Jamaican Creole or, in some cases, French Creole. The Creole dialects differ in vocabulary, syntax and phonology from Standard English so that they, like the Asian children, are likely to experience some degree of 'interference' between the two linguistic systems.

Le Page (1981) points out that all new language learners begin by 'hearing' everything in terms of the language they already know. Until they have a separate model for the new system in their heads, the native language is likely to interfere with the second language. Since non-standard dialects share similarities with Standard English, young West Indians may find it particularly difficult to keep the two systems apart. But in any case, the problems of interference would be accentuated, for both groups of minority children, by school learning where the knowledge which is transmitted must go beyond the range of personal perception and action.

Although all the children in our sample were competent English speakers, it is possible that some of them could have experienced difficulty in following oral lessons concerning events outside their experience, and out of the context of any on-going action. Moreover, teachers, like everyone else, subconsciously stereotype people on the basis of their language and dialect (see Giles and Powesland, 1975, for a review of studies on the social evaluation of speech styles) and may have come to have low expectations of Asian and Caribbean children.

However, although it is important that teachers should be aware of the difficulties which can be experienced by children who speak English as a second language and those whose speech styles markedly diverge from Standard English, we would not wish to overemphasize 'interference' as a factor in the cognitive development of these children. Most of the interference problems encountered by young children could be minimized if teachers relied less on telling out of context and more on showing within context. Certainly, the difference we found between the white and minority children in their abstracting and generalizing abilities were not such as to lend credence to the fears, expressed by some white parents, that their children were disadvantaged by attending multi-ethnic schools.

What the results do suggest, however, is that in the high-density districts, all children, regardless of ethnicity, are making slower progress in mastering the more efficient cognitive strategies, than those in the low-density districts. It is this remediable disadvantage, which the white children share with minority children, which should be the cause of parental concern.

7 Ethnic Identification and Preference

We have argued (Chapter 4) that central to the motives of children coming to share the attitudes and values of those around them is the fundamental need to understand their own identity. A critical part of our social identity is derived from the knowledge that we belong to certain social groups, but in order to understand how our group membership defines our place in society, we must know where our group stands in relationship to others. That is to say, the establishment of our social identity essentially involves the twin processes of social categorization and social comparison.

Nowhere have young children's sensitivity to the evaluative matrix in which they find themselves been more sharply delineated than in the early studies of black American children growing up in white society.

In the late 1930s and early 40s the seminal work of Kenneth and Mamie Clark (1939a, 1939b, 1940, 1947) demonstrated that young black children in both the northern and southern states of America had difficulty in accepting their blackness and had serious social identity problems.

While the Clarks were not the first investigators to study ethnic identification and preference, the role of their studies in the historic United States Supreme Court decision of 1954 to desegregate American schools and the impetus their work provided for later studies has given their research a pre-eminence in the literature on ethnic identification and preference.

Research with young children presents the investigator with a number of problems. Techniques which rely on spoken or written language depend too much on the individual child's linguistic competence. The instructions must be readily comprehensible and the task sufficiently inviting to ensure the child's willing participation.

The Clarks decided that it was practicable to attempt to determine the ethnic attitudes of young black children between the ages of three and seven by a modified form of doll play.

The Clarks (1947) individually presented 253 black children, aged three to seven, with four dolls which were identical in every respect except for hair and skin colour. Two of these dolls were dark brown with black hair and two were white with yellow hair. In the experimental situation the subjects were asked to respond to the following requests by choosing one of the dolls.

1. Give me the doll that you like to play with.
2. Give me the doll that is a nice doll.
3. Give me the doll that looks bad.
4. Give me the doll which is a nice colour.
5. Give me the doll that looks like a white child.
6. Give me the doll that looks like a coloured child.
7. Give me the doll that looks like a negro child.
8. Give me the doll that looks like you.

The first four requests were designed to reveal preferences, requests 5 to 7 to indicate knowledge of 'racial differences' and request 8 to show self-identification.

In brief, the Clarks found that the ability to recognize gross ethnic differences was well established by the age of three, progressing to a near 100 per cent accuracy by the age of seven. Approximately two-thirds of the children preferred the white doll to the brown doll and about a third of them identified with the white doll in response to question 8. Both the preference for the white doll and the identification with the white doll decreased generally with age, although the majority of children preferred the white doll at every age level.

Most of the subsequent studies which followed the Clarks' lead included a white comparison group. Moreover, the variations in methods, materials, chronology and geographical context often make detailed cross-study comparisons speculative. Nevertheless, the substantive findings of the Clarks were convincingly confirmed during the 1950s and 60s by the work of Goodman (1952), Stevenson and Stewart (1958), Morland (1958, 1962), Asher and Allen (1969), Porter (1971) and others.

Not all the partial replications and variations on the Clarks' work, however, were confirmatory. Gregor and McPherson (1966a) tested both black and white children in segregated schools in an unspecified area of the 'deep South'. The white group were consistently ethnocentric in their responses to the requests for the dolls but the own group identification of the black children was much stronger than in the Clarks' study and there was a slight increment in own-group preference.

These findings, however, must be set against those of Asher and Allen (1969) who reported a slight, but statistically non-significant, increase in white preference amongst black children in the three decades that separated their study from the original study of the Clarks. Asher and Allen set up two theoretical models in their prediction of change between their sample of children and that of the Clarks. The first predicted that because of social and economic progress there would be an enhanced feeling of competence and pride amongst the black children, particularly those from the middle class. The alternative hypothesis was that economic progress and greater social mobility would lead to frequent comparisons with whites who were generally more advantaged and that such social comparisons would lead to increased feelings of inferiority on the part of the black group.

The investigators administered the Clarks' preference questions, substituting puppets for dolls to a total of 341 black and white children who were divided into middle-class and lower-class groups according to the parents' occupation. The children, whose ages ranged from three to eight, were attending schools in New Jersey with varying degrees of racial integration.

The white and black children were consistent in their preference for the white puppets and rejection of the brown puppets and no differences in the proportion of own-race preferences occurred between middle and lower-class children. The authors interpreted the absence of a significant difference between their black sample and that of the Clarks to be in accordance with their social comparison hypothesis. They suggested that the apparent rise in economic status combined with integrated schooling contributes to more frequent comparisons with whites and to 'increased feelings of inferiority'. Such feelings are to be attributed to the relatively inferior position of the black community as a whole, rather than to attacks on personal competence.

One further study based on the Clarks' paradigm which questions their results needs to be summarized. Greenwald and Oppenheim (1968) suggested that the Clarks' misidentification results might be misleading. They pointed out that a greater proportion of light-skinned black children than dark-skinned children had misidentified and that this could be because they perceived the white dolls colouring to be actually closer to their own than that of the dark brown doll. They, therefore, administered approximations of the Clarks' questions to 75 black and white nursery school children using a mulatto doll in addition to white and dark brown dolls.

Almost equal proportions of light and dark-skinned black children chose the mulatto doll in response to the question: 'Is there a doll that looks like you?' Only 13 per cent of the black children chose the white doll. Moreover, the level of misidentification was greater amongst the white children than among the black children. The investigators suggested that this unanticipated result was perhaps due to the fact that the mulatto doll was the most appropriate choice for some white children who were darker skinned. This interpretation, however, ignores the fact that half the dark-skinned black children also chose the mulatto doll despite the discrepancy between its colouring and their own. It may well be as Porter (1971) has suggested, that Greenwald and Oppenheim inadvertently created a choice bias by using colour variations which were too small for accurate discrimination by four and five-year-olds.

No significant differences were found on the critical preference questions 'play with' and 'nice' between the Clarks' data and those of Green-

wald and Oppenheim. A majority of both black and white children preferred the white doll. Since more than 20 years separated the two studies
the authors interpreted the absence of discrepancy on the preference questions, despite methodological differences, as evidence of the 'high
reliability over time' of the phenomenon of out-group preference on the
part of black children.

It would appear that despite some discordant results the following broad
summary can be derived from investigations into ethnic preference and
identification in America during the 1950s and 60s. Ethnic group awareness is well established by the age of four or five. Identification 'errors'
persist to a later age with black children than white. Both white and black
children prefer representations (dolls, puppets, drawings or photographs)
of whites to those of blacks.

These, and similar observations derived from other methodologies,
were interpreted to mean that black children in the United States had a
negative or ambivalent attitude to their ethnic identity.

Non-American studies

During the same period, reports of investigations in other cultural settings
suggested that the apparent devaluation by some children of their own
ethnic group was not peculiar to American black–white relationships, but
was more likely to be related to the social norms governing the relative
position of groups in a particular society. It has been found, for example,
that children as far apart, and as culturally distinct, as the Maoris in New
Zealand (Vaughan, 1964) and the Bantu in South Africa (Gregor and
McPherson, 1966b) were less likely to identify with and prefer their own
group than the white children in those countries.

This interpretation is further supported by studies in contexts where
the phenomenon of own-group devaluation did not seem to occur. Using
photographs and variations of the Clarks' identity and preference questions, Morland (1969) compared the responses of Chinese children in
Hong Kong with those of black and white American children living in the
northern and southern states of America. Moreland describes Hong Kong
as a 'multiracial setting in which no race is clearly dominant' and 'one in
which the Caucasians and Chinese might be said to hold parallel positions'. Hong Kong is officially bilingual, there is no racial exclusion of any
sort, the Chinese are prominent in business, education, government and
social life and all the schools are 'integrated'.

In response to the 'play with' question Morland found that preferences
for their own group were expressed by 82 per cent of the white American,
65 per cent of the Hong Kong Chinese and only 28 per cent of the black
American children.

When asked which children in photographs they most looked like 12 per cent of the white American identified with a child of another race, 14 per cent of the Hong Kong Chinese did so but 45 per cent of the black American identified with Caucasians.

Thus, the Hong Kong children, unlike the black American children, predominantly prefer and identify with their own ethnic group. They do this less extensively than the American white children but this Morland takes to be reflective of a society in which there is no dominant ethnic group. Morland interprets this comparison between the Hong Kong and American children as supporting the normative theory of racial prejudice; that is, prejudice is a function of the norms of society which define the ways in which members of different groups ought to behave in relationship to each other. He concludes that implicit in his findings 'is the assumption that if the American social structure changes so that Negroes are no longer in a subordinate position, the racial preference and racial self-identification of Negro children will change' (p. 373).

Children, however, appear to be sensitive to subtle, social influences which can engender a belief in the relative inferiority of their own group even in social contexts which are not characterized by intense intergroup tensions or where there are no clear visible differences such as skin colour.

At the time of Tajfel *et al.*'s (1972) study in Haifa, a little before the Six-day War in 1967, about 60 per cent of the Israeli Jewish population consisted of people of Middle Eastern or North African origin, most of the remainder of the Jewish inhabitants were of European descent. Despite the efforts of the public authorities to promote social, economic and psychological integration some degree of strain exists between the two groups.

The subjects of the study were 400 primary school children, age six to eleven, drawn equally from those of European parentage and those of Oriental parentage, but most children of both groups had been born in Israel.

The children were presented with a set of photographs of young Israeli men, half of which were European and half of Oriental origin. On the first occasion they were invited to express their liking or disliking for each photograph. Some weeks later they were given the same photographs and asked to sort them into two boxes labelled, 'Israeli' and 'not Israeli'. Both groups of children judged a significantly greater number of European photographs to be likeable and both groups assigned a greater number of the European photographs to the category 'Israeli'. Both these trends increased with age.

Subsequently, a group of adults in Britain, who had never been to Israel, were asked to guess whether each photograph was of a European or Oriental Jew. The accuracy of their guessing was better than chance, which suggests that there were some physiognomic cues to be picked up if one was alerted to them. At the same time, the intergroup differences could not have been nearly so obvious or consistent as those between ethnic groups in America or Hong Kong. Moreover, the authors point out that it was unlikely that the physiognomy of the Oriental photographs would have been alien to the children since a majority of the Israeli Jews were by that time of Middle Eastern or North African origin.

The particular interest of this study is that it demonstrates that children can assimilate negative in-group evaluations even in conditions of reduced distinctiveness. The tension between the two groups in Israel is not nearly so acute as in other countries in which studies of children's ethnic preferences have been carried out, yet the children of Oriental parentage showed a fine sensitivity to the social context which creates these tensions.

In Britain during this period studies of group identification and preference were somewhat sparse and on a smaller scale than those in America. Inevitably, some of the results reflect the somewhat specialized samples of children employed.

Marsh (1970) for example, studied a sample composed of privately fostered West African children whose parents were studying at various Universities and other institutions of higher education in Britain. He compared their responses, by a series of Clark-type questions, to a set of coloured photographs with those of their white foster siblings and a white no-contact control group. There were no significant differences in accuracy of identification between the three groups but whereas some 64 per cent of the West African children said they would like to be white some 72 per cent of the white foster siblings said they would like to be black! Since 78 per cent of the white control group expressed an in-group preference Marsh attributes his unusual results to good fostering. He concludes that an awareness of ethnic differences does not lead to negative stereotyping unless children are exposed to a racially conscious form of socialization.

In a similar study involving fostered West Indian children Futcher (1972) found that black children reared in white families were no more confused or unrealistic about their group identity than West Indian children living in their own families.

Nevertheless, the more broadly based and large-scale studies of Jahoda and his co-workers (1972) and Milner (1973) leave little doubt that children in Britain, as in America, were learning as part of their induction into a multi-cultural society the hierarchical order of ethnic groupings in society.

Jahoda compared the identification and preference responses of Asian children and Scottish children in six Glasgow primary schools by means of a novel identikit technique. Each component of the face was represented in three shades of colouring. The children were asked, first to make up a face to look as much like themselves as possible and then to make up the face they would like to have. The children had been selected in two age groups (6 and 10 years) and it was found that the ability to represent themselves correctly improved with age. 30 per cent of the younger Asians mis-represented themselves at 6 but this dropped to 20 per cent for the 10-year-olds. The comparable figures for the Scottish children were 17 per cent and 10 per cent. On the preference questions, the Scottish group show a slight in-group bias at age 6 which increased significantly with age. On the other hand, whereas the Asian children preferred their own physical make-up at age 6, by age 10 they had shifted their perference towards the outgroup.

In a replication of the study, the introduction of a 'charming and attractive' (*sic*) Indian female experimenter had an insignificant effect on the identification choices, but on the preference item the outgroup choices of the Scots showed an increase while the outgroup choices of the Asian children decreased. Nevertheless, there was the same trend from the younger to the older age groups towards a greater outgroup preference. 46 per cent of the 10-year-old Asian children opted for the physical features of the indigenous population. As Jahoda observes 'still not a negligible fraction' and one which shows that: 'Asian children in Glasgow are definitely not insulated from the values of the host community and are, on the contrary, powerfully influenced by them' (p. 30).

Milner (1973), whose data was collected in the late 1960s, carried out one of the very few tri-racial studies in this area of investigation. A total of 300 West Indian, Asian and white children were presented with dolls and pictures and asked a series of questions of the same basic type as those employed by Clark and Clark. On the critical identity question, 'which doll looks most like you?' 48 per cent of the West Indian children and 24 per cent of the Asian children misidentified but not a single white child did so. On the ethnic preference questions, only a tiny proportion (6 per cent) of the white children favoured outgroup figures but over 70 per cent of both minority groups exhibited on outgroup preference. Milner notes that his results are qualitatively similar to earlier American studies and concludes that: 'many immigrant children feel distinctly equivocal about their group's identity in British society, in contrast to the English children's wholehearted identification with and preference for their own group' (p. 293).

Studies of self-esteem

Proceeding at the same time as these studies of group identity and preference has been a related series of investigations which have concentrated on the self-esteem of minority group children and adolescents. These studies, which have employed a different methodology from those previously discussed, have produced a diversity of findings which have not always been readily reconcilable either with each other or with those in the Clark tradition. (See Rosenberg and Simmons, 1972; Bagley, Mallick and

Verma, 1979, for useful overviews of the American and British studies respectively.)

The notion of self-esteem admits to numerous definitions but in the work of most researchers it has been investigated as the negative and positive feelings and attitudes a person has about him or herself. (See, for example, Coopersmith, 1975.) Thus a self-esteem rating scale typically consists of a 'self-checking' inventory of items by which people can make some appraisal of themselves. The shorter form of the Coopersmith scale which has been extensively used in British studies by Bagley and his co-workers includes such items as: 'I often feel ashamed of myself', 'My parents expect too much of me', 'I often feel upset at school', 'I can usually take care of myself'. Similarly the Rosenberg and Simmons scale presents the individual with such statements as: 'I feel I have a number of good qualities', 'I take a positive attitude towards myself', 'I certainly feel useless at times'.

A priori one might predict that where individuals belong to a social group which is low in prestige and the object of extensive prejudice and discrimination there would be a strong tendency for the individuals to be low in self-esteem.

The evidence, however, suggests that it would be a mistake to assume that the awareness by a minority of its depressed social image will necessarily be accompanied by low self-esteem on the part of its individual members. The great majority of the studies reviewed by Rosenberg and Simmons (1972), like their own investigation in 26 schools in Baltimore City, show that black youngsters (8–19 years) think no less well of themselves than whites of the same age. On this side of the Atlantic, Louden (1978a), using the scale developed by Rosenberg and Simmons, found no overall difference in the self-esteem of English, West Indian and Asian adolescents although the self-esteem of both West Indian and Asian girls was higher than that of the English girls. On the other hand, Bagley, Mallick and Verma (1979) in a study of 39 schools, have shown that the level of self-esteem in West Indian boys is below that of both white boys and West Indian girls.

The increasing number of self-esteem studies which report no significant difference between American black and white children is viewed with suspicion by Adam (1978). He detects an ideological bias both in the choice of the instruments of assessment and in the manner in which results are interpreted. Adam points out that the early studies in the Clark tradition which were interpreted to demonstrate 'black inferiorization', and which were used effectively as a lever in the struggle for black civil rights appeared, after the onset of black militancy, to take on the taint of racism, 'the "damage" inflicted by an oppressive society begins to look like a defamation of a people which is moving collectively against its oppressors' (p. 49). In consequence (in Adam's view) the psychometry inspired by the

Clarks became unfashionable and the journals began publishing self-esteem studies which in the words of one pair of investigators had the intention of 'putting to rest' the lower self-esteem-in-blacks tradition. 'Discrediting this tradition is we believe, necessary' (McCarthy and Yancey, 1971, p. 591).

The result, Adam complains, is that we no longer know what is going on under the self-esteem label. Self-esteem has become a psychological abstraction. It tells us nothing about how black people cope with restricted life chances in earning a living, going to school and so on. Sympathy with minority members, and a desire to free them from the stigma of low self-esteem have led to attempts to deny its existence. Analysis has become 'arrested in an ill-defined psychological state divorced from the original problematic and abstracted from the political context which made it meaningful. This obliteration of the problem ironically lends itself to the modern "benign neglect" policy toward black problems and to the rationale undermining "affirmational action" ' (p. 49).

Simmons (1978) in her own defence, and that of other investigators who have adopted the self-esteem approach, denies the charge of ideological bias. She agrees with Adam that the differences between the earlier and later studies could be due either to actual change in self-attitudes over time or methodological differences. However, later investigators she considers have employed a different approach, not because they wish to free minority members from the stigma of 'low self-esteem' but because the question that has been most relevant for self-esteem investigators has been the ways in which individuals' positive and negative attitudes towards themselves are affected by being minority group members. Nevertheless, since the Rosenberg and Simmons (1972) scale is actually designed, 'to exclude judgements about any specific characteristics of the self; race, for example, is not made salient' (p. 10), there is some justification for Adam's contention that studies of inter-ethnic self-esteem often 'rely on measures that have become far removed from the original problem' (p. 50).

Simmons goes on to argue that an individual's attitudes to him or herself are more likely to be influenced by the opinions of significant others in the immediate environment than by the 'larger society'. The black child tends to be surrounded by other blacks and 'comparing himself to other economically disprivileged blacks' the black child does not feel less worthy as a person on account of race and economic background. In fact, encapsulated in a de facto segregated environment, as are most urban black children, they may be less aware of society's pressure.

While this thesis might fit Rosenberg and Simmon's data well enough (and perhaps that of some other American investigators) where only 3 per cent of their black sample lived in predominantly white neighbourhoods, it is doubtful if it can serve as a universal explanation. Tenuous support for the argument could be derived from some studies on this side of the

Atlantic, where higher levels of self-esteem have been found to be associated with the higher concentration of black children in a school (Louden, 1978b; Young and Bagley, 1979). But against this evidence Stone (1981) found no difference in the self-esteem scores of West Indian children attending schools with a high proportion of West Indian children and those where the proportion was less than 50 per cent. Nor did she find any difference in the scores of children who attended West Indian Community Schools (official and self-help) and those children who went exclusively to local LEA schools where there were no special programmes or study groups for West Indian children.

Even in American segregated communities it seems improbable, as Milner (1981) has pointed out, that black people can insulate themselves from the valuation placed on their group by white people. 'Race attitudes enter into the whole spectrum of cultural media with which they have contact whether in a segregated or non-segregated environment' (p. 138).

Setting aside Adam's imputations of ideological bias on the part of some investigators who have favoured the self-esteem approach, a more general explanation of the discrepancies between the findings of this type of study and those based on the Clark paradigm can be sought along the lines put forward by Pettigrew (1978).

He accepts that oppression and subjugation do in fact have 'negative' personal consequences for minority individuals, but he gives considerable weight to Porter's (1971) discovery that there can be a sharp disjunction between the 'real' personal self and the 'racial' self. Thus, he maintains that proud strong minorities are possible despite the 'marks of oppression', 'and this strength will become increasingly evident as the minority itself challenges the repressive societal system' (p. 60).

While there may be doubts as to just how sharp the disjunction between personal self-esteem and group identity is in some social contexts, intrinsically there is no reason why the data from the two techniques should not be regarded as compatible. The common element of all the studies based on variants of the Clark paradigm is that members of minority groups are always required to make a comparative judgement between their own group and the majority group. As we have seen, this comparative assessment has frequently produced evidence of a bias towards the group consensually rated as 'dominant' in a particular society. On the other hand, the self-esteem technique invites people to take stock of their personal qualities and achievements and express attitudes towards them. This too requires a comparison process, but here the comparisons can be made between one's self and others in the same social group or the comparisons can be made within oneself, say, between oneself past and present or between achievements and aspirations. As Stone (1981) observes, following her discussion of black culture and consciousness, '. . . people derive the means to sustain a sense of self from many sources and do not rely on

negative and hostile views as their source of information about self'
(p. 233).

However, if this line of reasoning is to get beyond the somewhat banal
conclusion that if you ask different questions you get different answers, a
coherent theory is required which will bring the two kinds of data into
some sort of mutually illuminating relationship.

It will be recalled (Chapter 4) that a basic postulate of Tajfel's theory of
intergroup behaviour is that a critical part of our social identity is derived
from the knowledge that we belong to certain social groups which have
some value for us. Moreover, he maintains that a social group will only be
capable of sustaining an adequate social identity for its members if it
manages to retain a positively valued distinctiveness from other groups.
Given the centrality of a positive self-image for our general well-being,
then, what options are open to individuals who are members of social
groups which are consensually defined as 'inferior'?

Tajfel (1974; for an elaboration of the theory see Tajfel, 1978 and Tajfel
and Turner, 1979) proposes that where a group's relative position is
perceived to be so low that it can no longer contribute to those aspects of a
person's social identity from which satisfaction is derived, alternative
means to attaining positive distinctiveness will be sought. One solution
might be for individuals to leave the group, if this is possible, or to attempt
to dissociate themselves from it. Usually this implies some kind of upward
social mobility. While this is possible for members of some minority
groups the option of dissociating themselves from the low-prestige category is not open to those who are stigmatized by their pigmentation.
Although, one might argue that on the basis of the evidence, it is an option
fantasized by the very young.

An alternative solution, suggested by the self-esteem data, is to avoid
high-status group comparisons and either compare one's individual condition with that of other in-group members, or with that of other low-status
groups judged to be even less favourably regarded. In this respect, it is
worth noting that Louden (1978b) found the same tendency to disparage
other minority groups amongst his sample of black adolescents as we did
amongst primary school children.

With the possible exception of the last option described, none of these
individual strategies contribute to a group solution. Indeed, they may
actually be dysfunctional in so far as they destroy the subordinate group's
solidarity and may reduce the possibility of achieving a positive
reappraisal of the group as a whole.

Moreover, outside the insulation of a ghetto, the building up of a
separate and powerful image of personal worth is unlikely to be a totally
successful strategy. It is clear from Weinreich's (1979) painstaking case-
study approach that since individual identities are formed simultaneously
by daily interactions, both within and without the membership group, that

a degree of what he describes as 'identity diffusion' is likely to be experienced.

Ultimately, the economic, political and social requirements of the group and the task of regaining, or retaining, its self-respect cannot rely on individual strategems. Instead it must depend on some degree of consensus within the group to bring about a change in the manner in which it is treated, or regarded, by the dominant group.

The first group strategy which might be attempted is some form of integration with the dominant group. The danger here is that the minority group may lose its cultural distinctiveness and thereby its ability to contribute to the individual's sense of personal worth in this respect. Although some ethnic groups, both in Britain and the United States, have accepted a social and psychological merging with the majority this is not a realistic option for black minorities as long as the attitudes of the majority remain what they are. As Tajfel (1978) points out, attempts to obtain a straightforward integration into the wider society are now regarded by black Americans as a failure.

A second group strategy might be to seek a re-evaluation of the group by changing the criteria by which it is judged. 'Black is beautiful' for example, is an obvious attempt to change a previously negatively valued characteristic of the group to a favourable one.

A closely related strategy, to endow the group with new and positive attributes, is to search the past of the group for its traditions or ancient attributes and revitalize them. Rastafarianism and the use of the Creole dialect amongst West Indians are good examples of these trends. Louden (1978a) attributes the high self-esteem he found among West Indian adolescents to the 'awareness of the need to create and identify with a distinctive cultural heritage' (p. 51).

Any attempt to shift the group's social position by re-evaluating its attributes, or creating new ones, can only be successful if the group's new evaluation of itself receives wide and positive acceptance from other groups. The failure of such efforts to reduce discrimination and to improve the social and economic opportunities of group members is likely to lead to the more aggressive strategy of direct competition with the dominant group.

The aim of social competitive ethnocentrism is not simply to shift the group's position within a system of values but to change the values themselves and with it the social structure which supports them. The claim of the black militant movements which gathered momentum in the United States during the 1960s was not only for a recognition of the black minority's separate and positive cultural distinctiveness but also for economic and social parity. In so far as the strategy of social competition implies a redistribution of resources and a relocation of groups within the social structure, Tajfel and Turner (1979) predict that it will engender conflict and antagonism between the subordinate and dominant groups.

Social change and social identity

It can be seen that both the evidence from the self-esteem approach and that which requires aspects of identity to be defined in group terms can be accommodated with Tajfel and Turner's theory. What remains to be explained is the chronological shift in the emphasis of the results. Tajfel and Turner (1979) concede that discovering the precise conditions in which one set of strategies rather than another will be adopted by a subordinate group is a long-term research task. Nevertheless, their tentative proposals show a reasonably good fit with the data under discussion.

They suggest that where no alternatives appear to be available a subordinate group will do little to challenge the status quo but its members may well seek individual solutions to the problem of social identity. Where, however, there is a shared awareness that 'the existing social reality is not the only possible one and that alternatives to it are conceivable and perhaps attainable' (Tajfel, 1974, p. 82), then the problems of social identity will be resolved by challenging the legitimacy of the dominant group's position by one or more of the group strategies previously outlined.

The 1960s were a time when minority groups, not only in America but in other parts of the world, seemed to perceive that a change in the relationships between themselves and the privileged was attainable. Spurred on perhaps by the emergence of black African nations and other new independent states, there was 'a world-wide push towards differentiation originating from minorities which were often at great distances from each other geographically' (Tajfel, 1978, p. 7). The factor which was common to all these minority movements was the claim to the right to be different on their own terms and not as dictated by the majorities.

Although it is impossible to establish direct causal links, it is a reasonable hypothesis, given children's sensitivity to their social milieu, that this push towards positive differentiation would be reflected in their attitudes towards their group identity. This hypothesis would seem to be supported by American investigators who continued to use variants of the Clark social comparison technique to explore those aspects of identity which are derived from the social significance of group membership.

In the early 1970s it became increasingly clear, as report followed report, that the militant ethnocentrism of black adults together with their increasing involvement in politics, the mass media and education, had been accompanied by a greater probability that black children would prefer and identify with their own ethnic group than those of earlier generations. (Hraba and Grant, 1970; Ward and Braun, 1972; Fox and Jordan, 1973; Bunton and Weissbach, 1974; Epstein *et al.*, 1976, Moore, 1976).

Moreover, in New Zealand Vaughan (1978) who had pursued a consistent methodology throughout his researches since the early 60s, reported that for the first time there was a pronounced degree of in-group preference among Maori children. The shift away from the passive acceptance of ascribed group inferiority which was typical of the 60s was evident amongst the younger children (6 to 8 years) but most clearly established in the responses of the older (10 to 12 years) and cognitively more sophisticated Maoris. Vaughan attributes the change to the combined effects of urbanism and a new sensitivity to social underprivilege, accelerated in the 70s by a knowledge of minority group assertions elsewhere, particularly in the United States.

As part of a larger study concerned with a class-room intervention programme conducted in 1974 Milner (1979) repeated the identification tests from his earlier study carried out in the late 60s (Milner 1973). On the identification tests the proportion of West Indian children who identified with the white figure had significantly declined (27 per cent compared with 48 per cent five years previously). The Asian children exhibited a similar pro-white orientation to that which they had shown previously (30 per cent compared with the earlier 24 per cent). However, roughly 80 per cent of both West Indian and Asian children maintained they would *rather be* white.

There does, therefore, seem to be an appreciable amount of support for the presumption that the world-wide trends in the assertion of minority group identity would be reflected in the way black children regard their group membership. Although the shift away from out-group identification has been less in evidence in Britain than elsewhere, it has nevertheless long been obvious that minority groups in Britain were no longer willing to accept passively an underprivileged position. It was, therefore, of particular interest to us in the present study to ascertain whether the decline in own-group rejection, increasingly emphasized in the American results, was finding expression amongst children in Britain.

Perception of differences

We explored this possibility by two measures, one to assess ethnic identification and the other to assess ethnic group preferences. For both the identification and preference tests, full length photographs of primary school children were used. The photographed children were identically dressed, the boys in jeans and sweaters, the girls in jumpers and skirts, in order to minimize the selection of irrelevant cues. Black and white half-plate prints were used, in preference to coloured photographs since skin shade can be a critical factor for West Indian children and it was thought that good quality monochrome prints would allow them to project freely their preferred skin shade.

The identification test was carried out during the first visit to a school. The children were presented with three photographs of children of the same sex as themselves, one for each ethnic group, and asked: Which one looks most like you? For the preference test, presented after an interval of some weeks, the children were shown the same photographs but this time they were asked: If you could choose, which one would you most like to be?

Identification question results

The proportions of children from each ethnic group who correctly identified with the appropriate photograph are set out in Table 7.1 It is immediately clear that the results provide little support for the phenomenon of own-group rejection amongst minority group children.

Indeed if the West Indian and Asian proportions are pooled then, statistically, it can be said that it is no more probable that a black child will say that he looks like a white child that it is that a white child will say that he looks like a black child.

An interesting exception to the overall trend is provided by the white and Asian girls who were not only more likely than white boys to identify with an out-group photograph, but were also more likely than West Indian girls to make an out-group response. Their remarks during the test suggested that they ignored pigmentation and picked out similarities in small details of hair style and dress – despite the fact that all the girls in the photographs wore identical clothing!

No consistent trend towards a stronger out-group orientation was found amongst either West Indian or Asian children in schools where they constituted only a small minority. The only reliable difference between the high and low-density schools was provided by the Asian children; significantly more Asian children in schools where the concentration of Asians was small, than in those where it was 50 per cent of more, chose their own-group photograph. This difference is largely to be accounted for by the Asian girls, who showed a greater readiness in the low-density schools to identify with their own group.

For white children, the distribution of own-group choices was not significantly different amongst those in the two 'no contact' schools from those in schools with differing proportions of minority group children.

Comparisons between schools in the north and the south also yielded significant differences for the Asian children but not for the other two groups. The Asians in the London schools made more own-group choices than those in Yorkshire, but again, the girls were the principle contributors to the difference, with the boys failing to approach the conventional significance level.

An analysis was made of the West Indian children's responses according to their skin shade. There was a progressive, but non-significant, trend in

Table 7.1: *The self identification test. Percentage of children at each of four age levels making the correct response*

Race and sex of subjects (correct responses as % of group)

Age	White			West Indian			Asian			Total correct
	Boy	Girl	All	Boy	Girl	All	Boy	Girl	All	
7 +	90.6	75	82.8	75	100	87.5	87.5	68.8	78.1	82.8
8 +	93.8	62.5	78.1	93.8	100	96.9	93.8	75	84.4	84.4
9 +	87.5	75	81.3	87.5	87.5	87.5	93.8	81.3	87.5	84.4
10 +	93.8	78.1	85.9	100	93.8	96.9	93.8	81.3	87.5	89.1
Total correct	91.4	72.5	82	89.1	95.3	92.2	92.2	76.6	84.4	85.2
Total incorrect	8.6	27.5	18	10.9	4.7	7.8	7.8	23.4	15.6	14.8
N =	128	128	256	64	64	128	64	64	128	512

the frequency with which the white photograph was chosen by children judged as being of dark, medium and light pigmentation.

Preference question results

The results from the self-preference question (Table 7.2) present a very different picture. The responses of both the West Indian and Asian children differ markedly from those of the white group. Whereas some 86 per cent of the white children preferred their own group, less than half the West Indian and Asian children made own-race choices.

Taken as a whole, the choices of the small proportion of white children who preferred another group to their own, marginally favoured the Asians. This predilection was stronger for girls than boys, although none of the differences in the distribution of choices between West Indians and Asians was significant. The pattern of the white children's preferences was remarkably consistent. The magnitude of their own-race preference was relatively unaffected by either the ethnicity of the group with which they were in contact or by the size of the group, relative to their own, in a particular school. Again, the 'no contact' children did not respond significantly differently from the other white children in the frequency of their out-group choices, but in their case, *all* their out-group preferences were for the Asian photograph.

The out-group preferences of the two minority groups indicate that they had little desire to be like each other. 'I wouldn't want to be like her', said one West Indian girl pointing to the photograph of the Asian girl. 'She looks like a Paki or something'. Only 4 per cent of the Asian children preferred the West Indian photograph, and less than 5 per cent of the West Indians chose that of the Asian child. Overwhelmingly, their preference was for the picture of the white boy or girl.

Neither the size of the concentration of a particular group in a school, nor its location north or south, appreciably affects the general pattern of ethnic preference for minority group children. There is a trend for more West Indian girls in schools with a low concentration of West Indian children to prefer to be white, and significantly more Asian children in northern than the southern schools chose the white photograph.

The results do, however, suggest that for all groups, age brings a greater acceptance of one's own ethnicity, but only the difference between the 7 and 10 year old West Indians is statistically reliable. Girls, in general, tend to be more out-group orientated than boys, but within each ethnic group the difference between boys and girls is only reliable for the Asians.

As with the identification question the children of light and medium pigmentation made more white choices than the dark-skinned children. On this occasion, there was a considerably stronger relationship between skin shade and the choice of the white photograph, with 36, 45 and 56 per

Table 7.2: *The self preference test. Percentage of children at each of four age levels making the own-race response*

Race and sex of subjects (own-race responses as % of group)

Age	White			West Indian			Asian			Total correct
	Boy	Girl	All	Boy	Girl	All	Boy	Girl	All	
7 +	93.3	76.7	85	37.5	37.5	37.5	42.9	35.7	39.3	61.7
8 +	86.7	80	83.3	50	50	50	64.3	28.6	46.4	65.8
9 +	83.3	90	86.6	37.5	50	43.8	71.4	21.4	46.4	65.8
10 +	96.7	83.3	90	68.8	62.5	65.6	57.1	42.9	50	74.2
Total	90	82.5	86.3	48.4	50	49.2	58.9	32.1	45.5	66.9
Total of other race responses	8.3	15	11.6	46.9	50	48.5	37.5	62.5	50	30.4
Missing data	1.7	2.5	2.1	4.7	0	2.3	3.6	5.4	4.5	2.7
N =	120	120	240	64	64	128	56	56	112	480

cent of the dark medium and light-skinned children, respectively, stating a preference to be white. This trend just fails to reach the 5 per cent level of significance.

Concordance between identification and preference choices

Table 7.3 presents the distribution of the patterns of relationships between the self-identification and the self-preference choices for children in the three ethnic groups.

Overall some 63 per cent of the children present a concordant pattern, mainly by expressing an own-group choice on both the identification and preference tests, boys being more consistent than the girls. Very few children totally reject their own group by making two out-group choices. The degree of concordance is higher for the white children than for the two minority groups, although for all groups it is above 50 per cent.

The principal pattern of discordance is own-race identification accompanied by a preference for another group. 40 per cent of the minority group children responded in this way. The majority of the contributors to the alternative pattern, other race identification with own race preference, are white girls. Their choices account for nearly 63 per cent of the total responses under this heading.

Photo-preference and friendship

A full analysis of our study of the children's friendship patterns is provided in Chapter 10. However, it is useful at this point to compare the children's preferences expressed in the photo-choice situation with their response when a choice is made from a known group in their school.

A number of investigations have found that children exhibit more prejudice in projective tests than in reality-based situations (Radke *et al.*, 1950; Goodman 1952), and in a recent replication of the Clarks' study Hraba and Grant (1970) failed to find a correspondence between doll choice and friendship patterns.

For the purposes of this comparison between ethnic preference and sociometric choice only the results from schools in the high-density portion of the sample were used, in order to give every ethnic group an equal opportunity for having exclusively own-race friends. In the Hraba and Grant study, the proportion of black children in some of their schools was so low that it would not always have been possible for a child who preferred black friends to have behaved consistently with his choice on the projective test. It appears that, in schools where the ethnic mix is such as to allow children a more or less equal opportunity of choosing own-race friends or other-race friends, only a minority wish to confine their

Table 7.3: *The degree of concordance between the self-identification and self-preference tests*

Race and sex of subjects (number of respondents as % of group)

Self identification	Self preference	White			West Indian			Asian			Total
		Boy	Girl	All	Boy	Girl	All	Boy	Girl	All	
Concordant											
Own race	Own race	81.7	60	70.8	48.4	48.4	48.4	55.4	26.8	41.1	57.9
Other race	Other race	0.8	4.2	2.5	10.9	1.6	6.3	5.4	19.6	12.5	5.8
Total concordant		82.5	64.2	73.3	59.3	50	54.7	60.8	46.4	53.6	63.7
Discordant											
Own race	Other race	7.5	10.8	9.2	35.9	48.4	42.2	32.1	42.9	37.5	24.6
Other race	Own race	8.3	22.5	15.4	0	1.6	0.8	3.6	5.4	4.5	9
Total discordant		15.8	33.3	24.6	35.9	50	43	35.7	48.3	42	33.6
Missing data		1.7	2.5	2.1	4.7	0	2.3	3.6	5.4	4.5	2.7
N =		120	120	240	64	64	128	56	56	112	480

friendships exclusively to members of their own group. From a total of 238 children 66.5 per cent preferred to have some other-group friends. This sentiment is most pronounced among the West Indian children (78.5 per cent) and least often expressed by the Asians (55.4 per cent) with the white children falling between the two (63.6 per cent). Moreover, the fact that a third of the children appeared to be exclusive in their friendship patterns does not necessarily mean that they had no other-race friends: it may merely mean that these friends were not ranked high enough to be named amongst the top two on any of the three criteria with which the children were presented.

However, those children who named no other-race friends were more likely to have chosen their own race on the preference test. Considered independently, each of the ethnic groups exhibits the same trend, but the difference only reaches the 5 per cent level of significance with the white children.

Discussion

These results tend to diminish the importance that has been attached to the phenomenon of self-rejection amongst minority group children. The low frequency of misidentification by West Indian and Asian children, in fact, compares favourably with the incidence of misidentification amongst white children. These data are in marked contrast with those from many earlier studies, where as much as a third to a half of the children in the black samples have identified with the representation of a white child. It will be recalled that in the only other British study to make tri-racial comparisons in this field, Milner (1973) reported that 48 per cent of the West Indian children and 24 per cent of the Asian children misidentified, but not a single English child did so, although these proportions were modified by his partial replication in 1974.

Although there are differences in design and materials between Milner's study and the present one, it seems probable, in view of the recent American and New Zealand evidence and the fact that Milner's original study was carried out in the late 1960s, that the push towards positive differentiation on the part of the minority groups is the greatest contributor to the difference between the two sets of findings.

The results of the preference test give more cause for concern and suggest that the minority group children have little doubt as to who has the favoured place in the social pecking order. Altogether, some 45 per cent of the West Indians and Asians indicated that they would rather be white. Despite variations in geographical location and the different proportions of Asian or West Indian children concentrated in the schools, there is a considerable degree of within-group consistency in the results from both the identification and preference tests. There are, as has been noted, a few statistically significant exceptions to the general pattern, but these appear to be the product of particular interactions between sex, ethnicity and locale.

Louden (1978b) and Young and Bagley (1979), both working with self-esteem measures, have reported that West Indian children rated themselves more highly in schools and classes where there was a high proportion of minority group children. Louden, however, found the relationship to be curvilinear. It was the West Indian adolescents in schools with a medium concentration (between 30 and 50 per cent) of black pupils who had the highest levels of self-esteem. On the other hand, in Milner's (1973) investigation which was based on the social comparison approach, no significant differences emerged between schools with different concentrations of Asian and West Indian children. Similarly, Hartman and Husband (1974) in seeking to ascertain the attitudes of white adolescents towards the racial situation in Britain, systematically sampled schools with different concentrations of black children in areas of high and low immigrant settlement. Although there were some differences in how individuals felt about immigrants which could be accounted for by specific local experiences, there was a consensus across the areas regarding the general situation: 'immigrants' were a 'problem'; 'too many were coming in', and 'there would be trouble'.

These attitudes accord with those obtained from the parents of the children in the present study (see Chapter 11). Irrespective of ethnicity and the proportions of white or black in the particular area, the parents were pessimistic about the state of community relations in Britain, despite the fact that many of them reported the situation in their own neighbourhood to be satisfactory. They whites felt the fault lay with the immigrant groups, but the West Indians and Asians attributed the cause of the poor relationships to the attitudes and behaviour of the host community.

Given the range of geographical locations and the differing degrees of minority group representation collectively sampled by Milner, Hartman and Husband, and the present investigation, the consistency between the three studies suggests that the proportional representation of a group in a school or neighbourhood is not the primary determinant of an individual's attitude to his or her social group. Although specific local features can enhance or depress the quality of life for an individual, it is society's categorizing system, as transmitted by the statements and reactions of others, which determines in what manner his group membership defines his place in society.

Certainly many of the children's remarks, when explaining their choices, displayed both ethnocentrism and a lively awareness of the disadvantages of belonging to a group which was stigmatized by its pigmentation. For example:

'I don't like those ones. I don't like their skin'

(White boy, 9 years, choosing white photograph)
'Because she's white . . . and black people are nice sometimes but not all the time'
(White girl, 10 years, choosing white photograph)
'I like dark people, but I wouldn't like to be one'
(White boy, 9 years, in 'no contact' school choosing white photograph)

Conversely, the minority group children plainly perceived the advantages which accrue to membership of the dominant group.

'Because he's big and strong. No one would start anything with him!'
(Asian boy, 9 years, choosing white photograph)
'I like him. I think he is better than those two'
(Asian boy, 8 years, choosing white photograph)
'Then my face would be beautiful'
(West Indian girl, 8 years, choosing white photograph)

It therefore seems probable that it is the experience of being black in Britain, rather than black in Brixton or black in Bognor Regis, that is the critical factor behind the children's choices.

Since the modal response pattern for the sample as a whole is for the identification and preference choices to be in agreement with each other, the relatively high frequency of a discrepancy between the two responses amongst minority group children requires explanation. Two types of discrepancy are possible; first, other-group identification and own-group preference, secondly, own-group identification and other-group preference.

The first was favoured predominantly by white girls whose remarks suggest that they made a physical, or cosmetic match on the identification item but responded to the preference questions in ethnic terms. Remarks such as: 'She's got dark hair like mine', 'She has a fringe like mine' or 'I have a skirt like hers' were common amongst the white girls. Clothing, of course, was not a distinguishing feature as all the girls wore identical clothes, but perhaps some of the girls thought other group girls looked more attractive in the clothes. 'She looks nice and smart . . . her Mum looks after her' said one white girl. Obviously, since attractiveness may co-vary with ethnicity, and given that parents, literature, advertising and the mass media all encourage a female preoccupation with an appealing physical appearance, it seems plausible that this discrepancy could be due to differences in the socialization process of the two genders.

The second alternative, own-group identification and other group preference, accounts for only 9 per cent of the white children's responses but 42 per cent of the West Indian responses and 37 per cent of Asian responses. Fox and Jordan (1973), considered this particular response pattern to be indicative of self-rejection, but its relatively high frequency amongst minority group children in the present study, in conjunction with the magnitude of the own-group identification choices, suggests an alternative interpretation.

As inter-group attitudes in Britain become more intransigent, there is an increasing resistance within the minority communities to judging themselves by white values and adopting white goals. At the same time, pressure from minority group leaders in the mosques, in the churches, and in such self-help groups as Saturday schools, encourages the children to develop a pride in their own culture, which is manifest in the self-identification results. But self-pride and self-enhancement can only be achieved by comparison with the dominant group. This leads to a perception of the more favourable status of the white majority and the unequal competition for higher living standards and job opportunities, which in turn is reflected in the discrepancy between the results from the identification and preference tests. It is in this crevice between the heightened sense of personal worth and the sharpened perception of relative status that the seeds of intergroup hostility will germinate.

However, there is no indication from the sociometric data that a majority of children in any of the ethnic groups wishes to be entirely ethnocentric in their friendships. As one West Indian girl remarked pointing to the Asian girl's photograph: 'She's nice. She has a cute face and nice hair. I have three Indian friends.'

Contrary to the findings of Hraba and Grant (1970), there is a positive relationship between the preferences expressed in the photo-choice situation and desired friendship. The relationship is a weak one. It would be disturbing if it were not so. It seems likely, as Teplin (1977) suggests, that when children choose between photographs of unknown individuals the choices will reflect their ethnic stereotypes, since only visual cues are available. In contrast, when children choose from a known group, as in the sociometric test, their choice is not necessarily restricted by ethnic considerations since additional sources of information, relevant to potential friendship, are open to them. A close relationship between imaginary photo-choice and choice in a real-life situation would imply that the children's stereotypes were already so inflexible that the children were no longer amenable to the discovery of characteristics which conflicted with their own ethnic expectations.

On final comment needs to be made on the children's choices and that concerns the more pronounced out-group orientation, within the West Indian group, of the light-skinned children. The relationship between skin shade, other-group identification and preference has been noted by several investigators, for example, Clark and Clark (1947) and Fox and Jordan (1973) amongst black Americans, by Vaughan (1964) in New Zealand amongst Maori children and in Britain by Milner (1973) amongst West Indian children. Since lightness of complexion has been traditionally associated with social and economic advantage in the Caribbean Islands, especially in Jamaica, from where the majority of West Indian settlers in Britain came, skin shade is likely to be of particular significance for the West Indian children in our sample.

Researches carried out in Jamaica, cited by Young and Bagley (1979), show that fair-skinned adolescents express the greatest satisfaction with their physical characteristics and that the stereotyped beautiful girl or handsome boy has Caucasian features and is fair and clear in colour. Foner (1977), discussing the adaptation of young Jamaicans in Britain, observes that a white bias has permeated the entire Jamaican society since the eighteenth century, and suggests that it is mainly because being black stands for being poor in Jamaica that so many black Jamaicans place a negative value on a black skin.

It is therefore probable, as Milner (1973) speculates, that West Indian families settled in Britain, continue to transmit to their children the potential social advantages of a lighter skin and encourage them to think of themselves as more like the whites than they are like their dark skinned compatriots. Maybe, like many of Pryce's (1979) 'mainliners' – professional, middle-class, West Indian settlers – some of the parents would like to see their light-skinned children marry white.

Summary

Following the seminal work of the Clarks in America, evidence began to accumulate which indicates that, in a visibly multi-cultural society, ethnic group awareness is established by the age of four or five, self-identification 'errors' persist to a later age in black children than white, and that both white and black children are likely to reject representations of blacks (drawings, photographs or dolls) in favour of representations of whites. These, and similar observations, were interpreted as meaning that black children had a negative or ambivalent attitude to their ethnic identity.

During the 1960s reports of investigations in other cultural settings suggested that the apparent devaluation by some children of their ethnic group was not peculiar to American black–white relationships but was more likely to be related to the social norms governing the relative position of groups in a particular society. This interpretation is supported by both the negative results from cultural contexts where there is no obvious dominant group and the positive results from group interactions where there are no clear visible differences between the members of the groups.

In Britain studies of group identity and preference have been less extensive than in the United States and some of the work has been carried out on small or specialized samples. Nevertheless, the more broadly based studies convincingly demonstrated that children in Britain, as in America, had a good sense of the hierarchical order of the ethnic groupings in society.

There has also been a related series of investigations which have employed a different methodology focused on the self-esteem of minority group children. This approach has produced a diversity of findings, but in general the results indicate that the awareness and acceptance that one is a member of a low-status group is not incompatible with high self-esteem. Where a group's relative position is perceived to be so low that it can no longer contribute to those aspects of a person's social identity which are of value one solution might be to compare one's individual condition, not with that of the dominant group members, but with that of other in-group members.

Tajfel and Turner's theory, however, postulates that once group members who have an inadequate social identity become aware that the existing social reality is not the only possible one, and that alternatives to it are conceivable and perhaps attainable, they will begin to challenge the legitimacy of the dominant's group's position.

In America, the adult challenge to the traditional black–white relationship which gathered momentum in the 1960s, appeared to be reflected in the changed response of minority group children to tests of ethnic identification and preference. A similar change was evident in New Zealand.

In Britain it has long been obvious that minority groups are no longer willing to accept passively an underprivileged position and it seemed likely that a similar shift away from out-group identification would be manifest in the results of the present study.

Measures of ethnic identification, ethnic preference and sociometric choice were administered to a sample of white, West Indian and Asian children between the ages of 7 and 11 years. Overall, the results reveal that minority group children do not differ significantly from white children in the extent to which they identify with their own group, but their ethnic preferences demonstrated they perceived the advantages of being white: less than half of them preferred their own group. A positive but weak relationship was established between the children's ethnic preferences in the photo-choice situation and their desired friendship patterns.

8 Social Markers

It is obvious from the evidence presented in Chapters 4 and 7 that in visibly multi-ethnic societies, skin colour and other physiognomic characteristics will be amongst the most accessible criteria for constructing social categories. Almost any characteristic which is common to a collection of people is capable of being invested with social significance for this purpose and the potential range of cues, or social markers, is therefore enormous. Some are employed by minority groups to emphasize their distinctiveness, such as, for example, the maintenance of the purity of the Punjabi language by the Sikh community in Britain, while others are used by the dominant group as the stigmata of 'inferiority'. It is not unusual for the same marker to perform both functions simultaneously, or for a group to transform a supposedly negative criterial attribute into a positive one, as in the slogan: 'Black is beautiful'.

The significance particular personal attributes have as grouping criteria for children has been shown to vary both with age and the social context of their membership groups. Thus, for the children in the New York Bronx district interviewed by Hartley, Rosenbaum and Schwartz (1948), being a Jew or not a Jew was primarily a matter of doing something: 'going to Shul'; 'talking Jewish'; or 'going to a synagogue'. In Hawaii, Springer (1950) found that her sample of three to six-year-olds were influenced more by teeth, noses, mouths and the shape of eyes in their ethnic identifications than by skin colour. While in South Africa, Melamed (1968) has shown that skin colour is the most rapidly learned differentiator between groups, with the use of such subsidiary cues as hair type, lip shape and nose shape, varying as a function of the amount of contact between children of different ethnic groups. In Britain, Wilson (1981) has recently reported on a sample of children of mixed ethnic parentage, whose choice of grouping criteria included: skin colour, culture, place of origin, parentage and hair type. She suggests that these children attempt to form such complex categories because their own ambiguous position leads them to 'see the racial world in an unusually self-conscious, detailed and questioning way' (p. 40).

In order to make cross-group comparisons of the children's group identifications and preferences, we had presented them with photographs in which age, sex, dress and background had all been standardized. We now needed to answer two further questions. First, how would the children respond if they were given grouping tasks in which 'race' was only one of a number of possible grouping criteria? Secondly, would children in different ethnic groups and of different ages, demonstrate different orders of cue preference?

In seeking to discover how important ethnic characteristics were for children, we set them against the potential cues of dress, sex and age. That is, personal attributes which had been held constant in the preceding tests of group identification and preference were allowed to co-vary with ethnicity. We did this in two ways: first by a sorting task and secondly by a simple jigsaw puzzle technique.

Materials and procedure

The materials for the sorting task consisted of 16 monochrome photographs which varied along the following dimensions:

1. Sex   a. boy/man   b. girl/woman
   (photographs of Asian women wearing either Salwar Kamiz or a sari were used according to the predominant dress style of the local community.)
2. Age   a. child   b. adult
3. Dress   a. well-dressed   b. poorly-dressed
4. Race   a. Asian or West Indian   b. White
   (as appropriate to the subject)

As in the previous tests, the photographed children were identically dressed; the boys in jeans and sweaters, the girls in jumpers and skirts. They were first photographed with their clothes looking neat and clean, then photographed again with their clothes dishevelled and begrimed. The adult set of photographs had the same composition as the children's set, namely, 2 sexes, 2 races and 2 dress styles.

Each child was presented with a pack of 16 photographs, suitably shuffled, and two small wooden boxes and told: 'Half of these pictures belong in this box and the other half in that box. Can you put them in the boxes where they belong?' After each sort, half the cards, which had been classified by some criterion, were taken away and the child asked to divide the remaining cards between the two boxes. Since the photographs were equally divisible by race, age, sex and dress, the procedure was repeated three times to establish each child's rank order of the four cues.

In the puzzle test, the children were given sets of four photographs of children playing on a roundabout, which could be slotted together in pairs to make two complete pictures. After a demonstration and a learning trial with neutral material (a bus and a lorry and an elephant and a buffalo) the experimenter said: 'Here are some pictures of children. Look carefully at all the pictures. Choose the ones you want to go together to make two nice pictures'. Each set of two pairs could be fitted together in two ways to make a picture in which two halves of the roundabout were perfectly aligned, but on each trial one cue was always kept constant. For example, if the children in the four photographs were all well-dressed, then the child could either make a sex match, boys play with boys and girls play with girls, in which case there would be a race mix, or the child could make a race match and mix the sexes.

Altogether the children were presented with eight sets of four photographs. The last two sets in the series were designed to admit to either a straight sex match or a cross-race/cross-sex match. That is, a child could choose to put a white girl with a black girl, or a black girl with a white boy and vice versa. Since it was necessary to co-vary two cues on these trials it was not possible to determine which was the more salient and, therefore, the results were not used in calculating the final rank order of cues, although in the event most of the children made a straight sex match. However, to have denied the children the opportunity of making cross-race/cross-sex matches could have conveyed the impression that such combinations were in some way 'wrong'.

The sorting task results

The most outstanding feature of the results from the sorting task, as can be seen from Table 8.1, is the importance which the children accorded to ethnic characteristics as differentiating criteria in their sorting procedures. Of the four possible cues which they were offered for dividing the photographs into two groups of equal size, 'race' emerged at the top of the rank orders of all three ethnic groups. Conversely, 'dress' was the most consistently ignored cue. Less than a quarter of the children used 'dress' as the defining attribute for their first, second or third sortings.

The overall ranking of the cues, which is based on the frequency with which a cue was used in each of the four positions, conceals some interesting variations in the proportions of children who used the cues in a particular order (Table 8.2). Thus, 'race' occupies the first position for all three groups but, whereas 52 per cent of the West Indians used it first, 48 per cent of the Asians and 41 per cent of the white children did so. None of these differences are significant, but there are significant differences between the Asian children and the other two groups in the priority given to the 'sex' cue. Approximately a quarter of the white and West Indian children used it first, compared with only 7 per cent of the Asians. Yet, whereas 17 per cent of the white children ignored 'sex' as a possible cue, roughly a third of the West Indian and Asian children failed to use it. The overall effect was to push 'sex' into the third position for both these groups with a corresponding elevation of 'age' to second place.

Table 8.1: *Sorting task. Mean rank of each cue by the independent variables* (N = 512)

Independent variables			N	CUES Race	Sex	Age	Dress
	White		256	1	2	3	R
RACE	West Indian		128	1	3	2	R
	Asian		128	1	3	2	R
	White	Boys	128	1	2	3	R
		Girls	128	1	2	3	R
RACE	West Indian	Boys	64	1	3	2	R
AND		Girls	64	1	3	2	R
SEX	Asian	boys	64	1	3	2	R
		Girls	64	1	3	2	R
	White	Younger	128	2	1	3	R
		Older	128	1	3	2	R
RACE	West Indian	Younger	64	1	3	2	R
AND		Older	64	1	3	2	R
AGE	Asian	Younger	64	1	3	2	R
		Older	64	1	3	2	R
		High	128	1	2	3	R
	White	Low	128	2	1	3	R
		No Contact	32	3	1	2	R
RACE	West Indian	High	64	1	3	2	R
AND		Low	64	1	3	2	R
DENSITY	Asian	High	64	1	3	2	R
		Low	64	1	3	2	R
	White	North	128	2	1	3	R
		South	128	1	3	2	R
RACE	West Indian	North	64	1	2	2	R
AND		South	64	1	3	2	R
REGION	Asian	North	64	1	3	2	R
		South	64	1	3	2	R

'R' = The Residual Cue

Table 8.2 also shows that there were some variations within the main ethnic groupings in the relative priority given to the four cues. The rank orders for boys and girls, calculated separately within each group, do not deviate from the rank orders for their respective groups as a whole. Although, when the order of choices is broken down in this way, it can be seen that the boys' choices in each group contributed rather more than those of the girls to putting the 'race' cue into the first position.

The younger white children (seven and eight-year-olds) use 'race' for their first sort significantly less frequently than the white nine and ten-year-olds, but there is no corresponding difference between the younger and older West Indian and Asian children. This apparent earlier consciousness of ethnic characteristics as critical differentiators could be a concomitant of the different social implications which such characteristics have for white and minority group children.

Table 8.2: *Sorting task. Rank Frequency of each cue by race per cent* (N = 512)

CUES	Rank	Race		
		White	West Indian	Asian
RACE	1st	41.4	52.3	47.7
	2nd	16.4	13.3	9.3
	3rd	28.5	21.2	22.6
	Residual	13.7	13.3	20.3
	Total	100	100	100
SEX	1st	27.3	21.1	7.0
	2nd	35.6	24.2	35.2
	3rd	20.3	24.2	21.1
	Residual	16.8	30.4	36.7
	Total	100	100	100
AGE	1st	24.6	14.8	23.4
	2nd	31.6	39.8	22.7
	3rd	30.5	28.9	22.7
	Residual	13.3	16.4	31.3
	Total	100	100	100
DRESS	1st	2.7	6.2	4.7
	2nd	9.3	10.9	8.5
	3rd	11.4	12.5	7.0
	Residual	76.6	70.3	79.8
	Total	100	100	100
	N:	256	128	128

The concentration of minority children in a school appears to influence the prominence that ethnic attributes have as possible grouping criteria for the white children. In fact, the relative position of the 'race' cue corresponds to the proportionate size of the minority groups within the schools. That is, for white children in schools with a high concentration of minority children it ranks first; for those in schools where the concentration is low, it ranks second, and for the 'no contact' children it comes third. However, although there are overall differences in the relative position of the 'race' cue, the frequency with which it was chosen for the first sort does not differ significantly between the three groups.

Finally, there are some minor regional differences in the ordering of the cues. Overall, the white children in the north give less priority to the 'race' cue than those in the south, but again the difference in the frequency with which it is employed for the first sort does not reach statistical significance. There is, however, a significant difference between the proportions of white and West Indian children attending the northern schools, who used 'race' for their first division of the photographs; 40 per cent and 56 per cent respectively. The same West Indian children employed the 'sex' and 'age' cues with equal frequency, unlike the southern group of West Indians for whom the rank order of the cues is the same as for the West Indian group as a whole.

To summarize, the broad pattern which emerges from these results is for ethnic characteristics to be most frequently favoured as discriminative attributes; for 'dress' to be the least frequently favoured, with 'age' and 'sex' in between, alternating in second or third place.

The puzzle test results

The puzzle test was so arranged that each child could match the photographs by the same criterion on four out of the six sets. The most consistently used cue for all the ethnic groups was 'sex', with 'race' second and 'dress' coming a poor third. That is to say, in contrast to the sorting task where ethnic attributes were used as the primary differentiator, most of the children consider it more likely that girls would be playing with girls and boys with boys, rather than that children of the same ethnic origin would play together.

Table 8.3 gives the rank order of the cues derived from the total frequency with which each was used by a particular group as a matching criterion. It can be seen that the order 'sex', 'race' and 'dress' is remarkably unaffected by the gender or age of the children, the ethnic composition of the schools or their geographical locale. There are a number of minor differences, both within and between groups, in the pattern of usage, of which that of the 'no contact' children is probably the most interesting. Although their final rank order of cues does not differ from that of children in the multi-ethnic schools, the proportion of them who make a 'race' match on four trials out of six (34 per cent) is in significant contrast to the proportion of other white children (11 per cent) who match in this way.

The principal interest in the puzzle test results lies in their relationship with those from the sorting task. As we have seen, 'race' was the most favoured cue for the first division of the photographs but only some 14 per cent of those children who had used 'race' for their first sort went on to make the maximum possible use of the 'race' cue on the puzzle test. (Table 8.4) Approximately a third of these children matched by 'sex' on every possible occasion. Those children who had sorted by 'sex' first showed greater consistency across the two tests; over a half of them used 'sex' for four out of their six matches. Less than 6 per cent of them transferred to 'race' as their most preferred cue.

Table 8.3: *Puzzle test. Mean rank of each cue by the independent variables* (N = 512)

Independent variables				CUES		
			N	Race	Sex	Dress
RACE	White		256	2	1	3
	West Indian		128	2	1	3
	Asian		128	2	1	3
RACE AND SEX	White	Boys	128	2	1	3
		Girls	128	2	1	3
	West Indian	Boys	64	2	1	3
		Girls	64	2	1	3
	Asian	Boys	64	2	1	3
		Girls	64	2	1	3
RACE AND AGE	White	Younger	128	2	1	3
		Older	128	2	1	3
	West Indian	Younger	64	2	1	3
		Older	64	2	1	3
	Asian	Younger	64	2	1	3
		Older	64	2	1	3
RACE AND DENSITY	White	High	128	2	1	3
		Low	128	2	1	3
		No contact	32	2	1	3
	West Indian	High	64	2	1	3
		Low	64	2	1	3
	Asian	High	64	2	1	3
		Low	64	2	1	3
RACE AND REGION	White	North	128	2	1	3
		South	128	2	1	3
	West Indian	North	64	2	1	3
		South	64	2	1	3
	Asian	North	64	2	1	3
		South	64	2	1	3

There was no 'age' cue in the changed context of the play situation so it was of interest to see what the children who had sorted by 'age' first, would use as their criterion for matching play companions. The majority of the white and Asian children in this category predominantly used the 'sex' cue, while the West Indian children divided the choices more or less evenly between the 'race' and 'sex' cues.

Discussion

Although the results from both the sorting task and the puzzle test demonstrate the importance that children attach to ethnic characteristics when assigning people to social categories, they also show that the purpose for which they are choosing and grouping can change the relative values that different personal attributes have for them. When asked to sort and introduce some kind of order into a heterogeneous pack of photographs, differences in ethnic attributes appear to offer themselves as obvious and

Table 8.4: *Puzzle test. Score frequency of cues by race per cent* (N = 512)

CUES	Score	White	West Indian	Asian
			Race	
RACE	4	10.9	15.6	7.8
	3	19.9	19.5	21.1
	2	40.2	38.3	45.3
	1	18.3	14.8	21.1
	Nil	10.5	11.7	4.7
	Total	100	100	100
SEX	4	39.1	31.3	42.2
	3	16.8	17.2	17.2
	2	24.2	31.3	25.8
	1	14.8	11.7	11.7
	Nil	5.0	8.6	3.1
	Total	100	100	100
DRESS	4	6.6	10.9	1.6
	3	12.9	6.3	14.8
	2	22.3	26.6	21.1
	1	18.0	21.1	17.2
	Nil	40.2	35.2	45.3
	Total	100	100	100
	N:	256	128	128

readily available criteria for systematizing the collection – as indeed they might for ordering and simplifying their social environment. However, structure the task, make it more precise by giving a reason for sorting and sifting through the personal attributes of others and the attributes seen to be relevant to that task have a greater probability of being given priority.

Thus, when the children were asked to choose companions for a joint activity, playing on a roundabout in the park, what seemed most obvious to them was that boys would play with boys and girls would play with girls. The strong pull that single-sex groupings exert on children of this age has been extensively documented (see for example, Durojaiye 1969; Jelinek and Brittan 1975; Singleton and Asher 1979). In our own study of friendship patterns (Chapter 10), which involved some 4,000 children including those under discussion, we found that only 2 per cent of the 24,000 choices recorded were sexually mixed. In this context, the fact that the 'no contact' children used the 'race' cue on the puzzle test more frequently than the other white children, becomes particularly noteworthy. It would seem for these children, who had had no experience of playing with children from other ethnic groups, that the strangeness of cross-ethnic groupings often appeared greater than the strangeness of cross-sex groupings.

Taken together, the results from the two tests are consistent with those of other investigators who have pitted different factors against ethnic attributes in more restricted educational settings. Richardson and Green (1971), for example, found for their sample of white children in London schools that visible physical handicap was a greater deterrent to friendship than blackness. While in New York, Epstein, Krupat and Obudho (1976) demonstrated that cleanliness was a more salient dimension than race in determining the preferences of both black and white children. A sorting task given by Madge (1976) to a group of children in London infants' school, produced a cue rank order of race, sex and age, but in a stories test there was a marked tendency, particularly by the black children, to prefer the characters which had received adult approval, irrespective of skin colour. But perhaps the most encouraging of all the findings from this small group of studies are those of Durojaiye (1969) who reported that although ethnicity was a strong factor in the friendship choices of the children of a Manchester primary school, it became secondary to ability when the children chose leaders for various activities.

The critical feature of both our own results and those of these other investigators, is not that sex or cleanliness, or any other attribute *per se*, can be a more important determinant than ethnicity of children's preferences. Their usefulness lies in the demonstration that the context in which a choice is made, and the purpose for which it is made, can change the perceived relative value of personal attributes.

In the course of their school careers, children are repeatedly grouped, banded, streamed or classified for all sorts of reasons. Most of these arrangements are for the convenience of the educators and require no more of the children than that they should passively coexist for a time with those with whom they are grouped. But it is basic to the model by which Homans (1950) seeks to coordinate the phenomena of group activity, that when people come together to form a group their behaviour elaborates and complicates itself beyond that required by the original purposes of the group. He goes on to postulate that if the activities and goals of the group necessitate frequent interactions between the members, then, other things being equal, sentiments of liking will grow up between them, which will be expressed in further activities and interactions over and above those required for the continuation of the group.

While Homans freely admits that there are exceptions to his general proposition that frequent interaction leads to sentiments of liking, by and large his proposition accords with common experience. Friendship does not come about by willing it in a vacuum. For the most part, our friends are people we studied with, worked with or learnt to get along with in the course of some shared activity.

Given that purpose and context can change our evaluations of others, it should be possible for educators to devise cooperative learning situations in which mutual dependence becomes more important than ethnicity. Furthermore, by Homan's reasoning, it is at least conceivable that the interactions necessitated by the educational tasks will stimulate sentiments of liking which will be expressed in extra-classroom activities.

9 Liking and Disliking

The demonstration that children prefer their own social group to another, or that they attempt to reduce the complexity of their social environment to self-evident ethnic units, does not in itself constitute evidence of positive or negative attitudes. But since a critical part of our social identity consists of the knowledge that we belong to certain groups which are of significance and value to us (Tajfel, 1978), it is extremely probable that these comparison processes which are involved in segmenting the social environment will be associated with emotive ideas about our own and other groups.

The spontaneous remarks made by some of the children during the identification and preference tests clearly indicated that self-differentiation is frequently accompanied by negative evaluations about outgroups. For example: 'I wouldn't like to be black; I wouldn't like to live in their kind of country'. 'I don't like those ones; I don't like their skin'. 'Black people are nice sometimes, but not all the time'.

Our own experiences corroborate those of earlier investigators whose work we reviewed in Chapter 7. Shown a picture of a boy coloured brown, Goodman (1952) reports one of her children as exclaiming 'He's black, he's a stinky little boy'. Clark (1955) describes how a black girl, with a clear preference for white dolls, described the brown doll as 'ugly' and 'dirty'. Again, a white boy confidentially told Pushkin (1967) during his London study: 'If I have to sit near him (a black classmate), I'll have a nervous breakdown'.

The essential feature of an attitude is its affective or emotive core, that is, the feelings an individual has for or against a class of objects or persons. In an extensive series of cross-cultural investigations, Osgood, Suci and Tannenbaum (1957) asked people to rate objects or concepts on a series of bipolar scales, the ends of which were labelled by such adjectives as, good–bad, strong–weak, fast–slow. It is significant that it was invariably found that the primary connotation of an object or class of objects is an evaluative one. That is to say, a very large part of the meaning of a category, or its exemplars, will be determined by the position it is seen to have on a good–bad or pro–con continuum.

There seems to be little doubt that children learn the socially sanctioned value judgements which appertain to various groups in their societies, hand in hand with the assimilation of the visible cues by which individuals are categorized. Indeed, a study conducted by Tajfel and Jahoda (1966) suggests that, if anything, likes and dislikes develop before children have a very precise knowledge of the categories to which they apply. One of the tests in Tajfel and Jahoda's research consisted of presenting the children with 17 black plastic squares of different sizes. They were told that the square in the middle of the series represented the size of their own country and then asked to select squares which would represent the relative sizes of America, France, Germany and Russia. In another test their preferences for the same four countries were elicited by a series of paired comparisons.

One of the most important findings to emerge concerned the relationship between the development of preferences and the assimilation of factual information. At the age of six and seven, children in Britain agreed more that they preferred America and France to Germany and Russia than that both America and Russia were larger in size than both France and Germany. That is, the children had learned which countries were 'good' or 'bad' before they had learned practically anything else about them. Tajfel (1969) considers that there is no difference between learning the two kinds of 'fact', knowledge 'facts' or preference 'facts'. 'Good or bad' 'large or small' can be equally incontrovertible statements of fact for young children. He goes on to generalize his findings to the early development of negative evaluations of out-groups which exhibit the same simplicity in attaching preferences to rudimentary categories.

In the present study the children's feelings towards other groups relative to their own were assessed by three techniques which explicitly required them to make evaluative judgements. The first two, which we called paired comparisons and limited choices, were based on picture ratings and choice and were designed to provide an assessment of their attitudes towards a person. The third was a test of stereotypes and provided a measure of the emotional value of various statements which had as their referents members of the three ethnic groups.

Materials and procedure

For the paired comparisons each child was shown a pack of 12 photographs representing both sexes of the three ethnic groups, well dressed and poorly dressed. The photographs were presented in pairs in a predetermined order so that every photograph was compared with every other one. On the presentation of each pair the child was asked to say which one was liked best. In all 66 choices are made and a rank position between 1 and 12 was calculated for each photograph.

The limited choice technique required the child to share sweets between children photographed playing in the park. Since we had already established that the own-sex choice was paramount in play situations (Chapter 8) all the children in the photographs were of the same sex as the respondent. On each of three trials there were two sweets to be shared between four children from two different ethnic groups. The trials were arranged so that it was possible for a particular group to receive any number of sweets between none and four, but impossible for any one group to receive five or six sweets.

In the stereotypes test the children were shown four wooden posting boxes, three identified by photographs of adult couples from each of the three ethnic groups and the fourth boldly labelled 'Nobody'. Each child was asked to post 20 cards in the boxes on which were printed such statements as: 'These are clever people'; 'These people make trouble'. The administration of the test was so arranged that it was possible for a child to send the same negative or positive statement exclusively to one particular ethnic group, to a combination of groups, or to 'Nobody'.

The results from the three tests

On each of the three measures the majority of the children from all the ethnic groups showed a considerable degree of in-group bias, but this was more pronounced with the white children than in the other two groups.

All the children showed a significant tendency to prefer the photographs of members of their own ethnic group on the paired comparisons test. But whereas the white children assigned their own group photographs to the first four positions, both the West Indian and Asian children included a white child in one of top four positions (Table 9.1). The Asian children actually allocated the first place to the well-dressed white boy. Each minority group assigned the other's photographs to the last four positions, while the white children ranked all the West Indian photographs above those of the Asians.

Appropriately adjusted to ensure that comparisons were made between equal judgemental positions (for example, white judging black was compared with black judging white; boy judging girl was compared with girl judging boy, and so on) the rank orders of the three ethnic groups shows a significant degree of concordance. The only pairs of rank orders which did not prove to be significantly similar was the preferences of the white and Asian children. This, of course, does not mean that the Asians were not ethnocentric in their preferences, but simply that their pattern of liking and disliking was markedly different from that of the whites. Whereas the Asians include a white photograph in the top four ranks the whites allocated no other-group photographs to these positions. In addition, the whites ranked the West Indians next to themselves in order of preference but for the Asians the West Indians were the least preferred group.

Table 9.1: *Paired comparisons test. Rank order of each photograph (with cues) by race*

Cues				Race		
	Race	Dress	Sex	White	West Indian	Asian
PHOTOGRAPH	White	Well-dressed	Boy	1	5	1
			Girl	2	4	6
		Poorly-dressed	Boy	3	8	5
			Girl	4	6	8
	West Indian	Well-dressed	Boy	5	1	9
			Girl	6	3	10
		Poorly-dressed	Boy	7	7	11
			Girl	7	2	12
	Asian	Well-dressed	Boy	9	9	3
			Girl	10	10	2
		Poorly-dressed	Boy	11	11	7
			Girl	12	12	4
			N	256	128	128

Within each set of own-group photographs the well-dressed pair tend to be ranked higher than the poorly-dressed pair. The only exception to this was the high rank that the West Indians, particularly the girls, accorded to their poorly-dressed girl. Similarly, within each set of other-group photographs, the well-dressed are always preferred to the poorly-dressed. As we saw on the sorting and puzzle tests, dress was the least frequently chosen social marker. Nevertheless, it would seem that while one's own group members are to be preferred to those of another, if a choice has to be made between the children of another group then the well dressed are more likely to be favoured. But as far as the white children are concerned, a poorly-dressed white child is preferable to any member of another group no matter how they are dressed.

Despite a few minor variations, neither the sex or age of the children, the ethnic composition of the schools or their location in the north or south of the country, significantly changes the overall rank order for any of the three ethnic groups.

An examination of the differences in the frequencies with which the own-group photographs were chosen reveals that within each ethnic group the own-sex, well-dressed photograph was always the most favoured. Conversely, the other sex, poorly-dressed photograph was the least frequently chosen. This preference for the own-sex, well-dressed photograph is more in evidence with the white children than those in the other two groups; 84 per cent of them ranked it highest amongst their own-group photographs compared with 69 per cent of the Asian children and 68 per cent of the West Indians. In each ethnic group more boys than girls liked the own-sex, well-dressed photograph more than any other. The trend is not a strong one and fails to reach statistical significance. There is, however, a consistent and reliable trend within each ethnic group for girls to favour girls and for boys to favour boys in a well-dressed, poorly-dressed order; a gender bias which is corroborated by the sociometric study of friendship patterns (Chapter 10).

Turning now to the results of the limited choice test, in which the children were asked to share sweets between members of different ethnic groups, we find that the same patterns of in-group biases are in evidence. That is, all groups displayed a marked degree of ethnocentricity, but just as the white children were more exclusive in their preferences than the other two groups so they were in the distribution of their sweets.

The results yielded three broad groups of children; the 'ethnocentric', who gave at least three out of the four sweets to their own group, the 'fair-minded', who distributed two sweets to each of the three ethnic groups and the 'out-group preferers', who predominantly favoured another group at the expense of their own. On Table 9.2 these 'out-group preferers' have been categorized in two ways. 'Out-group A' is composed of those white children who favoured the West Indians, plus the minority children from both groups who favoured the whites. 'Out-group B' consists of white children who favoured Asians plus the minority group children who favoured each other's groups.

There were significantly more 'ethnocentric' children amongst the whites than either the West Indian or Asian groups. The two minority groups differed very little with respect to ethnocentricity. At the other end of the continuum, significantly fewer white children than minority children were out-group orientated. Those that were generous towards minority group children (15 per cent) were more or less even-handed between the two groups but there was a tendency for white boys to favour West Indian boys rather than Asian boys and for the white girls to favour the Asian girls.

There were significantly more 'fair-minded' children amongst the West Indians than in either of the other two groups. The Asians were only marginally more 'fair-minded' than the whites. Those West Indian

Table 9.2: *Limited choice test. Preference pattern by race and sex – per cent (N = 512)*

Race and sex of subjects

Preference pattern	White			West Indian			Asian			Total		
	Boy	Girl	All	Boy	Girl	All	Boy	Girl	All	Boy	Girl	All
'Ethnocentric'	60.2	59.4	59.8	50	32.8	41.4	43.8	35.9	39.8	53.5	46.9	50.2
'Fair-minded'	22.7	26.6	24.7	28.1	43.8	36	25	26.6	25.8	24.6	30.9	27.8
'Out-group A'	11.7	5.5	8.6	18.8	20.3	19.6	23.4	34.4	28.9	16.4	16.5	16.5
'Out-group B'	5.5	7.8	6.7	3.1	1.6	2.4	7.8	0	3.9	5.5	4.2	4.9
'Others'	0	0.8	0.4	0	1.6	0.8	0	3.1	1.6	0	1.6	0.8
Total	100	100	100	100	100	100	100	100	100	100	100	100
N	128	128	256	64	64	128	64	64	128	256	256	512

children who were out-group orientated significantly favoured the whites more than the Asians (20 per cent compared with just over 2 per cent). Similarly, the Asian 'out-group preferers' favoured the whites significantly more often than they favoured the West Indians (29 per cent compared with 4 per cent). This white-group preference was considerably more marked amongst the Asian girls than the boys. Indeed, the girls might be said to have an antipathy towards West Indians, since not a single Asian girl offered to share sweets with a West Indian girl.

Overall, there was a trend for boys to be more ethnocentric than girls and a corresponding trend for girls to be more 'fair-minded' than boys, but neither trend reaches statistical significance.

There was no significant increase in ethnocentricity with age, except for the Asian children who tend to become more 'ethnocentric' and less out-group orientated as they grow older.

The concentration of minority children in the schools does not affect the overall pattern of response for any of the ethnic groups. The proportion of 'no contact' children in the 'ethnocentric' category is a little greater than for the other two white groups, but not significantly so. There is a trend for children in the south to be more ethnocentric than those in the north, but this does not reach significance except for the West Indian group.

To summarize: there were more white children in the 'ethnocentric' category than minority group children but, regardless of ethnicity, boys tend to be more 'ethnocentric' than girls and girls more 'fair-minded' than boys. Both the West Indian and Asian children who are out-group orientated favoured the whites at the expense of each other.

The results from the stereotypes test complement those from the limited choice test. The in-group bias displayed by the white children in the distribution of sweets was matched by their readiness to assign favourable attributes exclusively to themselves. In contrast, the minority children described both the whites and their own groups in equally complimentary terms, but were reciprocally derogatory to each other.

As Green (1954) has pointed out, an attitude is a comprehensive concept which is abstracted from a large number of related and consistent responses which an individual makes with respect to a set of social stimuli. Therefore, in considering the children's assignments of the various belief statements with which they were presented, our interest lay primarily in the balance between their negative and positive assignments rather than in the allocation of any particular statement. The direction of each child's intergroup attitude was computed by taking the difference between the number of favourable statements and the number of unfavourable statements, which he or she allocated to each group, including dual assignments, and treating the 'nobody' and 'everybody' assignments as neutral. Thus, three 'net' attitudes, one for each group, were calculated for each child. The intergroup comparisons which follow are based on the frequency with which a particular negative or positive 'net' attitude occurs within a group. The descriptive tables 9.3, 9.4, 9.5 provide an exhaustive account of the children's assignments.

Table 9.3: *The stereotypes test. How the children used the traits: the white children* (percentages: N = 256)

Given to:	W	WI	As	Dual Assignments	All	Nobody	Total
Positive traits							
Work hard	48.8	13.7	8.6	2.4	19.5	7.0	100
Brave	24.6	30.9	16.4	1.2	10.5	16.4	100
Kind	36.7	18.0	19.1	1.6	21.9	2.7	100
Clever	40.2	22.3	11.7	3.2	18.4	4.3	100
Cheerful	25.8	21.9	32.4	1.2	13.7	5.1	100
Truthful	43.4	14.1	13.3	2.6	23.0	4.7	100
Clean	46.5	16.0	11.7	2.8	20.7	2.3	100
Quiet	37.1	14.1	29.7	0.8	14.1	4.3	100
Friendly	37.5	16.4	21.1	2.0	21.1	2.0	100
Positive average	37.8	18.6	18.2	1.9	18.1	5.4	100
Negative traits							
Lies	6.3	17.6	18.8	1.2	3.1	53.1	100
Stupid	3.9	12.1	19.5	0.4	2.3	61.7	100
Talkative	10.9	20.7	30.9	1.6	2.0	34.0	100
Lazy	11.7	10.9	24.2	0.4	2.0	50.8	100
Softies	5.5	14.5	26.6	0.4	1.6	51.6	100
Dirty	8.2	12.1	14.5	0	1.6	63.7	100
Noisy	12.1	25.4	22.7	1.2	1.6	37.1	100
'Better than'	16.4	23.4	20.3	0.8	1.6	37.5	100
Quarrelsome	24.6	19.9	18.4	1.2	2.7	33.2	100
Unkind	9.8	16.4	14.1	0.8	1.6	57.4	100
Make trouble	6.6	23.8	17.2	0.4	1.6	50.4	100
Negative average	10.5	17.9	20.6	0.8	2.0	48.2	100

(Figures may not sum to 100 due to rounding)

KEY:-	W	: to Whites
	WI	: to West Indians
	As	: to Asians
	Dual Assignments	: to Whites and West Indians
		: to Whites and Asians
		: to West Indians and Asians

The white children's attitudes were significantly more favourable to themselves than to the other two groups. Almost twice as many negative statements were allocated to the out-groups than to their own group. There is no significant difference in their negative attitudes towards the

West Indian and Asian groups, but if anything they appear to regard West Indians with marginally less disfavour than the Asians.

Table 9.4: *The stereotypes test. How the children used the traits: the West Indian children* (percentages: N = 128)

Given to:	W	WI	As	Dual Assignments	All	Nobody	Total
Positive traits							
Work hard	35.1	28.9	8.6	2.4	11.7	13.3	100
Brave	25.8	32.8	16.4	4.7	9.4	10.9	100
Kind	28.1	35.2	17.2	0.8	11.7	7.0	100
Clever	32.8	32.8	14.1	0	13.3	7.0	100
Cheerful	23.4	33.6	29.7	1.6	9.4	2.3	100
Truthful	32.0	32.0	10.9	3.1	14.1	7.8	100
Clean	34.4	34.4	6.3	0.8	17.2	7.0	100
Quiet	31.3	35.9	17.2	0	7.8	7.8	100
Friendly	25.8	38.3	12.5	0.8	16.4	6.3	100
Positive average	29.9	33.8	14.8	1.6	12.3	7.7	100
Negative traits							
Lies	8.6	8.6	26.6	0	3.9	52.3	100
Stupid	9.4	3.1	22.7	0	2.3	62.5	100
Talkative	12.5	13.3	42.2	0	3.1	28.9	100
Lazy	17.2	11.7	16.4	0	3.1	51.6	100
Softies	13.3	7.0	35.9	0	2.3	41.4	100
Dirty	8.6	5.5	25.0	0	0	60.9	100
Noisy	13.3	14.8	31.3	0.8	2.3	37.5	100
'Better than'	25.0	20.3	19.5	0	1.6	33.6	100
Quarrelsome	21.1	22.7	25.0	0	2.3	28.9	100
Unkind	10.9	8.6	24.2	0	0.8	55.5	100
Make trouble	16.4	10.2	25.0	0.8	0	47.7	100
Negative average	14.2	11.4	26.7	0.2	2.0	45.5	100

(Figures may not sum to 100 due to rounding)

KEY:- W : to Whites
WI : to West Indians
As : to Asians
Dual Assignments : to Whites and West Indians
: to Whites and Asians
: to West Indians and Asians

There is no significant difference in the balance of negative and positive statements which the West Indian children allocated to their own and the white group, although slightly fewer positive statements and correspondingly slightly more negative statements were allocated to the whites than to themselves. On the other hand, their attitude to the Asian group was decidedly negative. Less than half the number of positive statements and twice the number of negative statements which they allocated to them-

selves and the whites were assigned to the Asians. Very few dual assignments were made but where they were used they reinforced the negative
attitude towards the Asians.

The results for the Asian children provide a mirror image of those from
the West Indians. They have a significantly positive attitude towards the
whites and their own group and a strong negative attitude towards the
West Indians. More than twice the number of negative statements are
allocated to the West Indians than to themselves or to the whites and
correspondingly more than twice the number of positive statements are
assigned to the whites and their own group. Again, there are few dual
assignments, 23 in all, of which 18 were positive attributes seen to be
shared by Asians and whites alike.

There are no significant differences by sex in the general pattern of
assignments, both boys and girls within each group tend to respond in the
same fashion. There are, however, some interesting age differenes. While
the relationship between the allocations of negative and positive statements remains relatively constant for the older and younger Asian children, the older children (9 and 10) in the white and West Indian groups see
the out-groups as approximating more closely to themselves. In both cases,
the gap between the in-group and out-group image is narrowed, to some
extent, by the older children's more extensive use of the neutral 'All' and
'Nobody' categories.

An analysis by the ethnic composition of schools revealed no major
deviation from the general response pattern for each group except for the
white children attending schools in areas of high minority group settlement. Those in schools with a high proportion of West Indian children
were more favourable to West Indians than they were to Asians and those
that attended schools with a high proportion of Asian children were more
favourable to the Asian group. The children in the 'no contact' schools
responded in much the same way as the white group as a whole, that is,
they were more favourable to their own group than to either of the minority groups and made little distinction between Asians and West Indians in
their distribution of the negative and positive statements.

There were a number of minor within-group differences between north
and south but they are not readily interpretable. For example, the northern white children were more favourable to West Indians than Asians
while the reverse tendency was evident in the south.

When the positive and negative statements are ranked by frequency of
assignment it is possible to compare the way in which each group sees itself
with the way in which others see it. There are, of course, a number of
problems in trying to infer the children's views of their own and other
groups from the intrinsic meaning of the attributes contained in the statements. The statements were not generated by the children but by the
researchers. Nevertheless, the wide variation in the way in which the

statements were used suggests that the children did not treat them simply as negative and positive missives but took account of their semantic content. It must also be borne in mind that the frequency with which a statement is used can vary considerably for the same position in the rank orders of different groups. Within these limitations, however, a number of generalizations are possible.

As regards the favourable attributes there is a significant concordance between the self-perception of the white and Asian groups and their image in the eyes of others. Both the white children and the Asians describe white people as 'hard-working' 'clean' and 'truthful'; the West Indian children see them as 'hard-working', 'clean' and 'clever'. The Asian group is described by both themselves and the West Indians as being 'cheerful' 'quiet' and 'kind'; the whites consider Asian people to be 'cheerful' 'quiet' and 'friendly'. Neither of the other two groups, however, agree with the West Indians' conception of themselves. The West Indians see themselves as 'friendly' 'quiet' and 'kind'; the whites describe them as 'brave' 'clever' and 'cheerful', and the Asians as 'cheerful' 'brave' and 'clever'.

There is less intergroup agreement as to each group's most conspicuous negative attributes, although both the West Indians and the Asians agree with the whites' negative assessment of themselves as 'arrogant' and 'quarrelsome'. There is no general agreement regarding the unfavourable attributes of the West Indian and Asian groups but, in both cases, the own-group assessment and that of the whites are positively correlated. That is, the whites agree with the West Indians that their primary faults are that they are 'noisy' and 'arrogant' and with the Asians that they are 'softies' and 'talk too much'.

In so far that it could be said that there was a shared stereotype for each group it would be that the whites are 'hard-working' but 'arrogant', the West Indians 'brave' but 'noisy' and the Asians 'cheerful' but 'talkative'.

On the whole, the children seemed more willing to approve than disapprove, albeit that, on balance, the majority of them considered their own groups to be most worthy of approbation. On average, across the three groups, whereas 94 per cent of the positive statements were allocated to one or more groups and 6 per cent deposited in the 'Nobody' box, only 54 per cent of the negative statements were exclusively or jointly allocated and 46 per cent of them were assigned to the 'Nobody' box. To what extent this is the result of parental influence and admonitions it is difficult to say, but certainly the great majority of the parents we interviewed (Chapter 11) expressed strong disapproval of racially insulting behaviour and declared that they would unhesitatingly reprove their children if they became aware of it.

There was also a small group of children, some 10 per cent of the sample, who consistently allocated the favourable statements to all the ethnic groups while assigning all the negative attributes to 'Nobody'. This group of 'non-stereotypers' splits more or less evenly by sex and ethnicity but contains more than four times as many children from the upper age groups as from the lower age groups. This, coupled with the general tendency already noted, for the older children to perceive the ethnic groups as being more like each other than do the younger children, suggests that this mode of responding represents a deliberate evasion of stereotyping. On the other hand, it may have been a reluctance to lay bare one's biases for an investigator, since this group of children were no more likely than other children to respond in what has been described as a 'fair-minded' manner on the limited choice test.

Table 9.5: *The stereotypes test. How the children used the traits: the Asian children* (percentages: N = 128)

Given to:	W	WI	As	Dual Assignments	All	Nobody	Total
Positive traits							
Work hard	44.5	13.3	18.8	0.8	11.7	10.9	100
Brave	26.6	23.4	29.7	1.6	11.7	7.0	100
Kind	28.1	10.2	40.6	3.9	15.6	1.6	100
Clever	32.0	17.2	21.9	5.5	14.8	8.6	100
Cheerful	18.8	22.7	44.5	0	11.7	2.3	100
Truthful	36.7	9.4	29.7	1.6	17.2	5.5	100
Clean	45.3	9.4	21.9	2.4	17.2	3.9	100
Quiet	24.2	10.9	44.5	0.8	11.7	7.8	100
Friendly	36.7	7.0	27.3	3.9	22.7	2.3	100
Positive average	32.6	13.7	31.0	2.2	14.9	5.6	100
Negative traits							
Lies	6.3	34.4	7.8	0.8	0.8	50.0	100
Stupid	6.3	25.8	4.7	0	1.6	61.7	100
Talkative	12.5	32.0	23.4	0	5.5	26.6	100
Lazy	10.9	25.0	13.3	0	0.8	50.0	100
Softies	11.7	18.8	25.0	0	3.1	41.4	100
Dirty	7.0	26.6	4.7	0	0.8	60.9	100
Noisy	10.2	32.8	11.7	0	2.3	43.0	100
'Better than'	21.1	27.3	10.2	1.6	3.1	36.7	100
Quarrelsome	13.3	25.8	15.6	0.8	3.1	41.4	100
Unkind	14.8	31.3	7.0	0	2.3	44.5	100
Make trouble	10.2	41.4	4.7	0	2.3	41.4	100
Negative average	11.3	29.2	11.6	0.3	2.3	45.2	100

(Figures may not sum to 100 due to rounding)

KEY:-	W	: to Whites
	WI	: to West Indians
	As	: to Asians
	Dual Assignments	: to Whites and West Indians
		: to Whites and Asians
		: to West Indians and Asians

In summary, the white children regard their own group with significantly more favour than either of the other two groups, but neither of the minority groups concurs with the whites' view that they can be described in more attractive terms than themselves. Both minority groups, however, believe that the whites are to be preferred to each other.

The interrelationship between the three tests

The use of three separate tests of ethnic attitudes allowed for the possibility that there could be some variation in the children's responses according to the measure used. Therefore, in order to eliminate test-specificity and to establish the degree of response consistency, a single measure of ethnocentrism was derived from the individual scores on the

Table 9.6: *Own race preference scale. Deviation about the mean for each racial group* (N = 512)

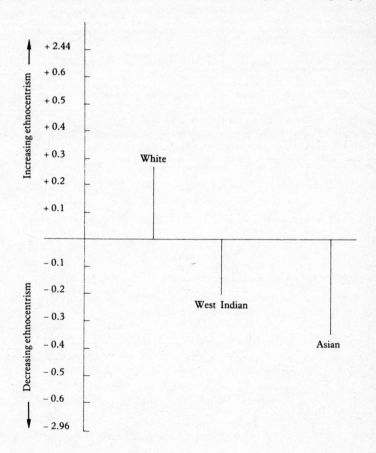

three tests by means of a principle components analysis. (Appendix III). This technique provided us with a standardized, intervally-scaled score for each child from which the Own-Race Preference Scale (ORPS) was constructed (Tables 9.6, 9.7).

Table 9.7: *Own race preference scale. Deviation about the mean by race and age* (N = 512)

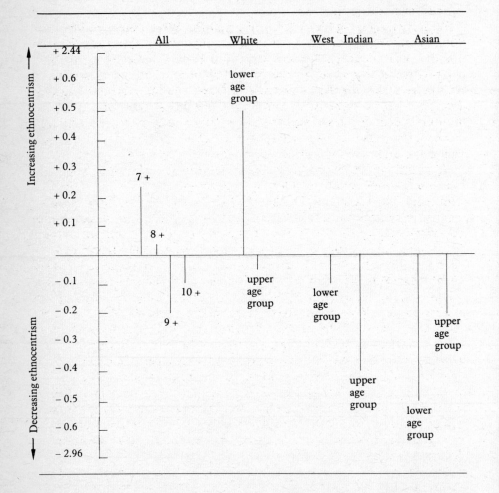

As would be predicted from their performance on the individual tests, Table 9.6 shows the white children to be markedly more ethnocentric than either of the minority groups. It also shows the Asian children as less ethnocentric than the West Indians. But while the difference between the white group and the minorities is significant, that between the minority groups is not and the evidence for greater ethnocentricity on the part of the West Indian children must be regarded as inconclusive.

The analysis also revealed a weak trend for girls to be less ethnocentric than boys, but none of the within-group comparisons reached the conventional level of significance. It is possible, therefore, that on the limited choice test, where the sex difference was most in evidence, that the 'fair-minded' girls were responding to some test-specific and non-ethnic cues.

With increasing age both the white and the West Indian children exhibit significantly less ethnocentrism but the reverse appears to be true for the Asian children. This is largely to be accounted for by the con trasting group responses to the limited choice and stereotypes tests. It will be recalled that the older Asian children showed a greater in-group bias than the younger Asian children in the distribution of the sweets. On the stereotypes test, both the older West Indian and white children appeared to take a more equitable view of other groups than the younger children in their respective groups.

The different concentrations of minority group children in the schools was not found to have any significant effect on the degree of ethnocentricity expressed by the children in any of the ethnic groups, nor did a contact/no contact comparison for the white children reveal a significant change in the level of ethnocentricity. The proportional representation of a group in a school is not a major determinant of children's ethnic attitudes. Their perception of other groups is more likely to be related to the history of discrimination in our society and to the assimilation of local norms which govern the relative status of groups in their area. It is possible that, in the present sample, there is a complex interaction between the effects of area norms and the effects of inter-group contact on the children's attitudes. The results from the stereotypes test indicate that of the two minority groups, white children in schools with a high concentration of minority children, rate more highly the group with which they are in daily contact. Nevertheless, although contact can bring about some reappraisal of a group's stereotypical image it is plainly not sufficient, in itself, to induce a desire for out-group friendship as our study of friendship patterns demonstrates (Chapter 10).

Finally, the Own Race Preference Scale indicates a weak trend for children living in the south to be more in-group biased than those in the north. For each group, the mean ethnocentricity score is higher for the southern children, but only for the white children does the difference reach statistical significance. These regional variations are difficult to interpret since they show no consistent pattern for the various groups and sub-groups over the three measures of affect, or on the other tests we have employed. The evidence for geographical differences has not been strong on any test and where they have occurred, it must be assumed that they are the product of interactions between local factors and other, possibly random, variables which have evaded the present analysis.

Nevertheless, despite these variations the relationship between the three ethnic groups on the Own Race Preference Scale is unambiguous. The white children are significantly more ethnocentric than the minority group children. They are more likely than the other children to make unfavourable comparisons between their own and other groups, more likely to be biased towards their own group in the distribution of sweets and more likely to see their own group as exclusively possessed of favourable attributes. Since, however, the younger children were more strongly in-group orientated than the older ones, the possibility exists that there will be some diminution of ethnocentricity with increasing age.

The West Indians are marginally more ethnocentric than the Asian children, but while the older West Indian children are less ethnocentric than the younger, the reverse is true of the Asian children. The most consistent feature of the response pattern of both minority groups is a tendency to favour the white group at the expense of each other. In making comparisons, each ranks the whites above the other, both are likely to be more generous to the whites in the distribution of sweets than they are to each other, and both entertain a more positive stereotypical image of the white group than they do of each other.

10 Patterns of Friendship

Many teachers believed, it appeared from their replies to Townsend and Brittan's (1973) questionnaire (see introductory chapter), that if young children were left to their own devices there would be no need to worry about how to promote good inter-ethnic relationships. Their observations, in their schools and classrooms, had convinced them (it seemed) that young children of different groups worked and played so happily together that 'it would be most unwise to put thoughts of racial differences into their heads'.

The assumption that young children do not notice skin colour nor take account of another's ethnicity when choosing friends and companions, is not, unfortunately, supported by the evidence from a number of investigations of inter-ethnic friendship patterns, carried out in different parts of the country. Rowley (1968) in a study of both primary and secondary school children in the West Midlands, found that across the age groups, 90 per cent of the white children chose their friends from within their own ethnic group, but smaller proportions of the West Indian and Asian children did so (75 per cent and 60 per cent respectively). The same trend towards ethnocentricity was observed by Kawwa (1968) in his investigation of friendship patterns in three London schools; a mixed junior school, a boys' secondary modern and a comprehensive school. Similarly, Durojaiye (1970), who studied the entire population of a Manchester junior school, reported a marked degree of in-group preference amongst both white and minority group children in all age groups, but only a small proportion of children in each class were of Asian or West Indian parentage.

One of the largest investigations in this field was carried out by Jelinek and Brittan (1975). Their national sample was drawn from 13 primary schools and 12 secondary schools where the proportion of ethnic minority pupils ranged from 18 to 84 per cent. In all, 1,288 primary school children and 3,012 secondary school children were questioned. The researchers found that even at the age of eight there was already a pronounced preference for friends of the same ethnic group and that the degree of in-group preference increased significantly with age, especially between the ages of 10 and 12- plus.

131

In short, there would seem to be a discrepancy between what these various investigations have revealed and the assumptions which many teachers make regarding the extent to which ethnicity functions as a criterion in the selection of friends. Perhaps teachers find it difficult to reconcile the research evidence with their experiences because their observations are only likely to be accurate at the extreme ends of the acceptance–rejection continuum: they spot the conspicuously isolated and the highly chosen, but not the children in between. Moreover, one cannot know by observation how children would like to associate.

In view of the low levels of intergroup friendship reported in the earlier studies, it was obviously important for us to ascertain how far the marked ethnocentricity, which the children demonstrated in other parts of our investigation, was manifest in their desired friendship patterns.

For this part of our study, the main sample of 512 children was augmented so as to include all the children in a sample child's class. The distribution of these children, by age and ethnic group, is set out in Table 10.1. Table 10.2 shows how they were distributed according to region and the overall concentration of a particular ethnic group within a school. For example, 363 children were seen in School 1, which is located in London and 50 per cent, or more, of the children on roll were of West Indian parentage.

Table 10.1: *The sample of pupils by age and ethnic group* (N = 3,953)

	Whites	West Indians	Asians	Total
7 Year olds	608	152	201	961
As % of Age Group	63	16	21	100
8 Year olds	600	184	181	965
As % of Age Group	62	19	19	100
9 Year olds	671	202	128	1001
As % of Age Group	67	20	13	100
10 Year olds	705	193	128	1026
As % of Age Group	69	19	12	100

While one researcher was teaching the class, each child was individually seen in a quiet corner of the room and asked:

Who are the two children you would most like to sit next to in this class?
Who are the two children you would most like to play with in the playground?

Table 10.2: *The sample of pupils by school, region and ethnic group composition* (N = 3,953)

School reference no.	Sample size	Ethnic composition	Density	Region
1	363			
2	181			South
3	182		High	North
4	383	White/		
5	232	West Indian		
6	96			South
7	360		Low	North
8	225			
9	136			
10	347			South
11	250		High	North
12	182	White/		
13	253	Asian		
14	310			South
15	163		Low	North
16	290			

Who are the two children in the school you would most like to invite home?

It can be seen that the questions change the social environment in which the desired interactions would occur, such that the possible influences or constraints on choice, move from the teacher and the classroom, through a comparatively free area, to the parents and the home.

In all, 3,953 children were questioned, yielding 23,718 pieces of information. Prior to the present study, with the notable exception of Jelinek and Brittan (1975), sociometric research on primary school children's inter-ethnic friendships has been confined to geographically restricted samples, sometimes from within a single school, and with only small numbers of minority group children.

The analysis of the results

Despite our declared intention not to burden the general reader with statistical and methodological technicalities, a short explanation on the way in which the children's choices have been analysed and presented will, we hope, make the results more readily comprehensible.

If one wishes to investigate the degree of attraction or cleavage which exists between ethnic groups located in different classes and schools, it is patently not sufficient simply to count the choices received by the individuals in one group and compare these to the number of choices received by individuals in another group. A measure is required which enables comparisons to be made between choice populations which vary both in size and ethnic composition.

It is also necessary that the measure takes account of the extent to which the observed pattern of preference deviates from the expected. For example, if a class consisted of 15 white children and 5 West Indian children, and the whites' choices split in the ratio of 3:1 in their own favour, it could not be argued objectively that the white choices indicated an in-group bias.

The Criswell Index of Self-Preference (Criswell, 1943) was chosen as a suitable measure as it allows for the variability in the size of groups, the number of choices made and the ethnic mix of the choice population. Basically, the index is the ratio of two ratios;

(i) The relative strength of the observed in-group and out-group choices and
(ii) the relative strength of the expected in-group and out-group choices on the basis of chance probabilities.

Thus:

$$\text{Observed ratio (O)} = \frac{\textit{Actual in-group choices}}{\text{Actual out-group choices}}$$

$$\text{Expected ratio (E)} = \frac{\textit{Expected in-group choices}}{\text{Expected out-group choices}}$$

$$\text{Criswell Index (CI)} = \text{O/E}$$

In Tables 10.3,10.4 and 10.5 an index greater than 1:0 indicates a tendency to select friends from the same ethnic group, a value less than 1:0 indicates that another ethnic group was favoured and a value of 1:0 indicates an absence of bias either way.

Since the children were asked to name two children with whom they would like to associate in various contexts, and given that an individual could not choose himself or herself, indices were only calculated when there were at least three members of a sub-group present. Where no meaningful index could be calculated this is shown by a dash in the appropriate column in Tables 10.3 and 10.4.

It will be seen that some of the indices relating to Question 1 (Tables 10.3 and 10.4) have values of zero or infinity. This is a peculiarity of the statistic, which is most likely to occur when sub-groups are small. If there are no in-group choices, then the numerator for the ratio calculation is zero so the index becomes zero. Conversely if there are no out-group choices the denominator is zero and the resulting index is infinity.

In the tables, those indices which would occur by chance less than 5 times in 100 are marked by an asterisk. (A note on the testing of Criswell Indices for statistical significance is included in Appendix III.) The size of an index required to reach statistical significance is directly related to the size of the choice population and its component sub-groups. Thus, within a school class, where the sub-groups can be very small or skewed, it is

Table 10.3: *Criswell indices (from question 1) for White/West Indian schools* (N = 2022)
(Question 1. Who are the *two* children you would most like to sit next to in this class?).

School ref. No:	1		2		3		4		5		6		7		8	
Ethnic group:	W	W.I.	W	W.I.	W	W.I.	W	W.I.	W.	W.I.	W.	W.I.	W.	W.I.	W	W.I.
7-Year Old Classes	–	1.2	1.3	1.4	4.3*	0	4.8*	4.3*	1.3	1.9	2.7*	0.3	1.5	2.7*	0.9	3.6*
	0	4.5*	1.1	3.6*	5.7*	5.6	4.7*	0	1.7	1.1			1.9*	5 *	2.6*	0
	1.3	1.1			4.7*	–	4 *	–					2.4*	0.7		
	1.5	3 *														
8-Year Old Classes	1.9	2.3*	0.7	2.7*	1.9*	4 *	2 *	0.2*	1.8*	2.2*	1.6	0.8	1	1.6	1.2	–
	–	–	2 *	1.1	1.8	0.5	7.7	41.2*	2.2*	3.8*	3.5*	3.5*	1	8.7*	1	–
	5.7*	5.7*	2.9*	5.6*	5 *	5.5*	6.5*	8.9*					1.5	1		
	–	2					9.5*	1.3								
9-Year Old Classes	8.4*	∝ *	1.2*	2.6*	2.7*	4.2*	2.4*	9 *	1.4	3.4*	2.4*	1	1.6	0.8	0.5	0
	2.9*	1	0.2*	4 *	4.5*	–	3.9*	2.4*	1	2.8*			2	1.2	1.5	11.5*
	–	3 *	1.6	3.6*	29.6*	0.2*	7	4.2*					1.4	2.1		
	4.8*	8 *					1.9*	7.7								
							7.3*	3.7								
							1.7*	8.3*								
10-Year Old Classes	2	1.1	0.7	1.6	1.2	1.5	1.7*	1.4	1.2	3.8*	2 *	1.3	1.1	2.7*	2.2*	3.8*
	9.2*	9 *	1	1.5	1.2	0.9	20.7*	0.6	1.1	5 *			1	2.5*	2	–
	–	2.1	1	1.9	1.2	2.1	2.8*	2.8*								
	2 *	2.6*					4.6*	2								
							22.5*	7.9								

* = Significant at the 5 per cent level

possible for one group to have a small index which is significant while another may have a larger index which fails to reach significance. On the other hand, in large samples with substantial sub-groups, as is the case where indices have been calculated for whole schools (Table 10.5), the magnitude of the indices provides a reliable guide to the relative extent of inter-ethnic cleavage. However, it must be borne in mind that, irrespective of population size, an increase or decrease between schools is not proportional: an index of four does not indicate twice as much in-group preference as an index of two.

In presenting the results, therefore, the following plan has been adopted. For Question 1, where a child's choice would be limited to a single classroom, Criswell Indices were first calculated on a class basis (Tables 10.3 and 10.4). For Questions 2 and 3, the potential context of choice is the school, and indices were calculated which take account of the relative proportions of the different ethnic groups in the entire school population (Table 10.5). Finally, in order to make comparisons between the three questions, indices for Question 1 were recalculated on a school basis (Table 10.5), and the non-parametric Sign Test was used (Siegel, 1956).

The results

None of the children was in a single-sex school and the children were free to choose from either sex, but only 1.8 per cent of the choices were sexually mixed. There were no significant differences between the three ethnic groups, nor were the figures appreciably affected by the geographical location of the schools. Question 2 produced the lowest number of inter-sex choices (1.4 per cent), and Question 3 the highest (2.3 per cent), with Question 1 falling between the two (1.7 per cent). The rate of desired inter-sex friendship is similar to that reported by Jelinek and Brittan (1975) for a comparable age group: in their sample it ranged from around 2 per cent in the primary schools to between 8 and 10 per cent at age 14.

It is immediately clear from the tables of Criswell Indices that there is a very low incidence of inter-ethnic choice. Of the 290 Indices calculated for Question 1, 170 (58.6 per cent) are significant and own-group orientated, while there are only 4 (1.4 per cent) significant other-group indices. In the following discussion the percentages and frequencies refer only to significant in-group indices.

On first inspection, the Asian children appear to be the most ethnocentric, since 64 per cent of their indices are in-group and significant, compared with 60 per cent of those for the whites and 52 per cent of those for the West Indian children. However, when the white sample is subdivided according to the minority group with which it is interacting, as had been done on Tables 10.3 and 10.4, a different picture emerges.

Table 10.4: *Criswell indices (from question 1) for White/Asian schools* (N = 1931)
(Question 1. Who are the *two* children you would most like to sit next to in this class?).

School ref. No.:	9		10		11		12		13		14		15		16	
Ethnic group:-	W	As.	W	As.	W	As.	W	As.	W	As.	W	As.	W	As.	W	As.
7-Year Old Classes	2.3*	1	2.8*	2.7*	14 *	∝ *	36.2*	∝ *	1.1	2.4*	4.1*	–	∝*	5.1*	1.8*	5.5*
			3.1*	0.8	9.6*	9 *	41.8*	2.2*	1.3	2.7*	5.5*	1			1.8	–
			9.9*	1.2	8.3*	5.5*					2.9*	2.4*				
8-Year Old Classes	6.8*	1.4	1.7	1.1	13 *	6.4*	42.9*	∝ *	1.8*	10 *	1.5	4.8*	4 *	0.9	1.8	1
			3.6*	2.5*	8.1*	1.1*	∝ *	∝ *	2.3*	0	8.2*	2.6			∝ *	–
			4.8*	2.1*	15 *	6.5*			1.8	1.8					∝ *	–
9-Year Old Classes	1	3.5*	4.8*	1.7	10 *	13.8*	20 *	30.8*	2	–	1.3	–	–	–	2	–
			9.1*	4.4*	∝ *	12.7*			3 *	–	2.1*	4.3*	8.2*	12.8*	1.2	0
			3.4*	0.9							0.9	2.3*			0.5*	0
10-Year Old Classes	5.8*	4.6*	3.9*	2.1*	∝ *	∝ *	∝ *	11 *	0.9	0	6.1*	–	–	–	3.3*	6 *
			2.8*	3.2*					2.4*	1.4	2	0	1.3	–	1	–
			3.5*	1.5					2.9*	4.6*	1.9	3.7*			∝ *	4.2*

* = Significant at the 5 per cent level

Whereas some 50 per cent white in-group indices are significant when they are in contact with West Indian children, the proportion increases to 71 per cent for whites interacting with Asian children.

Although there are variations by age, both within and between the ethnic groups, age has no consistent effect on the pattern of in-group friendship, either when the calculations are made across the ethnic groups, or when race–age interactions are taken into account.

On the other hand, the concentration of a particular minority group within a school has a uniform effect on the degree of ethnocentrism expressed by each ethnic group. In the schools where there is a low concentration of West Indian children (schools 5 to 8, Table 10.3) or Asian children (schools 13 to 16, Table 10.4), each ethnic group has fewer significant in-group indices than the corresponding group in the schools where the concentration of minority children is 50 per cent or more. The frequency for the white group, taken as a whole, almost doubles and for the Asians it increases from 56 per cent to 71 per cent. The trend is less marked for the West Indian children, but in the same direction, with an increase from 48 per cent to 54 per cent. In other words, when the white children are in the majority in a particular school, there is a tendency for them to be less ethnocentric, but when either of the minority groups is highly represented in a school they tend to be more ethnocentric.

Regional differences also show a consistent trend. Both groups of white children, those interacting with Asians and those interacting with West Indian children, make fewer in-group choices in London than in the north. The Asian children, too, exhibit this phenomenon. The location of the school, north or south, has no appreciable effect on the frequency of in-group choices made by the West Indian children.

The analysis of the school indices calculated on the responses to Questions 2 and 3 (Table 10.5) supports the main conclusions derived from the responses to Question 1. That is, white and Asian children mixing together in schools with a high concentration of Asians, especially in the north, display the greatest degree of ethnocentricity in their friendship patterns. However, although ethnocentricity is the norm throughout the sample, the application of the sign test to make comparisons between the three questions brought out some interesting and significant differences across the three projected situations.

The comparison of classroom choices with playground choices revealed few significant differences in the direction of bias, but the magnitude of the cleavage indicates that marginally more in-group preference is displayed in the playground by the two minority groups. In the northern schools, this directional trend is significant for both the West Indian and Asian children.

When the Question 1 choices were compared with those for Question 3, it would appear that children in all three groups are more reluctant to take

Table 10.5 *Criswell indices by school and ethnic group (all questions)* (N = 3,953)

School Ref. No.	Question 1			Question 2			Question 3		
	Whites	West Indians	Asians	Whites	West Indians	Asians	Whites	West Indians	Asians
1	3 *	2.3*		3 *	2.2*		3 *	3.8*	
2	1.1*	2.2*		1.1	2.1*		1.6*	2.9*	
3	2.8*	1.5*		3 *	1.9*		4.9*	2.1*	
4	3.8*	3.4*		3.2*	3.5*		4.6*	3.9*	
5	1.4*	2.6*		1.4*	3.1*		1.8*	2.9*	
6	2.4*	1.3		1.7*	1.6*		1.9*	1.2	
7	1.3*	1.9*		1.5*	2.3*		1.7*	2 *	
8	1.1	2.7*		1.3	2.2*		1.4*	3.6*	
9	2.7*		2 *	2.3*		1.9*	3.2*		3.1*
10	3.4*		1.7*	3.2*		1.6*	5.3*		2.2*
11	12.5*		8 *	8.6*		18 *	12.5*		16.8*
12	44.2*		14.9*	55.7*		22.6*	113.1*		45.8*
13	1.5*		2.4*	1.7*		2.6*	2.1*		3.3*
14	2.5*		2.8*	2.2*		2.6*	2.2*		4.1*
15	8.9*		6.1*	8.9*		10.7*	8.9*		6.8*
16	2 *		1.8*	2.2*		3.5*	2.4*		3.8*

Question 1:
Who are the *two* children you would
most like to sit next to in this class?

Question 2:
Who are the *two* children you would
most like to play with in the playground?

Question 3:
Who are the *two* children you would
most like to invite home?

* = Significant at the 5 per cent level.

home friends from a different ethnic background than they are to sit with them in class. This is largely unaffected by either the geographical location of the school or the concentration of a particular ethnic group within the school. All but two of the 17 comparisons made were statistically significant.

Furthermore, the trend towards a greater in-group bias when considering friends to take home is confirmed by the comparison of the responses to Questions 2 and 3. Overall, irrespective of ethnicity, the increase in own-group orientation is highly significant. In schools with a high concentration of minority group children, the comparisons for all groups reach significance. However, in schools where the concentration is low, the bias against taking home other-group friends persists, but the difference only reaches significance for the white children. Regional differences are negligible for all groups in these comparisons.

In summary, the responses to each of the three questions indicate very little desire for inter-ethnic friendship, but, where it exists, it is more likely to be evident in the context of school activities rather than those which centre on the home.

Discussion

The most outstanding feature of these results is, perhaps, the early age at which an awareness of ethnic differences begins to influence the choice of friends. Overall, 61 per cent of the indices calculated for the 7-year-olds indicate a significant own-group preference. The high level of own-group preference at 7, coupled with the limited age range investigated, may, to some extent, explain why no reliable age trend emerged. Jelinek and Brittan (1975) found a reliable increase in desired own-group friendship between their primary school sample (8-year-olds combined with 10-year-olds) and their secondary school children (12-year-olds combined with 14-year-olds) and a further significant increase between the 12-plus and 14-plus age groups. Unfortunately, they give no indication of whether the Criswell Indices themselves were tested for significance.

The age factor aside, the present results, like those of Jelinek and Brittan, leave little doubt that own-group friendship is strongly established at an early age in multi-ethnic primary schools. However, although all our results support this conclusion and all our comparisons are strictly confined to those indices which have less than 5 chances in a 100 of being in error, the case can be overstated. A Criswell Index is a summary statistic which can conceal individual differences. Not *all* the children in a group with an index greater than one will wish to be ethnically exclusive in their choice of friends.

It will be recalled that in Chapter 7 the choices of the main sample children who were in schools where there were high proportions of a particular minority group, were compared with their responses to the group-preference question. The scrutiny of the individual results revealed that only a third of these children wished to confine their friendships *exclusively* to members of their own ethnic group.

Clearly, some children do have other-group friends, but not as many of them as one would expect if ethnicity were not widely used as a social marker. The statistical result is that their out-group choices are rarely sufficient to pull the group index below one.

The effect of the size of the concentration of a particular group within a school also merits comment. The tables clearly show that two schools, 11 and 12, contribute disproportionately to the difference between high and low-density schools. Indeed, their indices reveal them to be the two most ethnically divided schools in the entire sample. The fact that both schools are in the north and both have a high proportion of Asian pupils suggests that there is a complex interaction between race, region and density. If we were to subtract the contribution of these two schools, the regional difference for Asians and for whites interacting with Asians, all but disappears as does the difference between Asians in high and low-density schools.

The very high degree of cleavage in these two schools was unexpected, but their similarities went beyond their geographical location and the concentration of Asian children. Both schools were designated as schools under stress, their intakes coming largely from economically depressed catchment areas; both had large classes and were struggling to cope with overcrowding; both favoured rather formal teaching styles. Furthermore, in the school with the more pronounced cleavage rating (School 12, Tables 10.4 and 10.5) there was little evidence, in terms of curriculum content, books, wall displays or assemblies, of any attempt to provide a multi-cultural education for the children. In contrast, however, School 11 seemed to be working very hard in this respect.

It would seem that a drive towards providing children with positive multi-cultural experiences can, to some extent, combat the effects of a school's social context and reduce ethnic cleavage. On the basis of the present investigation, this can be no more than speculation. Confirmation requires research specifically designed and directed towards the issue.

Differences in teaching styles, however, are unlikely to be the explanation of the greater in-group bias of white children in schools where the concentration of other-race children is high compared with schools where the concentration is low. This marked accentuation of own-group preference holds whether the high-density school is in the north or the south, and regardless of the ethnic group with which the white children are in contact. It might have been assumed that a high proportion of minority group children in the school would provide wider opportunities for the white children to form inter-ethnic friendships, but clearly contact *per se* is not enough.

All the schools with a high concentration of minority group children were situated in areas of high immigrant settlement, and it is possible that the reluctance of the white children to form inter-ethnic friendships is influenced by the area norms governing such relationships. This interpretation would be consistent with the findings of Hartman and Husband (1974) who reported that, although there was hostility to black children in their sample of 'high-density' schools, the hostility was more closely related to the level of immigration in the area as a whole rather than to localized concentrations of black people in the immediate environment and actual contact with them.

The present investigation did not include any direct measures of hostility, but some secondary evidence for believing that a similar process had taken place can be derived from the interviews we conducted with the parents, Chapter 11, and from the comparison of the responses to our three friendship questions. First, there was a trend, but not a significant one, for white parents in the areas of high immigrant settlement to express a more unfavourable attitude towards their neighbourhood than did those who lived in areas of low settlement. Moreover, those who lived in non-immigrant areas had a significantly more favourable view of their neighbourhood than either of the other two groups. Secondly, an examination of the children's responses shows that while only marginally more ethnocentricity is shown in the playground than the classroom, the increment in own-group choice between the playground and 'take home' questions is highly significant. For the white children, every comparison between these two sets of responses is significant. One way of summarizing these results would be to say that the greater the distance of the child from the teacher, the greater the influence of the area norms and the greater the own-group preference.

Despite some variations brought about by particular interactions between ethnicity, locale and the concentration of minority groups in some of the schools, there is a high degree of consistency in the level of ethnocentricity displayed by the majority of these children. The generality of the preference for own-group friends across the ethnic groups suggests that friendship is more determined by category membership than by personal characteristics.

Two critical facts can be extracted from this somewhat depressing survey of intergroup friendship amongst primary children. First, it is obvious that mere contact between white and minority group children will not automatically lead to good ethnic relationships. It may simply confirm the negative stereotypes that each group has of the other. The evidence reviewed by Amir (1969) indicates that positive outcomes are dependent upon such factors as the intimacy and pleasantness of the contact, the extent of the support by authority figures, the favourableness of the social context in which the contact takes place, the interaction between members of different groups in functionally important activities and the development of shared goals.

Secondly, these data show that by no means all the children wished to be entirely ethnically exclusive in their choice of friends. Furthermore, the fact that the children exhibited less in-group bias in the classroom than in the playground and out of school, suggests that teachers can be an important source of influence in the promotion of intergroup acceptance.

Taken together, these two facts imply that if educationalists wish to provide children with the values, knowledge and social skills for living in a multi-ethnic society, they need to make a thorough examination of the conditions propitious to such learning and to consider carefully the strategies they intend to adopt to promote inter-ethnic cooperation and friendship. This is an issue to which we will return in the final chapter.

11 The children's parents

Parents, or parent surrogates, are the primary agents of socialization and it is, therefore, commonly assumed that parents have a decisive and discernible effect on the development of their children's ethnic attitudes. Nevertheless, the effect a parent can have on a child's attitudes, once formal education has begun, can be overemphasized. For not only have the parental influences to contend with those of the school, the playground, the street, and what is learned through the various public media, but there comes a time for the child when the world is not as parents say it is but how the peer group says it is. It is not surprising, therefore, that many investigators have reported only a modest degree of agreement between parental beliefs and practices and the ethnocentrism of their children.

Broadly speaking, two principal directions of enquiry have been pursued. The first approach is derived from the work of Frenkel-Brunswick (1948) who reported that parents of highly ethnocentric children use rigid and harsh forms of discipline which frustrates the child and engenders a repressed resentment towards authority. The repressed resentment is later displaced from the original cause of the frustration, towards those outgroups which are perceived to be socially inferior and relatively unprotected. This view has led to the exploration of the general hypothesis, that parents who employ authoritarian child rearing practices are more likely to have ethnocentric children than parents who do not adopt such practices.

The second approach makes no reference to the inner dynamics of children, but seeks to discover the extent of the concordance between the ethnic attitudes of the parents and those of their children on the hypothesis that parental attitudes will be transmitted to the children by admonitions, prohibitions, precepts and practice.

The evidence for what might be called the scapegoat hypothesis is far from decisive. Harris, Gough and Martin (1950) by means of a questionnaire on the subject of 'child training' correlated the mothers' style of child rearing with incidence of ethnic bias in their children. They found a low, but positive, correlation between the ethnic prejudices of the children and maternal authoritarian attitudes, but no significant relationship between ethnic bias and maternal permissiveness. Lyle and Levitt (1955) also established a modest correlation between parents' punitiveness and their children's ethnocentrism. However, it is to be noted that Lyle and Levitt did not make a direct study of the parents' attitudes to child rearing but asked the children to report on their parents' punitiveness. Dickens and Hobart (1959) asked the mothers of 20 students showing high ethnocentrism on the Bogardus Social Distance Scale (Bogardus, 1933) and 20 students showing low ethnocentrism, to complete a questionnaire concerned with attitudes to child rearing. A significant association was established between parental dominance and ethnocentrism, but again, as the authors themselves point out, caution is necessary. The parental questionnaire did not assess the mothers' current views on child rearing, they were required to recall the way they felt when their child was of pre-school age. Thus, some 12 to 15 years had elapsed since the students had been pre-school children, so it is possible that forgetfulness and a change in attitudes influenced the strength of the association.

Mosher and Scodel (1960) also used a social distance scale and a parental child rearing questionnaire to study 400 children aged between 11 and 13 years old and their mothers. Their results lend no support to those of Dickens and Hobart, but modest support for the alternative hypothesis that attitudes to minority groups are learned by contact with the attitudes prevalent in their home. Their results demonstrated that, although there was a low but significant correlation between the children's ethnic attitudes and the ethnic attitudes of their mothers, there was no relationship between the children's ethnic attitudes and the mother's attitudes toward authoritarian child rearing practices. However, using a more complex experimental design, Epstein and Komorita (1966) found an interesting interaction effect between parental punitiveness and parental ethnocentrism. Their results indicate that high parental ethnocentrism associated with moderate punitiveness is most likely to lead to a similarity between the parent and the child's ethnocentric attitudes. The authors suggest that 'love-orientated' discipline, which lies midway between permissiveness and punitiveness, engenders a desire for parental approval but creates some doubt as to its attainment. The child seeks to reduce the doubt by internalizing parental attitudes and values. On the other hand, the avoiding tendencies and excessive autonomy, elicited respectively by high punitiveness and permissiveness, inhibit the process of identification.

The results from studies which have been primarily concerned with the transmission of ethnic attitudes from parent to child as a social learning process present an equally mixed picture. Allport and Kramer (1946) found that of the 437 undergraduates they questioned, 69 per cent of them thought they had been influenced by their parent's attitudes towards minority groups. There was a tendency for the more prejudiced students to report that they had taken over their parents' ethnic attitudes more or less unchanged.

However, investigators who have sought contemporary evidence, rather than retrospective evidence, of the transmission process, have failed to establish an association as strong as that reported by Allport and Kramer. Bird, Monachesi and Burdick (1952a) obtained a significant but weak correlation between parental and child attitudes but the parents resembled each other more than they did their children in attitudes toward black Americans. In a further study (1952b) they reported a stronger association between children and mothers who openly admitted that they discouraged inter-ethnic play activities.

In Britain, Pushkin (1967/1983) found no reliable relationship between children's ethnic attitudes and the child-control attitudes of the mothers in his sample, or between the ethnic attitudes of the mother and those of the child, except in cases of extreme hostility. Those children who were rated 'consistently unfavourable', on his various doll-choice tests, tended to have mothers who were rated 'very hostile' in their ethnic attitudes.

Hartman and Husband (1974) in the course of their study which examined the influence of the mass media on the beliefs and attitudes of white secondary school children and their parents regarding black people in Britain, constructed measures of hostility towards black people (the H scale) and of authoritarianism, which were administered to both parents and children. The correlation between the H scores of the parents and their children was very weak, but a strong association was found between the children's H scores and the attitudes they attributed to others, particularly their parents. It would seem that a degree of selective perception was operating, with the children's own attitudes persuading them to believe that their parents' attitudes were more like their own than they actually were. These findings provide a cautionary commentary on the results of those investigators who have relied only upon children's reports, sometimes retrospective reports, of their parents' attitudes.

The correlations between the measures of hostile attitudes and authoritarianism were even lower than those between the parents' and children's H scores. The authors, however, had established the existence of strong area norms of hostility towards black people, especially in areas of high immigrant settlement. The design of their investigation was such that they were able to estimate, in correlational terms, the influence of area norms on the development of hostile attitudes. The correlations between area and hostility were well above the authoritarianism–hostility correlations for both parents and children. The authors, therefore, felt justified in concluding that, 'area norms are far more important determinants of attitude to coloured people than authoritarianism' (p. 87).

In summary, it would appear that while there is some evidence of a resemblance between the ethnic attitudes of parents and their children via the determining effect of certain kinds of child rearing, a direct relationship has proved to be very difficult to establish. The low and variable

Table 11.1: *Family Background:* parental occupations, working hours, family structure and family size by race and density (per cent).

	Whites			West Indians		Asians	
	High	Low	No contact	High	Low	High	Low
Sub-sample totals	128	128	32	64	64	64	64
Not interviewed	0.8	3.9	nil	14.1	1.6	1.6	6.3
Father's occupation							
Non-manual	25.8	41.4	37.5	9.4	14.1	34.4	21.9
Skilled	29.7	18.0	25.0	17.2	25.0	17.2	17.2
Semi- or unskilled	28.1	25.8	31.3	43.8	48.4	37.5	51.6
Unemployed or dis-abled	3.9	3.1	6.3	3.1	1.6	7.8	3.1
No Father	11.7	7.8	nil	12.5	9.3	1.6	nil
Mother's occupation							
No occupation outside home	40.6	32.0	34.4	10.9	14.1	59.4	57.8
Non-manual	21.9	28.9	6.3	21.9	32.8	14.1	10.9
Manual	36.7	34.4	59.3	53.1	50.0	25.0	25.0
No Mother	nil	0.8	nil	nil	1.6	nil	nil
Time worked by mothers outside home							
None	40.6	32.0	34.4	10.9	14.1	59.4	57.8
Occasional	1.6	0.8	6.2	nil	nil	nil	nil
Part-time day	27.3	39.1	53.1	23.4	9.4	10.9	6.2
Part-time evening or night	7.0	6.2	3.1	9.4	10.9	nil	1.6
Full-time day	21.9	17.2	3.1	37.5	59.4	26.6	21.9
Full-time night	0.8	nil	nil	4.7	3.1	1.6	6.2
Family structure							
Two parents	87.5	87.5	100	73.4	87.5	96.8	100
Fathers only	nil	0.8	nil	nil	1.6	nil	nil
Mothers only	11.7	7.8	nil	12.5	9.3	1.6	nil
Family size							
One child	3.1	8.6	12.5	6.2	6.2	1.6	1.6
Two children	44.5	32.8	50.0	10.9	18.8	31.3	17.2
Three children	25.8	28.1	21.9	17.2	20.3	21.9	17.2
Four children	14.8	18.0	12.5	20.3	20.3	10.9	12.5
Five or more children	10.9	8.6	3.1	31.3	32.8	32.8	45.3

(For discussion see pp. 60–61)

correlations which have been reported point to the fact that the parental influence on children's attitudes to other social groups can only be one among many. Nevertheless, although the influence of parents may not be as decisive as some young adults believe it to have been, nor the undisputed force which perhaps some parents would like it to be, it is highly improbable that any child's ethnic attitudes will be wholly uninfluenced by parental beliefs and practices. It is to be expected, as Radke-Yarrow, Trager and Miller (1952) argued, that even in the absence of deliberate attempts to inculcate in children a particular point of view, that children's attitudes towards minority groups will be fashioned indirectly through the kind of social education in human relationships provided by parental example, and the beliefs and sentiments implicit in their reactions to various cultural differences.

In constructing an interview schedule for our children's parents it was therefore decided to select those topics on which their beliefs and opinions were likely to influence their children's perception and understanding of group differences.

The interview procedure

After careful piloting, an interview schedule of open-ended items was assembled which contrived to make the questions and their probes flow as normal conversation. As explained in Chapter 5, the parents had previously indicated their willingness to be interviewed. They had been introduced to the study as one concerned with children growing up in a multicultural society, but there were no direct questions on inter-ethnic issues until two-thirds of the way through the interview. The questions, however, were so framed that they could be answered in racialistic terms if racial issues were amongst the respondent's principal preoccupations. Primarily, we were interested in the parents' relationships with their children's school and their opinions on a multicultural curriculum; any restrictions that they imposed on the children's social relationships; their style of response to their children's questions about race and religion; how they would handle an incident of racial hostility between their own child and another; their opinion of their neighbourhood; their notions of an ideal neighbourhood and their views on inter-ethnic relationships in the country as a whole.

The interviews were conducted by experienced own-group (and for the Asian parents own-language) interviewers who were sensitive to the emotions which this area of research can arouse. Once the interviewing programme had begun in a particular neighbourhood the families were visited in rapid succession in order to minimize the possibility of a discussion of the questions between respondents.

In reporting our findings, the data are discussed according to the main issues which the interview schedule (Appendix II) was designed to elucidate and not necessarily in the order in which the questions were asked. In some cases more than one approach to the same topic was adopted. These approaches were sometimes separated in the interview by questions on a different topic, or by filler and linking questions, in order to ensure a smooth exchange between the interviewer and the respondent. The responses to every question are, therefore, not always represented by a sub-heading in the tables of results and the numerical results under a sub-heading can represent the computations derived from several questions. In

In each section the sample is discussed as a whole and according to the three main ethnic groupings. Sub-group data are discussed only when important differences were found.

Parents and schools

Like Rex and Tomlinson (1979) we found very little evidence to support the much-repeated assertion that parents of minority group children cannot be induced to take interest in their children's education. The majority of the parents in each of the three ethnic groups reported having frequent contact with their children's school (Table 11.2), although for many of them this meant going along when invited to parents' evenings, school plays, jumble sales or displays of work. Those who took an active orga-

Table 11.2: *The parents' opinions of their child's school: contact and opinions*: by race and density (per cent).

	Whites			West Indians		Asians	
	High	*Low*	*No contact*	*High*	*Low*	*High*	*Low*
Sub-sample totals	128	128	32	64	64	64	64
Not interviewed	0.8	3.9	nil	14.1	1.6	1.6	6.3
Contact							
Active	21.1	26.6	nil	3.1	7.8	1.6	nil
Less active	75.0	69.5	100	81.2	89.1	89.1	75.0
None	3.1	nil	nil	1.6	1.6	7.8	18.8
Opinion of school							
Approval:							
no race mention	57.8	82.0	90.6	81.2	85.9	82.8	90.6
positive race mention	1.6	nil	nil	nil	nil	nil	nil
negative race							
mention	13.3	2.3	nil	nil	nil	nil	nil
Disapproval:							
no race mention	17.2	9.4	9.4	1.6	7.8	15.6	3.1
negative race							
mention	9.4	2.3	nil	3.1	4.7	nil	nil
Opinion of multi-racial schools							
Approval	49.2	53.1	84.3	84.4	87.5	95.4	85.9
Non-committal	6.2	3.9	9.4	1.6	4.7	nil	7.8
Disapproval	43.8	39.1	6.2	nil	6.2	3.1	nil
Opinion of multi-religious schools							
Approval	35.9	41.4	68.8	65.6	46.8	68.7	67.1
Not concerned	47.7	39.1	21.8	9.4	18.8	3.1	9.3
Disapproval	10.1	14.0	6.2	7.8	26.5	26.6	17.2
Anti-religion in schools	5.4	1.5	3.1	3.1	6.2	nil	nil
Education on race and religion							
In favour	79.7	73.4	53.1	78.1	75.0	60.9	78.1
Non-committal	7.8	10.2	12.5	3.1	6.2	nil	9.4
Against	11.7	12.5	34.3	4.7	17.2	37.5	6.2

nizing part in school events or who were active members of Parent Teacher Associations were mainly in the white group. Only 5 per cent of the West Indian parents, and less than one per cent of the Asians did so. In fact, a quarter of the Asian parents in the north had never visited their children' schools, apart from the routine taking and collecting of children.

Since less than 2 per cent of the white, West Indian or Asian parents in the south fall into this category, it must be assumed that there are some constraining factors which are peculiar to the Asian parents in the north. One possibility could be family size. 61 per cent of Asian families in the north had five or more children compared with 17 per cent of Asian families in the south. But this cannot be the only inhibiting factor since, regardless of ethnicity, there is a consistent and significant inverse relationship between family size and school visiting. It will be recalled, however, that in Chapter 5 we noted that whereas some 70 per cent of Asian mothers in the south went out to work, less than 5 per cent of those in the north did so. The concurrence of a higher proportion of mothers who do not visit their children's schools, with the low incidence of work outside the home and the greater frequency of large families, suggests that they are facets of a more traditional family style than that of the Asian families in the southern portion of our sample.

More than 80 per cent of the parents in each ethnic group approved of their child's primary school, although the white parents in the areas of high minority group settlement were less enthusiastic than those in districts where the concentration was low. There was also a small percentage of white parents who qualified their approval with some reservation about the multi-ethnic character of the school.

> 'It's all right', said one southern white parent, 'The head and teachers are all right but it's packed out with coloureds. The head is very nice and has been very helpful.'

A northern white parent was more expansive on the same theme:

> 'I went there, and my father and grandfather. It's a good school but a lot of good teachers have left. They left because of Mr X. The only reason he got the headship was no one else would take it because of all the immigrants. He will push good children but he won't have a PTA. . . . He seems to be more for the immigrant children than for the whites.'

Apart from the parents who overtly objected to the multi-ethnic character of the school most of the complaints concerned discipline or a dislike of modern educational methods.

> 'I'm not very satisfied. There's too much play. I would like to see a bit more work and a bit more discipline. There's no corporal punishment here but a quick smack would help sometimes.' (White parent)

'I think it's a bit rough but it's nearby and convenient for me.' (White parent)
'The school could offer the children more. They could be stretched more.'
(West Indian parent)
'It could be better. I feel sorry that Solina is there, it's a bit rough.' (West Indian parent)
'Very poor. There is no homework for them. There's no teaching more than half a day.' (Asian parent)
'It's not good. Not as good as it could be.' (Asian parent)

These responses have been taken from parents with children in different primary schools but they must be balanced against the fact that the majority of the parents in all the ethnic groups approved of their child's school.

It is worth noting, however, that although the majority of Rex and Tomlinson's (1979) sample of parents in Handsworth, Birmingham, were also satisfied with their children's schooling, the small group of West Indian and Asian young people (aged 16–21) they questioned were less approving. About half of his group of 50 believed that their teachers had not been interested in their progress and had not pushed them to work enough.

Later in the interview we asked the parents to give their opinion about multi-racial and multi-religious schooling. The question was couched in very general terms: 'Some people think it is a good thing that children of different races should be in the same school. What do you think?' Followed by: 'How about different religions in the same school?'

Asian and West Indian parents were overwhelmingly in favour of children of different ethnic groups being educated in the same schools, but more than 40 per cent of white parents had various reservations about this and said they would prefer separate schools. There was no significant difference between the areas of high and low immigrant settlement, but the parents in the 'no contact' area responded very differently, only two of them were in favour of separate schools.

However, although some 40 per cent of the white parents with children in multi-ethnic schools said that, in general, they believed that different ethnicities should be educated separately, nearly 80 per cent of this same group of parents had expressed satisfaction with their child's school. There may be something of what Aronson (1972) has called 'the psychology of inevitability' about this seeming contradiction. That is to say, people tend to make the best of something they know is unavoidable. They try to convince themselves that things are not as bad as they had previously thought. An alternative interpretation, however, could be that many multi-ethnic schools are doing a better job than they are sometimes given credit for.

There was much less concern about children of different religions being educated together. The strongest objections came from the Asian parents in the north, where nearly half of them (compared with a single Asian in the south) favoured schools devoted to a particular form of religious teaching. In part, this was no doubt due to the fact that during the interviewing programme the question of separate schools for Muslim children had become a very contentious issue in the local Asian community.

It is clear that some parents differ in their enthusiasm for multi-racial and multi-religious schooling. Only a tiny percentage of parents, in each group, consistently disapproved of both multi-racial and multi-religious schooling (5 per cent whites, 2 per cent West Indian and 1 per cent Asian) but a more interesting picture emerges when we extract the consistent approvers. 32 per cent of the white parents, 60 per cent of the West Indian and 70 per cent of the Asian parents approved of both multi-racial and multi-religious teaching.

The figure for the whites is low because of their indifference to religious teaching and the relatively high percentage who felt strongly on the issue of ethnic separation. It is interesting to speculate, however, how much of the Asian parents' apparent confidence in multi-religious and multi-ethnic schools is due to the fact, as Rex and Tomlinson (1979) suggest, that society has learned to recognize separate Asian religions and the claim they have to be taught in school. 'By contrast the West Indian is thought to have no culture and as having no claim to have his culture taught in schools' (Rex and Tomlinson p. 171).

Parental aspirations

We also asked the parents what they would like their children to do when they left school. 54 per cent of the white parents (37 per cent in the 'no contact' area) compared with 22 per cent of the West Indians and 11 per cent of the Asian parents said they would leave the choice to their children. These proportions are in the inverse order to those obtained by Rex and Tomlinson (1979) when they asked a similar question in Handsworth. Of their sample of parents, 87 per cent of the Asians, 65 per cent of the West Indians and only 32 per cent of the whites said they would leave the decision to their sons. (Somewhat lower percentages were obtained for daughters but the rank order remained unchanged.) However, in contrasting these two sets of results it must be remembered that our parents were being asked to consider the futures of children still in the primary school whereas, Rex and Tomlinson's parents were asked for their job expectations of their *eldest* son or daughter. It is quite possible that if we were to return to our sample of parents when their children were near the end of their secondary school careers, that many more of those who now say that it is the child's choice would be more precise in their aspirations.

It would be a mistake to interpret the 'child's choice' response as indicating that these parents were indifferent or that they did not know what their children wanted to do. Many of the answers showed the parents knew quite well what their children wanted to do and, for the time being at least, were prepared to indulge them. For example,

Table 11.3: *Parental aspirations for their children:* by race and density (per cent).

	Whites			West Indians		Asians	
	High	Low	No contact	High	Low	High	Low
Sub-sample totals	128	128	32	64	64	64	64
Not interviewed	0.8	3.9	nil	14.1	1.6	1.6	6.3
Skilled manual work	7.9	7.0	12.5	1.6	9.4	6.3	3.1
Clerical work	6.3	2.5	6.3	1.6	6.3	3.1	1.6
Professional	14.8	18.8	34.4	21.9	37.3	40.6	48.4
Further/Higher Education	8.6	7.8	3.1	21.9	6.3	21.9	3.1
Child's choice	55.0	53.1	37.5	25.0	20.3	12.5	9.4
Get married	nil	nil	nil	nil	nil	4.7	12.5
Don't know	6.6	7.0	6.3	14.0	18.8	9.4	15.5

'What pleases them. I wouldn't want to push them into something they didn't want. Mark wants to be a dust-bin man!'
'It's their choice but I hope they can have a career. Michelle thinks she wants to be a nurse looking after little babies.'
'Simon wants to be a professional cricketer. I don't think he'll make it. It's a bit dangerous to have strong ideas about their careers at this stage, you might push them the wrong way.'
'There is a long way to go yet. She is set on dancing at the moment. I wouldn't plan for them, I'll let them follow their own course, they're developing all the time.'

The significantly lower frequency with which the 'child's choice' type of answer was given by parents in the minority groups suggests that their awareness of the uneven competition which their children will face for good jobs and social status prevents them, even at this early stage, from adopting a relaxed attitude towards their children's occupational hopes and aspirations. Many of those who concede a role for the child's opinion see the choice being made within a constricted range of occupations:

'Whatever he wants to become, a doctor, an engineer, or a lecturer.' (Asian parent)
'At the moment they both want to be firemen, but we want them to go to university so that they get a good chance of being a barrister or a doctor or a well-qualified teacher.' (West Indian parent)

Amongst those parents who had specific ideas about their children's future careers, very few of them mentioned skilled manual or clerical work. The majority of them, 25 per cent of the whites, 44 per cent of the West Indians and 57 per cent of the Asians wanted their children to go into some form of higher education or a profession. The fact that the proportion of minority parents specifying further education or a profession is about twice that for the whites cannot, of course, be taken to mean that the white parents were more realistic in their expectations, since significantly more of them said they would defer to their children's wishes. What the difference does suggest is that the minority parents feel a greater urgency than the whites to attempt to secure their children's future at an early age by orientating them towards high occupational achievement.

Attitude to children's friends

The opinions which parents express about their children's social relationships, and any restrictions they might attempt to put upon them, are likely to constitute an important influence on the way in which children perceive people and their attitudes towards other social groups. We therefore asked the parents a series of questions about their children's friends, both in school and out of school, and asked their opinion about the children in the neighbourhood in general. In evaluating the parents' responses it is important to bear in mind that all the questions were ethnically neutral. It was left to the parents, for example, as to whether they referred to a child's friend as say, Robert, or 'the little West Indian boy', and whether they described the children of the neighbourhood in terms of their ethnic groupings or by other characteristics.

The majority of parents had no difficulty in identifying their children's friends but whereas little more than a fifth of the whites and West Indians commented on the ethnicity of the friends some 73 per cent of the Asian parents did so. (Table 11.4) Such comments occurred less frequently where the children were in schools with a low concentration of minority children except in the case of the Asian parents. For this group there is a significant increase from 64 per cent in the high-density schools to 83 per cent in the low-density schools.

It will be recalled that when we examined the children's friendship patterns (Chapter 10) the children showed a greater ethnic exclusiveness in the friends they would choose to take home than they did in their choice of school friends. It could, perhaps, be expected therefore that fewer parents would comment on the ethnicity of their children's out-of-school friends. Overall, with the 'no contact' group excluded, this proved to be the case. The proportion drops from 33 per cent to 17 per cent between the two sets of responses. There was, however, very little difference between the two questions in the frequency with which the West Indian parents commented on the ethnicity of their children's friends, but the Asian percentage dropped sharply from 73 per cent to 24 per cent.

When we examined the nature of these unsolicited ethnic references elicited by these questions, we found that only a small and insignificant

Table 11.4: *The parents' attitudes to their child's friends:* by race and density (per cent).

	Whites			West Indians		Asians	
	High	Low	No contact	High	Low	High	Low
Sub-sample totals	128	128	32	64	64	64	64
Not interviewed	0.8	3.9	nil	14.1	1.6	1.6	6.3
School friends							
Known: race not mentioned	68.8	81.3	100	23.4	67.2	21.9	9.4
Known: race mentioned	25.8	12.5	nil	26.6	15.6	64.1	82.8
Not known	4.7	2.3	nil	35.9	15.6	12.5	1.6
Out of school friends							
Known: race not mentioned	70.3	69.5	84.4	28.1	42.2	62.5	32.8
Known: race mentioned	12.5	8.6	nil	31.2	18.8	17.2	31.2
Not known or sibs only	16.4	17.9	15.6	26.6	37.5	18.8	29.6
Opinion of neighbourhood children							
Approval: no race mention	48.4	43.8	68.8	60.9	64.1	62.5	45.3
Approval: race mention	9.4	5.5	nil	3.1	1.6	nil	nil
Non-committal	25.0	28.9	9.4	9.4	23.4	28.1	45.3
Disapproval: no race mention	12.5	12.5	21.8	12.5	6.2	6.2	nil
Disapproval: race mention	3.9	5.5	nil	nil	3.1	1.6	3.1
Action taken to influence choice of friends							
None: not applicable	66.4	60.1	87.5	57.8	73.4	82.8	73.4
Verbal discouragement	21.9	23.4	9.4	23.4	14.1	7.8	nil
Active prohibition	10.9	12.5	3.1	4.7	10.9	7.8	20.3

proportion of them could be classified as derogatory. But whereas the white and West Indian parents' references were mainly to 'other group' friends, a significantly greater proportion of the Asian references were to their own ethnic group. It was as if the white and West Indian parents wished to stress that their children mixed freely with other groups whereas the Asian parents wished to emphasize that their children played within their own ethnic group.

Some typical responses from the three groups of parents illustrate this difference in emphasis:

'He mixes with all kinds, colours and creeds. It's the united nations round here. There are 10 there now' (pointing to the garden where there was a miniature football pitch) 'a Maltese, a Jamaican, two Indian boys, one with plaits, and a Chinese. They're all football mad. It's home from home for them here.' (White parent)

'The friends come and go all the time. It's open house. She doesn't like Indians. I think she realizes the differences between the races and colours. To be honest, she may get it from me. We don't like them.' (White parent)

'They play with all nationalities. They get on with most children even with nationalities like Pakistanis. Their parents tend to put them off our children.' (West Indian parent)

'The neighbours children mostly, black and white. They're friendly and good

children. I don't like those who try to be too grown up.' (West Indian parent)
'Mostly Asians live round here so she has Indian and Pakistani friends.' (Asian parent)
'Mostly Asian boys. They are all Muslims and all well taught and good behaving types.' (Asian parent)

Most of the parents, in all three ethnic groups, took a favourable view of their children's friends but rather more were critical of the children in the neighbourhood and a substantial minority were non-committal or evasive on this topic.

Usually the objections concerned the children's behaviour; stealing, roughness, bad language and so on, but a few parents accompanied their objections with overt ethnic references:

'They are not very nice. Some are Irish and very dirty.' (West Indian parent)
'They're rough round here. They throw bricks at night at Indians.' (White parent)

The parents were also asked specifically if there were any children with whom they did not like their children to play and whether they did anything about it. The majority of them either said there was no one to whom they objected or considered it a matter of little importance.

'I've never objected to anyone who comes here but I don't like bad manners.'
'They must find their own friends. They are all welcomed here.'
'Some are a bit quarrelsome but it's usually when there is too many of them.'

The Asian parents, however, rather more frequently than those in the other two groups, denied the relevance of the question on the grounds that their children stayed at home and played with their siblings.

Of the parents who admitted that there were, or had been, friends to whom they objected, a few in each ethnic group did nothing about it: 'You can't really stop them', 'Friends come and go', 'Let it take its course'. Most of those who had taken any action had been content with verbal discouragement but the majority of the Asian objectors favoured some form of active intervention.

In summary, it would appear that most parents are aware of their children's friends, both in and out of school, and have a favourable attitude towards them. Parents tended to be more critical of the neighbourhood children than they were of their children's companions, but only a minority of them had made any attempt to control their children's social relationships. Asian parents, especially in areas of low immigrant settlement, displayed more consciousness than the other two groups of the ethnicity of their children's friends and showed themselves as more ready to intervene in those relationships of which they disapproved. This should not, however, be interpreted as inter-group antipathy, since there was no evidence of derogatory inter-group attitudes, but rather as a desire to keep their children attached to their own cultural and religious traditions.

Racial incidents

In order to assess how parents might respond to intergroup hostility involving their children, we presented them with three hypothetical incidents. The first posed the problem of a teacher faced with a child (of the same ethnic group as the respondent) who refused to sit next to a child of a different ethnicity. The parent was asked to suggest what action should be taken by the teacher. The second concerned verbally insulting behaviour directed at the parent's child, while the third asked them how they would react to their own child indulging in racial insults. We were concerned to learn how much support the parents were likely to give a teacher confronting discriminatory behaviour and how they might use the incidents to impart some understanding of intergroup relationships.

Table 11.5: *Parental handling of racial incidents:* by race and density (per cent).

	Whites			West Indians		Asians	
	High	*Low*	*No contact*	*High*	*Low*	*High*	*Low*
Sub-sample totals	128	128	32	64	64	64	64
Not interviewed	0.8	3.9	nil	14.1	1.6	1.6	6.3
The 'sitting together' incident							
No teacher action	57.8	52.3	37.5	20.3	28.1	21.5	7.8
Prompt teacher action	23.4	21.1	56.3	54.7	57.8	50.3	28.1
Consult parents	4.7	7.8	6.2	1.6	3.1	1.6	1.6
Teacher's discretion	13.3	14.8	nil	9.4	9.4	25.0	56.2
The receiving of insults							
Ignore	61.7	60.2	50.0	35.9	34.4	32.8	20.3
Retaliate	10.2	8.6	12.5	25.0	45.3	7.8	1.6
Explain and investigate	23.5	25.0	37.5	20.3	18.8	54.6	70.3
Don't know	3.9	2.3	nil	4.7	nil	3.1	1.6
The giving of insults							
Do nothing	7.0	4.7	nil	9.4	6.2	nil	1.6
Investigate	7.0	1.6	3.1	3.1	3.1	1.6	nil
Reprove	68.0	72.7	87.5	53.1	78.1	75.0	39.0
Punish	15.6	9.4	9.4	15.6	7.8	14.1	34.4
Deny	1.6	7.8	nil	4.7	3.1	7.8	18.8

On the first incident, the majority of the white parents, with children attending multi-ethnic schools, took the view that the teacher should not force the issue:

'It would depend on the reason. I wouldn't force them but I'd spend a lot of time trying to explain.'

'I would explain that they were the same except for colour. I'd try to persuade him but not force him.'

On this issue the parents in the 'no contact' area differed significantly from the rest of the white parents and responded in a similar way to the West Indians. The majority of these parents considered that the teacher should act promptly and decisively:

'I would try to explain we were equal if I were the teacher. I think I would have to insist if reason failed. It might spread to the other children.' (White parent)
'The teacher should make him understand, he shouldn't be like that. It would be giving strength to prejudice if she moves them.' (West Indian parent)
'The teacher should make him sit there or make him stand there if he won't sit.' (West Indian parent)

The Asian parents living in the areas of high settlement responded in a significantly different way from those living in areas of low settlement. Whereas the majority of the former group favoured prompt teacher action, the majority of the latter effectively side-stepped the issue by saying that it was a matter for the teacher's judgement. 'That is for the teacher to solve', 'The teacher should find a simple solution without fuss'.

The response pattern of the Asian parents in the north differed very little from those in the south and, taken as a whole, the Asian parents are more or less evenly divided between those who would leave the matter to the teacher's discretion and those who favoured an immediate resolution of the problem by the teacher.

When it came to the exchange of racial insults, the majority of the white parents would urge their children to ignore the behaviour but some 25 per cent would investigate what led up to the incident. Only one in ten of them said they would advocate any form of retaliation. Thus:

'Like I handle all problems of name calling – ignore it. I never encourage retaliation.'
'I'd ask him what he did first. If he hadn't done anything I'd leave it and see how it went. If there was more trouble I'd go to the school.'
'Find out what he called the black child. There must be a reason.'

On this issue the views of the 'no contact' parents were very similar to those of the other white parents, except that a rather greater proportion of them said they would investigate the incident in some way.

Fewer West Indian than white parents advocated ignoring the insulting behaviour and a much greater proportion of them (35 per cent) would advise their child to retaliate in some way. The parents who had children in schools where West Indian children were in the minority were more likely to adopt this view than those whose children attended schools with a high concentration of West Indian children. As one mother put it: 'To be truthful I always say don't start anything first but if they call you names, say something back'.

In contrast, less than 5 per cent of the Asian parents were likely to recommend retaliation. A substantial minority would advocate ignoring the behaviour but nearly two-thirds of them said they would, in some way, investigate the incident.

'When in this country, or whatever country, you've got to learn to live with dirty words. I'd advise my children to take no notice whatsoever.'

'I would forget it the first time but if it continued I would go to the parents.'

When asked how they would deal with racially insulting behaviour on the part of their own children the majority of parents in all three groups said they would reprove the child. Most of the parents thought they would be more upset if their child were the culprit rather than the victim, and some of them would have used the opportunity to help their children to a better understanding of human relationships.

'I'd be very cross. I would ask him if he knew what the words meant and reduce it to nonsense. Then I'd use it as an opportunity to explain race relations.' (White parent)
'Well, my eldest said he had a Sambo in his class. No prejudice – he plays with him. But I explained it is a term of disrespect and that he shouldn't do it. He admitted it right away. He understands now how it downgrades another boy.' (White parent)
'I would not like it, no, I would talk to them about it. I'd tell them that what's not good for the goose is not good for the gander.' (West Indian parent)
'I'd say stop that! and tell the other child to call him a name to see how he would like it.' (West Indian parent)
'We'd teach them it's wrong and make sure they don't repeat the nasty name.' (Asian parent)
'I would be cross. I teach them the correct manner on how to live with people.' (Asian parent)

Although the majority of parents would express disapproval, twice as many Asian parents (24 per cent) as in the other two groups said they would resort to some form of punishment, extra household chores or the stopping of pocket money, but three times as many of them than in the other two groups said they could not believe that their children would even do such a thing.

In summary, the white parents, with the exception of those living in the 'no contact' area, were more likely to advocate persuasion rather than insistence in a classroom confrontation. They would advise their children to ignore the offensive behaviour of others and would reprove them if they behaved in a similar way themselves. The West Indian parents are more likely than the whites to support firm, insistent teacher action. They were equally divided between those who would tell their children to ignore racial insults and those who would urge them to retaliate, but the majority of them would unhesitatingly reprove their children for similar behaviour. The Asian parents in the areas of high settlement expected firm action from teachers in dealing with classroom behaviour, but those in the areas of low settlement were less confident on the issue and suggest that it be left to the teachers' judgement. Very few of them would advocate that their child should reciprocate in the matter of insults, but the majority of them would investigate the incident. Most would reprimand their children for abusive behaviour towards other children and about a quarter of them would resort to some form of punishment.

Children's questions

If we consider the parents' reactions to the three hypothetical intergroup incidents there is little doubt that, overall, they are concerned to demonstrate to their children that they would not support discrimination. Nevertheless, children need more than occasional prohibitions and admonitions if they are to resist succumbing to the many intergroup prejudices which they encounter in their daily lives. Children need information and guidance in interpreting their experiences of intergroup relationships if they are to develop positive and accepting attitudes. We were, therefore, interested in what questions children asked about other groups, how their parents answered them and to what extent parents recognized they had a responsibility to help children understand the relationship between their own and other groups.

When we asked the parents what kinds of questions their children asked about other ethnic and religious groups we found that a surprisingly high proportion of them reported that their children never asked such questions. 50 per cent of the white parents with children in multi-ethnic schools, 38 per cent of the West Indian parents and 46 per cent of the Asian parents could recall no questions from the children about race or religion. However, considerably more children in the 'no contact' area were said to ask questions about other groups and significantly more Asian parents in the south than in the north (66 per cent compared with 34 per cent) reported dealing with such questions.

It seems improbable that so many children, especially in the areas of high immigrant settlement, have failed to seek information from their parents on group differences. Almost certainly a degree of selective recall was operating. Perhaps some parents only reported their children's most recent questions while others suppressed the questions which had challenged their adequacy as source of information.

Most of the questions from Asian children appear to be concerned with matters of religion:

Table 11.6: *Parental responses to their child's questioning about race:* by race and density (per cent).

	Whites			West Indians		Asians	
	High	Low	No contact	High	Low	High	Low
Sub-sample totals	128	128	32	64	64	64	64
Not interviewed	0.8	3.9	nil	14.1	1.6	1.6	6.3
Type of question							
None	51.6	49.2	34.3	43.8	32.8	48.4	43.8
Colour and race	14.1	18.8	46.9	12.5	17.2	4.7	14.1
Religion	21.9	15.6	9.4	4.7	23.4	37.5	35.9
Language	nil	nil	nil	nil	1.6	nil	nil
Clothes	1.6	2.3	3.1	1.6	nil	nil	nil
Behaviour	nil	1.6	3.1	nil	1.6	6.2	nil
Multiple question	7.0	7.8	nil	23.4	15.6	1.6	nil
Countries of origin	3.1	0.8	3.1	nil	6.2	nil	nil
Type of answer							
Egalitarian explanation	11.7	13.3	31.2	32.8	18.8	12.5	15.6
Realistic explanation	43.0	30.5	50.0	28.1	40.6	25.0	28.1
Refer to other authority	2.3	3.1	nil	1.6	nil	4.7	3.1
Explain as far as able	32.8	34.4	3.1	18.8	21.9	48.4	31.2
Children 'fobbed off'	4.7	7.8	15.6	4.7	17.2	6.2	14.1
Other group rejected	4.7	7.0	nil	nil	nil	1.6	1.6
Degree of parental responsibility							
Sole parental responsibility	47.7	51.6	65.6	15.6	57.8	43.8	53.1
Shared responsibility with School	30.5	31.2	18.8	64.1	35.9	46.8	23.4
Uncertain	21.1	13.3	15.6	6.2	4.7	7.9	17.2

'He asks about God and death.'
'She wants to know the difference between the Christian and Muslim religions.'

The questions of the white and West Indian children were more evenly divided between those concerned with religious differences and those concerned with differences of ethnicity but very little curiosity about differences in customs, language or countries of origin was reported.

The children's questions on ethnic differences were mainly requests for information on what they observe around them:

'Why are some people black and some people white?' (West Indian)
'Why is their hair so curly?' (White)
'Why do Paki girls wear trousers and why do some of the women cover themselves up?' (White)

A few of the questions from the 'no contact' children, who have only encountered black people via the media, or on occasional visits to relatives in other parts of the country, show a remarkable naivety:

> 'He once asked me, when we were travelling on the top deck of a bus in London, if there were a lot of coal mines near here and I had to tell him that it was the natural colour of their skins'.
> 'Steven saw a black boy in York and thought he had a dirty face. I had to explain about colour'.

Other questions go beyond visible differences and a few reflect the transmission of adult prejudices.

> 'He asks me why there are so many blacks here that they make trouble.' (White parent)
> 'They ask how you can tell the difference between an Indian and a Pakistani.' (West Indian parent)
> 'He's interested in the colour problem and wants to know why people of different colours can't get on together.' (Asian parent)

The children's conception of their own group and where it stands in relationship to others will inevitably be affected by the kinds of explanations they are offered for the group differences they observe and the extent to which these explanations carry with them implications of acceptance, rejection or superiority.

For the most part the parents' attempted an egalitarian or quasi-realistic style of response:

> 'About colour I say they come from a country with a lot of sun. I don't know how to answer why some are brown and some are black.' (White parent)
> 'I say they are just the same as us apart from a different coloured skin.' (White parent)
> 'I try to explain we have different ways of cooking and dressing and that we are all the same regardless of colour.' (West Indian parent)
> 'I tell them about Jamaica and why we came to Britain. The most important message I tell them is that in spite of differences in colour all people are equal and have the same rights.' (West Indian parent)
> 'We try to help him. He now knows that different races are different colours but that in a real sense they are all human beings and created by the same God.' (Asian parent)
> 'In my opinion, I say, all human beings are created by God but every religion and race has good things and bad things.' (Asian parent)

Very few of the parental responses could be said to imply a rejecting or disparaging attitude to other social groups but a small percentage of parents in each ethnic group admitted to protecting themselves with some such reply as 'Ask your teacher', 'Go and read a book', or with such obvious 'fob offs' as: 'You go to school, you know as much as I do about it'. About a third of the parents overall frankly admitted the inadequacy of their knowledge about group differences and relationships, but said they tried to answer their children's queries as far as they could.

Nevertheless, just under half of the parents accepted that they had a responsibility to provide some form of guidance in these matters for their children. In this respect, the parents in the 'no contact' area appeared to be more confident than the white parents with children in multi-ethnic schools; while amongst the minority parents, those in the areas of low settlement seemed more willing to undertake the task than those in the areas of high settlement. Some of the typical comments were:

> 'It's the parents' job. You can't leave everything to the schools.' (White parent)
> 'Schools can only teach the basic facts. It's up to the parents to show the day-to-day practice of religious ideas and how to treat people. It's a very responsible duty for parents.' (West Indian parent)
> 'Parents should give information about their own religion and customs and teachers about other things. They have more faith if they hear it from their own parents.' (Asian parent)

Many parents, however, felt insecure in the teaching role and half the West Indian parents and a third of the white and Asian parents expressed the hope that the schools would help:

> 'Schools should do it really. If Roddy asks I try, but what can I say?' (White parent)
> 'Parents must make an effort to get linked in with the school and vice versa. That would be good for the children.' (West Indian parent)
> 'Schools should help. My eldest daughter, she tells him, but we don't know very much ourselves.' (Asian parent)

Furthermore, in response to a question on the desirability of a multi-cultural curriculum (Table 11.2), some 73 per cent of the parents said they believed that schools should teach children about other races and religions. On this issue, there was no significant difference between the three groups of parents.

We may conclude, therefore, that the majority of parents recognized the importance of giving their children some guidance in the understanding of group differences. With very few exceptions, they see their task as one of developing accepting attitudes towards other social groups. The quality of the parents' explanations, however, indicates a profound lack of knowledge about cultural and ethnic differences and many of them are conscious of an inability to communicate with their children on these issues. Thus, while few parents would approve of discriminatory attitudes on the part of their children they are ill-equipped to use their children's questioning as opportunities for teaching intergroup understanding.

Neighbours and neighbourhoods

A series of questions were asked to assess how our sample of parents felt about their neighbours and the kind of district in which they lived. The questions were open-ended and bland. No reference was made to the social or ethnic composition of the neighbourhood, they were simply asked how they liked the area, what sort of people lived there and what it was like bringing up children in their neighbourhood. Our object was to see in what terms they discussed their neighbours and what they considered to be the most important features of their neighbourhood. At a later stage, towards the end of the interview, they were asked what kind of district they would look for if they had to move. (Ideal neighbourhood, Table 11.7.) Only at this point, if no mention was made of the ethnic composition of the district to which they would like to move, were they pressed to express their attitude towards living in a multi-ethnic area.

In general, the majority of parents in all three ethnic groups liked their neighbours and their neighbourhood but, with the exception of the parents of the 'no contact' children, more of them expressed objections to their neighbourhood than to their neighbours (Table 11.7).

Amongst the white parents with children in multi-ethnic schools, those living in areas of low minority group settlement were marginally more approving of their neighbours than those in high-density districts (54 per cent compared with 51 per cent) and their neighbourhood (55 per cent compared with 48 per cent). There was, however, no difference between the two types of area in the proportions of parents who objected to either their neighbours or their neighbourhood in ethnic terms. Taking the two questions, neighbours and neighbourhood, together there were as many approving ethnic references as there were disapproving (61 compared with 57). Examples of this mixed response were such remarks as:

> 'Lots of coloured people. The Indians are particularly charming. The Pakistanis are not so like us, so many in their families. The Irish are all right. I love it here. I'd only move for a bigger house.'
> 'It's going downhill. I blame it on the Indians. They have so many relations. I try not to but I get het up about it.'
> 'Working-class families mostly. Rather a lot of immigrants now, but those next door but one are smashing. They're all hard working people.'
> 'Very cosmopolitan. Asians, Irish, not so many West Indians.
> Immediate neighbours are Asian. Don't mix much, can't speak English and their children don't play out.'

As can be seen, references to the social class of neighbours were sometimes intermingled with ethnic references, but only 9 per cent of the white parents described their neighbours solely, or primarily, in terms of their social class.

West Indian parents, especially those living in areas of high West Indian

Table 11.7: *Parental attitudes to their neighbours and neighbourhood:* by race and density (per cent).

	Whites			West Indians		Asians	
	High	Low	No contact	High	Low	High	Low
Sub-sample totals	128	128	32	64	64	64	64
Not interviewed	0.8	3.9	nil	14.1	1.6	1.6	6.3
Attitude towards neighbours							
Approval: no race mention	21.9	38.3	56.2	17.2	18.8	12.5	10.9
Approval: race mention	28.9	15.6	nil	54.7	43.8	67.2	51.6
Disapproval: no race mention	10.2	3.9	25.0	nil	1.6	nil	nil
Disapproval: race mention	10.9	11.7	nil	4.7	12.5	6.2	6.2
Class mentioned	6.2	12.5	3.1	nil	10.9	3.1	12.5
Non-committal	21.1	14.1	15.6	9.4	10.9	9.4	12.5
Attitude towards neighbourhood							
Approval: no race mention	46.9	52.3	93.8	54.7	56.2	75.0	64.1
Approval: race mention	0.8	2.3	nil	nil	nil	3.1	nil
Disapproval: no race mention	33.6	22.7	3.1	20.3	14.1	6.2	3.1
Disapproval: race mention	10.2	11.7	nil	nil	1.6	3.1	nil
Non-committal	7.8	7.0	3.1	10.9	26.6	10.9	26.6
Bringing up children in the neighbourhood							
Approval: no race mention	45.3	49.2	75.0	37.5	50.0	78.1	59.4
Approval: race mention	1.6	1.6	nil	nil	nil	nil	nil
Disapproval: no race mention	29.7	24.2	25.0	23.4	26.6	6.2	6.2
Disapproval: race mention	9.4	10.9	nil	nil	nil	3.1	1.6
Non-committal	13.3	10.2	nil	25.0	21.9	10.9	26.6
Ideal neighbourhood							
Same as this	21.1	29.7	59.4	26.6	14.1	34.4	39.1
Improved amenities	67.2	53.1	37.5	54.7	60.9	39.1	40.6
Negative race mention	10.2	13.3	3.1	4.7	23.5	10.9	10.9
Positive race mention	0.8	nil	nil	nil	nil	14.1	3.1
Possible racial mix in ideal neighbourhood							
Refusal of mixed area	21.1	19.5	18.8	nil	4.7	nil	3.1
Acceptance:							
with reservations	18.8	21.1	28.1	nil	10.9	nil	nil
no reservations	49.2	43.0	40.6	84.4	68.8	96.8	89.0
Preference for mixed area	0.8	4.7	9.4	1.6	3.1	1.6	1.6
Evasive or resigned	9.4	7.8	3.1	nil	10.9	nil	nil

settlement, were more enthusiastic about their neighbours than the whites (72 per cent compared with 63 per cent in the low settlement areas) and fewer of those in the areas of high settlement objected to their neighbours in ethnic terms (5 per cent compared with 18 per cent). However, a slightly higher proportion of the parents in the high-density area expressed dissatisfaction with their neighbourhood (20 per cent compared with 15 per cent).

The Asian parents, more than any other group, seemed content with both their neighbours and neighbourhood. On both issues those who lived in areas with a high concentration of Asian families were more approving than those in low-density districts: 80 per cent compared with 63 per cent in the case of neighbours and 78 per cent compared with 64 per cent were pleased with their neighbourhood. A negligible number of Asian parents said they disliked either their neighbours or their neighbourhood, but 11 per cent of those in high-density districts and 27 per cent in low-density districts were non-committal in their response to the neighbourhood question.

The difference in the degree of satisfaction expressed by those parents in districts of high and low Asian settlement suggests that these parents were, not unnaturally, very conscious of the advantages of living in a community with a reasonably homogeneous cultural orientation.

This is supported by the large number of Asian parents (59 per cent) who accompanied their approval of their neighbours by some reference to their shared ethnicity or their pleasure at having other Asian families around them:

> 'Mostly working-class Indians. Very quiet and friendly. I have friends here. I like it very much.'
> 'Mostly Asian people. They are nice neighbours, very friendly.'
> 'They are all nice and proper people. A lot of nice young Asian people.'

When the parents were asked how they regarded their neighbourhood as a place for bringing up their children there was no significant change, within any group, in the relative proportions of approvers and disapprovers. Nor was there any appreciable change in the small proportion of parents who objected to the ethnic composition of their neighbourhood. In other words, there was a strong concordance in each ethnic group between those who liked their neighbourhood and those who thought it to be a good place for bringing up their children. There was also a significant and positive relationship between those parents who liked their neighbourhood and those who approved of their child's school.

When they were asked what kind of district they would look for if they had to move, most of those parents who wanted some kind of change enumerated various improvements in amenities and conditions:

> 'I'd like the kids to have a bit more room. I think I'd like a small town with a few shops and a swimming bath and that sort of thing. But you've got to go where the work is.' (White parent)
> 'I'm worried about schools. The junior school is all right but I'm frightened of them being too big. I'd like something like this village but with more amenities and shorter commuting distances.' (White, 'no contact' parent)
> 'It would be nicer to have a garden than a back street, but it would have to be somewhere with plenty of amenities, playing fields, swings, clubs etc.' (West Indian parent)
> 'I'd like somewhere safer for the kids. That main road is like a bloody motorway.' (West Indian parent)

'I'd like somewhere for them to play but it would have to be somewhere respectable and clean.' (Asian parent)

'Somewhere not too noisy and dirty, but near the school. We have to watch the traffic all the time.' (Asian parent)

Only 12 per cent of the main group of white parents and three per cent of the 'no contact' group spontaneously referred to ethnically mixed districts as something to avoid when seeking a new place in which to settle. The figures increased, to 20 per cent and 19 per cent respectively, when the respondents were pressed to say whether they would object to an ethnically mixed district. There was also a small number of parents in the two minority groups who expressed a wish not to live in areas with a large minority group population. This type of response came most frequently from West Indian parents living in the areas of London with a small minority group settlement. One assumes that the combination of disadvantages suffered by their compatriots in the more densely settled areas was all too obvious.

In general, however, it would appear that most of these parents do not object to their neighbours and judge their neighbourhoods by whether they have good schools, are good places for bringing up children and have reasonable amenities, rather than by their ethnic composition.

Community relations

When the parents were asked to give their opinions as to the general state of community relations in Britain only a minority of them (12 per cent of the whites, 16 per cent of the West Indians and 30 per cent of the Asians) thought we were getting along quite well with each other (Table 11.8).

Table 11.8: *Parental attitudes to community relations*: by race and density (per cent).

	Whites			*West Indians*		*Asians*	
	High	*Low*	*No contact*	*High*	*Low*	*High*	*Low*
Sub-sample totals	128	128	32	64	64	64	64
Not interviewed	0.8	3.9	nil	14.1	1.6	1.6	6.3
Good	11.7	11.7	15.6	14.1	17.2	31.3	29.7
Locally fair, elsewhere poor	14.8	5.5	nil	7.8	10.9	3.1	4.7
Poor: blames minorities	27.3	33.6	21.9	nil	3.1	nil	nil
Poor: blames majority	3.1	6.2	18.8	18.8	21.9	14.1	23.5
Poor: blames all groups	13.3	12.5	12.5	4.7	20.3	12.5	3.1
Deteriorating	7.0	10.2	nil	4.7	nil	12.5	3.1
Non-committal	21.9	16.4	31.3	35.9	25.0	25.0	29.7

These reasonably optimistic views were expressed with roughly equal frequency, within each ethnic group, both by those living in areas of high and low minority group settlement. Overall, however, there was significantly more pessimism amongst the white parents than amongst those in the other two groups. More than 56 per cent of whites consider intergroup relationships to be poor or deteriorating compared with some 35 per cent of the minority group parents.

An important feature of the white and West Indian parents' responses was that more of them living in areas of low minority group settlement than in the areas of more concentrated settlement consider the relationships between communities to be poor or deteriorating. A possible interpretation of this difference is that whereas the opinions of people in the areas of high settlement are likely to be informed by direct experience, the views of those in the low settlement areas will be more dependent on secondary sources, in particular media reporting on immigration, minority group crime and disturbances in which minority group members are involved. Hartman and Husband (1974), for example, found that the media were more frequently cited as the source of information on intergroup relations by people living in areas of low settlement than by those in high settlement areas. This interpretation is further reinforced by the fact that one in eight of the white and West Indian parents, living in the 'high' areas, consider the situation in their own locality to be satisfactory but community relations in other parts of the country to be poor. These views are exemplified by such statements as:

'Not too bad here really. Just at certain times things seem to blow up. But it's not race, it's pressure from the environment. If there's a lot out of work they say they've got our jobs. But I don't think it's bad, compared with a lot of places it's good.' (White parent)
'Areas vary, we've had no trouble with anyone round here, but if you go to Southall or the Oval then you'd find trouble.' (White parent)
'It's not bad. It's OK round here but I wouldn't like to go down south.' (West Indian parent)
'I don't find it bad. We're getting on well here. It can be tense in some places. There's so much distinction.' (West Indian parent)

Although the parents were not asked to give an opinion as to who they felt to be responsible for the general state of community relationships in Britain, most of those who adopted a pessimistic view did so. On the whole, the whites were more inclined to blame the minority groups than the minorities were to blame them. 30 per cent of the white parents (22 per cent in the 'no contact' area) had such complaints as:

'They don't fit in.' 'They take the houses needed by the whites.' 'They won't learn the language.' 'They don't like us, they just tolerate us because they have to live here, they should ship them back.' 'They don't mix, they pretend to be tolerant but they're not.' 'There's too many of them.' 'They do their toilet in the street, they take houses and turn them into slums.'

In their turn 20 per cent of the West Indian and 19 per cent of the Asian parents made such statements as:

'Blacks seem to be synonymous with barbarians'. 'Too many black kids are relegated to ESN schools, they see us as inferior.' 'Parliament pays lip service to equality, we are dominated by whites they treat us like second-class people.' 'They say we take their jobs, they think only of themselves.' 'We're picked on by the police.'

Very few parents blamed their own group for the poor state of affairs which they considered to exist, but some 13 per cent of both the white and West Indian parents and eight per cent of the Asians thought that both the majority group and the minorities were at fault.

Many of the parents who looked for some improvement in intergroup relationships pinned their hopes on a change in attitudes, but one of the reasons why attitudes are often so resistant to change is that they tend to form interlocking and mutually supporting clusters. It was not surprising, therefore, to find that the cross-tabulations between the responses given by the white parents, living in multi-ethnic areas, to this general question on community relationships, revealed a number of significant connections with their responses to more specific questions on intergroup living. Those parents who blamed the minority groups for the poor state of community relations were more likely than other white parents, to object to multi-ethnic schools, to be dissatisfied with their present neighbourhood, to object to their neighbours in racialistic terms and to desire a move to an all-white area.

Parents and children

The next stage in our investigation was to ascertain whether there was a reliable relationship between the children's attitudes to group differences and the beliefs and values manifest in their parents' responses to our questions. In order to do this a single measure of ethnocentrism was derived, by means of Principal Components Analysis (Appendix III) from the children's tests of affect (Limited Choice, Paired Comparisons and Stereotypes). This technique provided us with an internally valid, intervally scaled score for each child, the Own Race Preference Scale, which enabled us to compare the degree of a child's ethnocentricity, as shown by his or her scale position, with the parental responses on a number of critical questions.

No strong overall link was found between the intergroup attitudes of the parents and those of their children but a number of interesting relationships were established between those children whose scores fell at the extreme ends of ethnocentricity continuum, that is the upper and lowest tenths, and the attitudes of their parents.

Parents who approved of multi-ethnic education tended to have children who were more tolerant towards the other ethnic groups than did those who disapproved. This relationship was particularly marked for the white group, in which parents who approved of multi-ethnic schooling had almost twice as many children in the lowest ethnocentric category compared with those who favoured ethnically discrete schools. A similar result emerged with regard to parental attitudes towards the teaching of comparative religion in schools.

A majority of parents in all the ethnic groups expressed a favourable attitude towards their neighbours, but there was a clear and reliable trend for those who disliked their area, and thought it an unsatisfactory place in which to rear their children, to have children high on the ethnocentrism scale. The reverse trend was also in evidence among the whites; children in the lowest ethnocentric category tended to have parents who liked, or who accepted, an ethnic mix in their neighbourhood and who would willingly move to another of the same type.

The parental data, as already described, revealed differences between the white and minority group parents in their approach to hypothetical racial incidents involving their children. Only within the West Indian group, however, was there a discernible relationship between parent and child attitudes. The parents of children at the higher end of the ethnocentricity scale were likely to express 'helplessness', or to recommend 'retaliation' over racial incidents. In contrast, the parents of children low in ethnocentricity were more likely to explain to their own children the other child's behaviour, or to investigate the incident and initiate some preventive action. Furthermore, those West Indian parents who advocated 'on the spot' justice from teachers in response to discriminatory behaviour in the classroom had fewer highly ethnocentric children.

The extent to which parents felt responsible for their children's attitudes and their strategies for dealing with the child's questioning on racial matters showed no reliable relationship with the degree of ethnocentricity expressed by their children, again with the exception of the West Indian group. Of those children at the low end of the ethnocentrism scale some 82 per cent had parents who acknowledged that they had a responsibility for inter-group education. This is especially interesting when considered in relation to the attitudes of the rest of the West Indian parents who, more firmly than either of the other two ethnic groups, placed the primary responsibility for multi-ethnic education in the hands of the schools.

Summary and conclusions

The popular assumption that parents exert a decisive influence on the formation of children's intergroup attitudes implies that the parents themselves will have well formed and highly crystallized intergroup attitudes and, furthermore, that they will be prepared to expend a considerable amount of effort transmitting similar beliefs and sentiments to their children.

Reviewing all the data from the parental interviews we feel justified in concluding that inter-ethnic issues were not a preoccupation of many of these parents. Indeed it would seem that in some cases the interview led to an awareness of some aspects of group relations which had hitherto received little sustained consideration. The low priority which most of the parents accorded to inter-ethnic relationships agrees with the findings of Little and Kohler (1976/77) and Anwar (1980) and partly explains why the relationship between their attitudes and the ethnocentricity of their children was not a strong one.

Nor did we find evidence of any consistent attempt to inculcate children with intergroup antipathies. For the most part the parents were approving of their children's multi-ethnic schools, liked their neighbourhood, did not object to their neighbours in racialistic terms and did not interfere with their children's choice of friends.

On the other hand, if there was no conspicuous emotional investment in intergroup hostility, it is equally true that there was little evidence of any deep commitment to intergroup equality and social justice. To be sure, most of the parents acknowledge a responsibility to help their children to understand and respect group differences, but it was clear that few of them had given the matter more than *ad hoc* attention.

Their reactions to the hypothetical incidents presented during the interview, and their reported style of response to their children's questions, suggested that many of them were unable to offer their children more than a superficial explanation of cultural differences, and were failing to equip them to resist the prejudices which they would inevitably encounter. They felt inadequate for what is, admittedly, a demanding task and looked to the schools for help.

Given that, across the three ethnic groups, more than 73 per cent agreed that their children should be taught more about their cultural and religious groups in school, it would appear that the schools have an implicit parental mandate for doing more than many of them attempt to do in the area of community relations. Neither parents nor teachers alone can resolve the problems presented by the need for intergroup education, but a lot could be achieved by parents and teachers working in concert. But it is the schools which must take the lead in involving all the ethnic groups in their neighbourhood in planning a programme of intergroup education. In this way they would not only make a valuable contribution to the welfare of the children but provide the potential for the self-evident need for parent-to-parent education.

12 A Summary and some implications

This study was undertaken to investigate the acquisition of ethnic awareness of primary school children growing up in a multi-ethnic society. In general terms, our findings provide good evidence that young children make extensive use of ethnic distinctions in their attempts to structure the social world and to understand their place within it. Furthermore, their growing consciousness of ethnic differences was accompanied by a marked degree of ethnocentricity which had a profound effect on how they regard members of other ethnic groups and their choice of companions. A more detailed summary of the results can most economically be presented in terms of the principal explanatory variables.

By far the most important predictor as to how children would respond to the various tasks with which they were presented was their ethnicity. In contrast with many earlier studies, which have stressed the importance of own-group rejection by minority children, our findings demontrate that both minority and majority group children have a strong sense of group identity. On the other hand, the pattern of ethnic group preferences showed that the minority children clearly perceived the advantages of being white. A well defined sense of personal worth, accompanied by a sharp perception of depressed relative status. is likely to prove a socially explosive mixture, unless we are more successful than we appear to have been in educating children for living in a multi-ethnic society.

When the children were offered a variety of personal attributes by which people could be grouped together, the most significant fact to emerge was the primary importance which the great majority of them, regardless of group membership, attached to ethnic characteristics as differentiating criteria. These results were somewhat softened by those from the puzzle test, which showed that the three groups of children were equally likely to consider the sex of their companion as of more importance than his or her ethnicity when contemplating a joint activity.

On the three tests of liking and disliking, each group of children exhibited a strong in-group bias, although the white children were considerably more ethnocentric than either of the minority groups. They decisively rated themselves above the other groups, favoured their own group in the distribution of sweets and showed a greater readiness than the minority children to attribute favourable characteristics exclusively to themselves. In contrast, although the two minority groups conceded a place for the whites in their hierarchy of preferences, showed some generosity towards them in the sharing of sweets and were willing to describe them in equally favourable terms as themselves, they were reciprocally ungenerous and derogatory towards each other's groups.

We found little desire for intergroup friendship amongst the children in any of the three groups. Moreover, all three groups appeared more reluctant to take home friends from a different ethnic background than they were either to sit with them in class or play with them in the playground. Of course, six choices for companions, in three different social contexts, is unlikely to have exhausted the children's capacity for sociability and there was evidence that the children did not wish to be entirely ethnically exclusive in their choice of friends. Nevertheless, the extent and consistency of the cleavage between the three groups, taken in conjunction with the data from the other tests, suggests that the social images attached to the categories 'black' and 'white' were so salient for these children that they had become a serious impediment to intergroup friendship.

For primary school children, gender differences are strong competitors to ethnic differences as obstacles to friendship, although the social identities associated with gender categories are very different in content from those associated with ethnic categories (Schofield, 1981). Less than 2 per cent of the extended sample of nearly 4,000 children recorded any desire for cross-sex friendship.

Sex-related differences in the children's social perceptions and in the way in which they feel about other groups relative to their own, were less consistent and found to occur only between some groups of boys and girls in conjunction with particular tasks.

White girls and Asian girls made fewer own-group choices on the identification test than the respective groups of boys, and Asian girls were more likely than Asian boys to prefer another group to their own. There were no significant differences in the use boys and girls made of 'race' and 'sex' as social grouping criteria; on the puzzle test, the expectation that boys would play with boys and girls would play with girls was common to both sexes. Similarly, on the pair comparisons test, in each ethnic group, girls preferred girls and boys preferred boys in a well-dressed, poorly-dressed order. However, in the distribution of sweets there was a trend, particularly strong among the minority group girls, for girls to be less 'ethnocentric' and more 'out-group orientated' than boys. Overall, therefore, the evidence for sex-related differences in the degree of ethnocentricism must be regarded as weak and inconclusive.

The effect of age on the children's cognitive skills is unambiguous. Growth brings an increasing mastery of the more complex grouping strategies in all three groups. The effect of age on ethnocentricity is less certain. There were no significant differences between the four age levels in the frequency of own-group identification, possibly because that by the age of seven, own-group identification was already well established in all the ethnic groups. Amongst the minority children there was some increase in own-group preference from the youngest to the oldest children in each group. On the sorting task, the youngest white children showed themselves to be less conscious than the older children in their group of ethnic attributes as critical social differentiators, but there were no such differences amongst the minority children. The overall effect of chronological growth on intergroup attitudes, as shown by the own-race preference scale, suggests a complex interaction between ethnicity and age. The white and West Indian children showed less evidence of ethnocentricity with increasing age, but the reverse was true of the Asian children. In neither case, however, was there a corresponding change in the children's friendship patterns.

With regard to regional differences, the location of the children's schools, in the north or the south, did not prove to be a critical determinant of their intergroup perceptions and attitudes. For the most part, regionally related effects were weak and occurred only intermittently in between-group and within-group comparisons. They were most strongly associated with the children's affective response to other groups and the own-race preference scale shows the children in London to be more ethnocentric than those in the north. On the other hand, white and Asian children in London, but not the West Indians, were less in-group orientated in their friendship choices. In neither instance is the difference very great and both would need to be replicated before any reliable generalizations could be made.

The ethnic composition of the schools attended appeared to have little effect on the way in which the children regarded their own or other groups, although some minor differences did occur between particular groups of children. White children in schools with high or low proportions of minority children, or with no minority children at all, did not differ significantly in the extent to which they preferred and identified with their own group. Similarly there was no consistent trend for the strength of the minority children's own-group identification, or the magnitude of their own-group preference, to vary with the size of their group's representation in a school. There was some evidence that white children, in schools with a high proportion of minority children, were more ready than the other white children to use ethnic attributes as primary grouping criteria. These children also showed a greater in-group bias in their friendship patterns than white children in schools where the concentration of minority children was low. On the other hand, both minority groups were more ethnocentric in their choice of friends when they were highly represented in a school.

Growing up in a multi-ethnic society

The generality of the children's ethnocentricity across groups, genders, schools and localities, lends little support to the beliefs entertained by some teachers that 'most primary school children have no thoughts of race' (Jelinek and Brittan, 1975). Nor does it lend much credence to the idea that the genesis of ethnic prejudice in children can be explained by some kind of personal malfunctioning. To be sure, the multi-faceted nature of the enquiry has revealed some variability in the children's intergroup biases, but broadly speaking it does not seem to matter very much whether they are boys or girls, in schools in the north or south of the country, whether they attend multi-ethnic schools or schools where no West Indian or Asian child has yet been seen.

The crux of the matter is that children perceive, categorize and evaluate each other in the way they do because they are judging, choosing and reacting to each other within a society in which that sort of classification works and is daily reinforced. They see others treated with respect or as inferior; they hear them described in complimentary or uncomplimentary terms and they notice the roles assigned to them in books, comics, the public media and in society in general. What they learn in one situation is likely to be confirmed in another.

It might be argued that the children's consistent tendency to favour their own group more than others is quite harmless, since it indicates no more than that they like people who are like themselves. However, ethnocentricity – as Sumner (1906) saw it – has a reflexive function, involving on the one hand, feelings of in-group superiority and on the other, a dislike, distrust or fear of the out-group. The principal objective is to secure for the group and its members a positive differentiation from others. Moreover, it would appear from a series of experiments carried out by Tajfel and his co-workers, that the most common route to the elevation of one's own group is to depress the position of another's.

Tajfel *et al.* (1971) have demonstrated that the assignment to groups on the most trivial criteria, such as a preference for certain paintings, or even randomly on no criterion at all (Billig and Tajfel, 1973) is all that is necessary to bring about in-group favouritism and out-group discrimination. In neither of their experiments were there any ethnic differences or a history of conflict amongst the boys concerned. 'It seems that the mere mention of "groups" by the experimenters was sufficient to produce strong intergroup discrimination' (Billig and Tajfel, p. 48).

Their interpretation of the results is by no means bland in its implications. In accordance with Tajfel's theory of intergroup relations (see Chapter 4), it is postulated that the fundamental problem in any intergroup situation is that of defining one's social identity by placing oneself in relation to others. Since an individual's social identity is seen as those aspects of the person's self-image which are derived from a consciousness of belonging to certain social categories, it follows that the construction or maintenance of a social identity can only take place through comparisons between the person's own group and other groups. Moreover, a group can only contribute to the positive aspects of a person's self-image if it can be positively differentiated, on some value-laden dimension, from other groups. In the minimal group situations just described, inter-personal cues which could have provided a basis for comparison were absent and the only way in which the boys could establish distinctiveness was through the distribution of monetary awards. Thus the intergroup discrimination which ensued is interpreted as being due not to a conflict over monetary gains, which in any case brought no personal advantage, but to differentiations based on comparisons made in monetary terms. This is supported by the fact that absolute in-group favouritism was not as important as relative in-group favouritism. That is to say, the boys were more concerned that the other group should get less than their own group, than they were with the absolute amounts of money they awarded to in-group members.

Tajfel and Billig consider that our need to define and place ourselves in the social world activates similar comparative and discriminatory processes. Certainly, the basic proposition that because individuals strive to maintain a positive social identity they experience pressure to evaluate their own group favourably through intergroup comparisons, offers some explanation of the mutually disparaging attitudes of the minority groups in our sample towards each other.

If the aim of social differentiation is to enhance the social identity of the group members, it follows that the lower the status of a group the less it is able to contribute to its members' positive self-image. However, the relative status of the West Indian and Asian children's groups is determined by the white majority who give absolutely no indication that they are prepared to have their hierarchical position upset or even to concede parity. Indeed, so unassailable did the whites' position appear to our minority children, that less than 50 per cent of them felt able to compare their own group's status favourably with that of the whites (Chapter 7). One way out of this dilemma suggested by Tajfel and Turner (1979) is for minority groups to avoid high status out-group comparisons and to seek positive distinctiveness by comparisons with other groups which the dominant group has relegated to an equally low status. It would seem that a successful outcome to the social comparison process is dependent on being able to perceive that there is a social layer beneath your own. This interpretation would fit both our own data and those of other investigators who have recorded the same phenomenon of mutual disparagement between disadvantaged groups. (See for example, Berry *et al.*, 1976; Louden, 1978b; Bagley *et al.*, 1979).

The processes of social categorization, self-evaluation and intergroup comparisons are inherent to social interaction and social life. We must accept that just as children use differences in objects and people as the bases for their categorizations so, in a visibly heterogeneous society, they will note differences in skin colour, hair form, dress and other ethnically related attributes, and these too will stimulate a classificatory process. However, children construct their categories and make their comparisons within a framework of values which is not of their own creation.

There is an implicit consensus in our society as to where the various groups stand in the order of things. It is from within this consensual perspective that the children learn what to notice, how group differences should be evaluated and acquire the notion of an ethnic group as a social collectivity sharply bounded by a consistency of physical and behavioural attributes. People can be categorized in innumerable ways and it does not follow from the inevitability of the need to categorize that the present divisions of society must be seen as fixed and immutable, nor does it follow that the recognition of group distinctiveness involves conflict. What is certain, however, is that the convenience of ethnic classifications will prove irresistible tools for children in their attempts to order and simplify their social world, unless there is a considered and coordinated drive to introduce them to the potential fluidity and interdependence of human groups and to promote intergroup acceptance and friendship.

Schools and the multi-ethnic society

The intergroup relationships between children in our schools have been fashioned by history and the relative economic, political and social advantages and disadvantages which have accrued to their membership groups. Is it not then naive to expect that white and minority group children in our schools will spontaneously form close mutual relationships? Schools, of course, respond to society; they cannot by themselves bring about a social reformation. If the inequalities in Britain are to be narrowed there must be radical and effective legal, economic and political policies directed towards such problems as unemployment, low pay, institutionalized discrimination, poverty, poor housing and the deteriorating fabric of the inner cities. Nevertheless, as Gill (1982) has argued, teachers must be prepared to take seriously the 'knowledge' which the children bring to school regarding other groups in their community and endeavour to work towards a different perception of social life.

The beliefs and practices of teachers are of crucial importance not only in determining the educational aspirations and achievements of the children they teach, but also in creating a social climate in which all can feel confident and secure in their group identity. This is not only a matter of adjusting teaching techniques and curricula to meet the needs of children from different cultures, but of helping all children to understand those with whom they share their lives and enabling them to respond to the diversity of human groups without fear or hostility.

If teachers are to respond effectively to the educational and social needs of children growing up in a multi-ethnic society, then they will require the resources and support of both the Department of Education and Science (DES) and the local education authorities (LEAs). In 1977 the DES issued a discussion document which emphasized that the presence of minority ethnic groups in Britain has implications for the education of all children and that all schools, whatever their ethnic composition, should give their pupils a 'sympathetic understanding of the different cultures and races that now make up our society' (para 10.11).

It is evident from the increasing number of courses on various aspects of multi-cultural education provided by the colleges and departments of education, and the in-service initiatives of HMI's and LEA advisors, that there is a growing consciousness of the implications of a multi-ethnic society for teacher training. How students and teachers interpret the information they receive, however, depends very much on their self-conceptions and their own group's frame of reference. It follows, therefore, that any educational programme designed to prepare teachers for working in a multi-ethnic society, should begin by helping them to discover their own habitual ways of thinking about such social categories as gender, ethnicity and social class and the manner in which their group membership has structured their perception. For any of us overcoming the ethnocentricity of our own enculturation is a difficult and emotional experience. Nevertheless, as Ehrlich (1973) has suggested, to understand that we are part of the problem is an important preliminary to contributing to the solution.

Although there has been an appreciable change in attitude to curriculum development and teacher education since Townsend and Brittan's survey in the early 1970s, Little and Willey (1981a) reporting on their large-scale investigation carried out for the Schools Council, recorded less progress in terms of action in the schools. The survey reveals 'a considerable gap between the views and policies about what should be happening and some aspects of practice' (p. 10). In particular there appears to have been insufficient coordination of effort and resources to enable much curriculum development to take place. In areas where there were few or no minority group pupils there was little evidence that such development had been given systematic consideration. Commenting on their report in another paper (Little and Willey, 1981b), the authors conclude that there is a need for decisive leadership and that without national and local authority action 'we will be guilty of asking professionals and schools to do too much and holding them responsible for problems that are not of their making' (p. 8).

The prospect, however, is not entirely bleak. The Schools Council has endorsed the recommendations of Little and Willey's report and is funding a number of projects on different aspects of multi-cultural education. In addition, initiatives by organized groups of teachers and resource teams committed to such issues as development education (Storm and Richardson, 1980), multi-cultural education (Street-Porter, 1978), peace education (Haavelsrud, 1976; Hicks, 1980) and world studies (Heater, 1980; Selby, 1983), are beginning to influence curriculum planning.

There are differences of emphasis amongst these approaches but they share common objectives in seeking to foster an understanding of the interdependence of human groups and a respect for cultural diversity. Hicks (n.d., World Studies Document No. 6) in his clarification of their similarities and differences suggests that world studies, multi-cultural education, development education and peace studies, should not be seen as distinct fields but as offering organizing concepts for curriculum planning. Certainly, the practitioners in each of these groups, through their publications, resource centres and expertise have a great deal to contribute to an anti-ethnocentric curriculum in all types of schools, no matter what their ethnic composition. It is worth noting that much of the pioneering work for the World Studies Project, which is now attracting Schools Council support, was carried out in an all-white school. (Selby and Cox, 1978; Aucott *et al.*, 1979; Selby, 1980).

Teachers and parents

It is imperative that schools should make every effort to incorporate parents into their thinking and planning, but Townsend and Brittan (1972) reported that home–school relations appeared to be 'one of the most unsatisfactory areas of life in multi-racial schools' (p. 89). A decade later, Little and Willey continued to stress the overriding need to secure the participation of parents in all aspects of school life. Our own data show that across the three ethnic groups, more than 70 per cent of the parents agreed that their children should be taught more about other cultural and religious groups in school, but that it was principally the white parents who took an active organizing part in school events.

Schools which embark on some form of curriculum reform to counter ethnocentrism, without enlisting the cooperation and participation of the children's parents, not only deprive themselves of a valuable source of support against the attacks of extreme right-wing political minority groups (Norburn and Wright, 1982), but undermine their own credibility. Stone (1981), for example, complains of the disenchantment of some parents and community groups with what schools have to offer; 'white schools try to compensate children by offering black studies and steel bands; black parents and community groups are organizing Saturday schools – to sup- plement the second-rate education which the school system offers their children' (p. 11).

It is not sufficient that schools should merely keep parents informed as to what they are doing or hoping to achieve. They need to get the parents actively involved in the school's affairs and provide a forum for parent-to- parent exchanges, as well as for a continuing parent–teacher dialogue. On the one hand the parents need to assure themselves that their children are receiving sound and effective teaching, on the other, the teachers need feed-back from the parents and support for their endeavours in the home.

Some schools are achieving considerable success with such partner- ships. Winkley (1981), a head teacher in Handsworth, has described how he and his staff have weekly parents' evenings throughout the year with something like a 90 per cent attendance rate. The meetings give the families an opportunity to meet each other and the staff informally, discuss the children's work and admire their efforts. The parents are encouraged to see the school as a community resource. The school remains open every evening for supervised activities, and provides teas for the children of working parents. The parents are also offered help with family, money and housing problems.

If, in these and other ways, schools can provide the means for produc- tive intergroup relationships among parents, there are good reasons for believing that the probability of friendly interpersonal relationships between their children will be enhanced (see, for example, Orive and Gerard, 1975).

Cooperative learning

Whatever the emphasis or orientation of the multi-cultural programme adopted by a school, it is unlikely to have a great deal of influence on peer relationships unless what is taught is in harmony with how it is taught. There is, for example, an exquisite irony in attempting to instruct children in the ideals of some interdependent multi-ethnic society when they are divided by the apartheid of ability groupings, or expecting them to appre- ciate the value of human rights when they are denied freedom of speech.

Purging the text books of black stereotypes, boosting the minority groups in the teaching materials and adjusting the curriculum to accom- modate cultural diversity, will have little impact on how children treat each other, if teachers make rules without explanation, if they command needlessly and assume their authority to be established by convention. We learn to cooperate with one another, not by hearing about cooperation, or by reading about cooperation, or even by discussing cooperation, but by living in a community in which cooperation is practised and rewarded. If the aim of multi-cultural education is to help children to become responsible, productive people who can effectively participate with each other in joint enterprises, then teachers have an obligation to create a context for learning in which cooperative skills can be learnt and practised. They need frequently to re-examine whether the way in which they group children together for different purposes, the manner in which they negotiate with them and the extent to which they are prepared to share their authority with them, is likely to foster or inhibit intergroup friendship.

The development and refining of cooperative learning techniques aimed at encouraging good peer relationships have been the subject of a considerable amount of research activity and a variety of approaches to collaborative learning have been explored. Aronson and his co-workers have sought to foster peer cooperation through a jigsaw technique. A different portion of a learning task is assigned to each of five or six members of a group so that the completion of the task is contingent on mutual cooperation and peer tutoring. (Aronson *et al.*, 1978).

The approach of DeVries and Slavin (1978) also relies on team learning and peer tutoring. Groups are composed to reflect a cross-section of academic ability as well as to have representatives of both sexes and different ethnic groups. The function of the team is to prepare its members, through peer tutoring, for participation in learning-game tournaments.

The group-investigation model functions very differently. It concentrates on having pupils gather information from a variety of sources in collaboration with each other. Learning proceeds through cooperative group enquiry, discussion and interpretation of collected material, problem solving and the synthesis of individual contributions into a group product, (Johnson and Johnson, 1975; Sharan and Sharan, 1976; Barnes, 1977).

Currently in Britain, Salmon and Claire (1984) have completed a study of collaborative learning using mixed ability, mixed gender and ethnically mixed partnerships. The Schools' Council *Language in the Multicultural Primary Classroom* project team (Hester and Steedman, 1983) is also investigating children's learning through collaborative group work in different parts of the country. The emphasis is on teachers working as their own researchers, initiating activities and observing and recording their children's social learning.

These group learning methods differ in a number of important respects but they all embody features which could foster good peer relationships and inter-ethnic attraction. First, they all require some reorganization of the traditional classroom into small groups of pupils who interact with each other for mutual assistance. Secondly, they all imply some decentralization of authority, insofar as the teacher ceases to be the fount from which all knowledge flows. Thirdly, they share an emphasis on process rather than academic content. Each technique aims to influence peer and ethnic relationships through the medium of the interaction and communication processes within groups of children cooperating on some learning task. They are thus easily adapted to a wide range of curricula.

Sharan (1980) has recently carried out a review of a number of evaluative investigations designed to assess the effectiveness of some of these cooperative group techniques. Although the gains in academic achievement are not consistent for all the group methods or on all the measures employed, the results reported demonstrate the superior performance of pupils in small collaborative groups, as compared with that of pupils in traditional classrooms. Moreover, the studies repeatedly confirmed that under cooperative group learning conditions, helping behaviour increased, the children felt more liked, more accepted and felt more concerned about each other. As a result, many reported themselves as feeling better able to cope with their work. Most of the studies which assessed inter-ethnic relationships as a function of interaction and peer cooperation, reported positive effects, but in many cases there was only a modest improvement. Sharan considers that many of the evaluative studies were too short-lived to make a proper assessment of the effects of cooperative learning on inter-ethnic relations. If cooperative methods had been employed for a greater part of the school day and over a more prolonged period of time during the school year, then more decisive findings would have been expected.

Sharan's review reveals many gaps in our knowledge as to how to employ these techniques to maximum advantage, in particular very little is known of the effects of collaborative learning on our-of-school relationships. Nevertheless, collectively the evaluative investigations present a very positive picture of cooperative group learning. Certainly it offers more promise for the improvement of peer relationships and intergroup acceptance than the passive learning processes of the traditional classroom.

If teachers can create a context for learning in which each child is respected as a contributor and a communicator, and in which each child's social and affectional needs are recognized as equally legitimate, then they will not only make schools more egalitarian, but they will make an immediate contribution to each child's welfare and *that* is an end in itself. To rely on mere physical proximity to work a social alchemy, accompanied by some vague laissez-faire policy of treating everyone alike, is to do no more than collude with an unsatisfactory status quo.

Appendix I: **Administration of the children's tests**

1. *Concept formation*
    1. Place the 42 test cards in six rows of seven, left to right, by numbers.
    2. Ask the child to name the object on each card to ensure that he sees every card.
    'Tell me what this is?' Correct the child if necessary.
    3. Say to the child: 'Look at them all again. Choose the cards which belong together. Any way you do it is fine, but tell me why they go together. You can choose as many as you like.'
    4. Replace the chosen cards in their correct position by number. Say: 'Choose some more cards which go together.'
    5. Repeat the test five times.

2. *Picture identification*
This is a test of the accuracy of the child's self-identification.
    1. Present the child with three same-sex children's photographs, one for each race.
    2. Ask: 'Which looks most like you?'

3. *Picture preference*
This second test of social perception is designed to assess the extent to which the child's perceived identity corresponds with the person he/she would like to be.
    1. Present the child with the three same-sex children's photographs, one for each race.
    2. Ask: 'If you could choose, which would you most like to be?'

4. *Sorting task*
This is a test of cue saliency, designed to indicate the extent to which colour, sex, age and dress-standard are important to the child for classifying people.
The test materials are the adult and children master sets, using the appropriate ethnic group for the school under study.
    1. Present the child with the master set between two boxes right and left.
    2. Say: 'Half of these pictures belong in this box and the other half in

that box. Can you please put them into the boxes where they belong.'

3.   Take away half of the photos that are inappropriate for the particular child, e.g. if he/she sorts into adults/children, take away the adults; if a white child sorts into white/black, take away the black photographs.

4.   Present the appropriate half of the array again between the two boxes. Repeat as above.

There are four variables: sex, race, age, dress. The procedure must, therefore, be repeated three times to get the salient cues.

Haphazard sorting

(i)   If the child sorts haphazardly, say: 'That's good; now let's sort them out another way.'

(ii)   After three consecutive haphazard sorts, abandon the test. If after one or two haphazard sorts the subject then sorts 'rationally', proceed as above, disregarding the 'false starts'.

(iii) If after a 'rational' sort, the next is a haphazard one, tip the cards out again and say: 'Can you sort them another way?' (Abandon the test after three consecutive haphazard sorts).

5. *Puzzle test*

This is a second test of cue saliency, the cues being race, sex and dress. In each presentation, one of the variables is kept constant and a choice has to be made between the other two.

Demonstration trial

1.   Using the four bus/lorry cards, present alternate bus and lorry cards in a line.

2.   Show the four cards. Say: 'I have four cards here. See if I can make two pictures.'

3.   Show the mismatch and say: 'That doesn't make a very good picture, does it?'

4.   Show the match and say: 'This is all right, isn't it? Now you try.'

Learning trial

1.   Use the four elephant/buffalo cards. Present alternate elephant and buffalo cards in a line.

2.   Say: 'Now you put these together to make two nice pictures.'

3.   Accept the same animal sequence, the wrong way round, without comment. If the subject gives an incorrect match, explain and demonstrate. Say: 'Now you try.' No further help is to be given with any matching.

Test trials

1.   Present the set of four cards randomly on the table.

2.   Say: 'Here are some pictures of children playing. Look carefully at all the pictures. Choose the ones that you want to go together to make two nice pictures.'

3.   Repeat for each set of four cards.

6. *Paired Comparisons*

This is a test of affect where all the variables are presented to the child and a complete ranking of the child's preferences is obtained. It is thus essential that each card is compared with every other one in the set.

1. Divide the photographs into two piles, nos. 1–6 on the left, and 7–12 on the right.

   (NB Throughout the test, always keep the small numbers on the left. The left-hand pile is always the moving pile.)

2. Instructions to child:

   'I'm going to show you some photos in twos, and each time I want you to say which you like best.'

3. Ask the child to compare 1 with 7, then turn both of these face down and repeat with 2 and 8, 3 and 9, etc., until the piles are exhausted.

4. Take card no. 1 and place it at the bottom of the left-hand pile. Repeat the above method, now comparing 2 and 7, 3 and 8, etc.

5. Then put card no. 2 at the bottom of the left-hand pile. This whole process is repeated until card no. 1 is again at the top of the left-hand pile.

6. Take the left-hand pile and divide it into two, cards 1–3 on the left and 4–6 on the right.

7. Repeat exactly as above, moving the cards in the left-hand pile until card no. 1 is agin at the top.

8. Compare cards 1 and 2, 1 and 3, 2 and 3;

   4 and 5, 4 and 6, 5 and 6.

9. Take cards 7–12 and divide into two. Repeat the procedure until card no. 7 is again at the top of the left-hand pile.

10. Compare cards 7 and 8, 7 and 9, 8 and 9;

    10 and 11, 10 and 12, 11 and 12.

7. *Limited choice*

This is a second test of affect. The child is presented with all the variables, but his/her positive choice is limited.

We have already established that same-sex choice is paramount Therefore use six same-sex puzzle test cards, two White, two West Indian and two Asian (different children of the same race).

Trial 1. Present two same-race cards with two of the first other race.

Trial 2. Present two same-race cards with two of the second other race.

Trial 3. Present the two sets of two other-race cards.

Instructions to the child on each trial:

'Suppose you had a bag of sweets and there were three left. You have one and so now there are two left. Who would you give the other sweets to?'

8. *Stereotypes test*

The child must have the opportunity of applying *each* of one of the ethnic groups, all of them, or to none of them.

1. Place the four boxes on the table. The end flaps with the ethnic photographs and the 'nobody' label are placed one in front of the each box.

2. Say: 'We are going to play a posting game. You see, I've got a lot of little cards with messages written on them.' 'I shall read you what each of them says, and I want you to post them to the people on these boxes that you think they fit best of all.'

   'If the message on the card doesn't fit anyone, you put it into "nobody".'

   (Point to the box with the 'nobody' written on it.)

3. Say: 'Sometimes you might think that the message fits more than one lot of these people. If it does, don't worry, give it to me.'

4. Say: 'Is that OK? If the message fits one lot of these people best, post it to them. If it doesn't fit anyone, put it in the "nobody" box. If it fits more than one lot of people, give the card to me.'

5. Start the test.

6. At the end of the test, pick up the cards that have been given back by the child. Say: 'These cards that you've given me, you think these messages fit more than one lot of these people? How about this one?' (Read out message). 'Who does this message fit?'

7. Repeat this for the other returned cards.

9. *Sociometric choice*

This test is carried out on a class basis, involving all the children in the classes from which the sample children are taken. The test is designed to show the 'known group' choices of the sample children and their peers.

1. Have the class register to refer to if possible, in order to ascertain whether the children named in questions 2 and 3 are in the class or not. If they are not, a note must be made and details found out about them later.

2. Introduction to the class (teaching experimenter):

   'My name is (researcher 1), and this is (researcher 2) We're going to take this next lesson. While I'm reading you a story (researcher 2) is going to ask each of you to come out one at a time and will ask you some questions. These are very easy questions but we're going to keep your answers a secret'.

3. Instructions to second experimenter:

   Ask each child the following questions:

   (i) Who are the two children you would most like to sit with in this class?

   (ii) Who are the two children in the school you would most like to play with in the playground?

(iii) Who are the two children in the school that you would most like to invite home?

4. If the child asks if he has to have the same children for the different questions, say: 'No, you can choose any child.'

Appendix II: **Parents' Interview Schedule (abbreviated form with filler and flow questions omitted).**

Introduction

'I'm (researcher). I'm connected with the study that (child) took part in at school, about children growing up and their ideas.

Do you mind if I take notes? You do understand that this is completely confidential. We're not using anyone's names. We just want to compare the ideas of parents in London and Yorkshire about children growing up.'

We've met (child)

1. Have you any other children? Ages?
2. Can you tell me what work your husband does? Where? What?
3. Do you work? Where? What?
4. How many hours do you work?
5. Do you ever go down to (child) 's school?
    If yes: what sort of things have you been to the school for?
6. What do you think of the school?
7. Who does (child) usually play with at school?
8. What about after school? Who does he/she play with?
9. Who are they? What sort of children are they? What are they like?
10. Do (child's) friends come here? Does he/she go to their house?
11. Are there any children you don't like him/her to play with? Why is that?
12. Do you do anything about it?
13. What kind of people live round here? What are they like? What are the children like?
14. How do you like this area?
15. What is it like bringing up children round here?
    You know that we're interested in how children's ideas change as they grow up. One of the things we're interested in is their ideas about different kinds of people.
16. Does your child/Do your children ask you questions about different religions and races? What sort of things do they ask?
17. What do you say? (Or if no: If they did, what would you say?)
18. Some people think it's a good thing that children of different races should be in the same school. What do you think?

19. How about different religions in the same school?
20. Some people think it's a good thing for schools to teach children about other religions and races. What do you think? Why is that?
21. How about parents? Do you think they should try and explain these differences to children, or leave it to the schools?
22. How do you think people of different races are getting on in this country?
23. Supposing a white/black child (same colour as parent) refused to sit next to a white/black child (opposite colour to parent) at school, what do you think the teacher should do?
24. If your child came home and said he/she had been called nasty names by a white/black child (opposite colour to parent), what would you say?
25. Suppose you heard your child call a white/black child (opposite colour to parent) names, what would you say to him/her?
26. If you had to move, what kind of district would you look for?
    (If no mention of race, ask: Would you mind if there were different racial groups in that district?)
27. What school would you like (child) to go to when he/she leaves (school)? Why?
28. What would *you* like your child/children to do when he/she/they leave school?

Appendix III: **The Quantitative Analysis Contributed by Paul Mullin**

The statistical tests

Chi-square was the most commonly used statistical test and was applied to all the children's tests, except stereotypes and sociometrics, and the data arising from the parental interviews.

In order to analyse the results of the stereotypes test we used the sign test, for it makes fewer assumptions about the structure underlying the data (see below). Spearman's rank order correlation coefficient was used to examine the data from the paired comparisons test.

When the investigation produced intervally-scaled data, as was the case with certain components of the puzzle and limited choice tests, we were able to apply the more powerful, multivariate technique of analysis of variance. This technique was also used to investigate the relationship between the attitudes of parents and their children, and experimentally, to examine further the structure of the concept formation data (see below).

Methodological notes

Certain of the children's tests produced specific methodological problems to which attention should be drawn.

The concept formation test posed particular problems of presentation and analysis by virtue of comprising five trials. Repeating the test in this way produces more stable figures, less affected by 'freak' outcomes. However, subsequent structuring of the results by the independent variables produced five tables per trial, or 25 tables in all. A summary measure was required which rendered the information manageable, but did not distort or waste information. It was decided that the best way to achieve this was to average the results within each category.

While aggregating data in this manner is fine as regards presenting descriptive summary tables, it is not legitimate in terms of the statistical analysis, for two reasons.

First, significance testing requires the independence of observations, but it is unlikely that the outcome of the fifth trial in a series is totally unrelated to those which have gone before. Such observations are clearly not independent but are conditional probabilities of unknown magnitude.

Secondly, aggregating the data would mean that the same child could appear in more than one category of results. Furthermore, the resultant artificially-inflated sample size would increase the likelihood of producing spuriously significant results.

Therefore, the initial analysis had two stages. Each trial was analysed individually and the results compared so that any trends contained therein could be identified. Then, the average results were converted to integers based on a sample of 512 and this 'mythical trial' was analysed. Having completed the analysis of the data as nominally-scaled, we experimented further by treating it as though it were an interval scale and applying the Analysis of Variance technique. As we hoped, the outcome was the same substantively, but stronger statistically.

The stereotypes test also proved to be less than straightforward. The difficulty in the analysis arose because, not wishing to create a position of artificial exclusivity, the children were allowed to make dual assignments (as well, of course, of assigning traits to all the groups or none of them). This meant that the resulting data did not fall into simple, mutually exclusive and exhaustive categories independent of one another, since the same child could occur in more than one category. Thus, it would not have been legitimate to use, for example, the chi-square test and so it was decided that in order to analyse the complete data set resulting from the test, we should use the nonparametric sign test which requires fewer assumptions about the data than does chi-square.

Further, this technique permitted the aggregation of data – both as regards children into groups and as regards the individual traits into a collective indicator of each child's ethnic attitudes, as revealed by use of the traits. Three 'net' attitudes, one towards each group, were calculated for each child by taking the difference between the number of favourable traits and unfavourable traits which had been allocated to each group, including dual assignments, and treating the 'nobody' and 'everybody' assignments as neutral. The sign test was then applied to the results.

The own-race preference scale (ORPS)

To facilitate comparisons, a single measure of ethnocentrism was required, and was derived from the three tests of affect by principal components analysis. This measure is the own-race preference scale (ORPS).

Use of principal components analysis provided the solution to the problems: how to legitimately combine the three heteroscedastic scores into a single measure, intervally-scaled; how to eradicate, or minimize at least, test specific influences on the measure; how to assess the extent to which the three affect tests are internally valid and are actually measuring the same phenomenon, ethnocentrism.

Principal components analysis is one of a range of factor-analytic techniques, which enables us to see whether some underlying pattern exists in data, such that it may be arranged into a set of factors or components that may be taken as 'source variables' accounting for the observed inter-relations in the data.

The raw data from the three affect tests, upon which the analysis was based, were: (a) limited choice test: the number of own-group sweet allocations made by each child; (b) paired comparisons test: the number of own-group cards ranked by a child in one of the top four positions; (c) stereotypes test: the number of favourable traits each child allocated exclusively to his/her own group.

The analysis produced the following results:

Correlations between variables and factors

		Factors		
		3	2	1
	(a)	0.5062	−0.4946	0.7065
Variables	(b)	−0.6317	−0.1599	0.7585
	(c)	0.1964	0.7605	0.6189

Percentage variance explained by each factor

	23.1292	28.2844	48.5864

Note that only factor one is both highly correlated with each test and, more importantly, unidirectional. This is the ethnocentric component and it accounts for about half of the observed variance in the affect tests.

The analysis produced a score for each child on the ethnocentric component. This is the own-race preference scale, which was explored further using analysis of variance and 't' tests with pooled variance estimates.

Sociometric choice and Criswell Indices

A sociometric measure was included to assess the extent to which friendship patterns are confined to ethnic groups, or cross inter-ethnic boundaries. All the children in a sample child's class were asked three questions regarding friendship patterns, which involved nearly 4,000 children and yielded nearly 24,000 pieces of information.

To obtain a measure of own-group preference, the investigator requires, ideally, a method which allows for variability in size of groups, number of choices made, and the ethnic composition of the choice population. The Criswell Index (Criswell, 1943) was chosen as satisfying these requirements.

The Criswell Index is a measure of group preference representing a ratio of two ratios. The relative strength of the observed in-group and out-group choices; and, the relative strength of the expected in-group and out-group choices, based on probability theory.

Thus: observed ratio (O) $= \dfrac{\text{actual in-group choices}}{\text{actual out-group choices}}$

$$\text{expected ratio (E)} \quad = \frac{\text{expected in-group choices}}{\text{expected out-group choices}}$$

Criswell Index (CI) = O/E

To calculate E, let a = the number of individuals in a group, t = total number of choices made by a group, N = number of individuals in the test population.

If a population consists of groups 1 and 2 making t_1 and t_2 choices respectively, then:

$$\text{expected in-group choices} \quad = \frac{t_1(a_1 - 1)}{N - 1} \tag{1}$$

Notice that 1 is substracted from 'a_1' and 'N' since an individual cannot choose himself).

$$\text{Expected out-group choices} \quad = \frac{t_1(N - a_1)}{N - 1} \tag{2}$$

(This assumes that the out-group is equal to the entire population minus the sub-group 'a_1').

Dividing expression (1) by expression (2), we obtain the group 1's expected ratio equation (E):-

$$E \quad = \frac{a_1 - 1}{N - a_1} \tag{3}$$

Group 2's equation is, of course, obtained in the same manner, substituting a_2 for a_1 in expression (3).

To calculate CI,

$$CI = O/E$$
$$= \frac{T_1/T_2}{a_1 - 1/N - a_1}$$
$$\therefore \quad CI = \frac{T_1(N - a_1)}{T_2(a_1 - 1)} \tag{4}$$

where: T_1 = actual number of in-group choices, T_2 = actual number of out-group choices, N = number of individuals in test population, and a_1 = number of individuals in group 1.

Again, group 2's preference index (CI) is obtained by substituting a_2 for a_1 in expression (4), and using the appropriate observed in-group and out-group choices.

An index greater than 1.00 indicates that the group preferred themselves to the other group: less than 1.00 indicates that the other group was preferred. Absence of preference is indicated by an index approximating to 1.00. However, as Criswell (1943), notes: '. . . the size of the final index is not in itself an indication that preference is present in statistically significant degree'. For this purpose, she uses 'routine chi-square methods', when the figures are 'large enough'.

It is important to note that Criswell Indices do not follow an interval scale. Consequently, it is not possible to say, for example, that a group with an index of 4 is twice as in-group orientated in its choices as a group with an index of 2. Criswell does, however, claim that the index produces 'measures comparable for different populations to which the same sociometric test was given, even though these populations varied in size and in the percentage of each race present'. In other words, as Jelinek and Brittan (1975) put it: '. . . the larger the value of the Criswell Index the greater the own-group preference'.

The above claim, together with the usefulness of the index itself for certain samples, were thrown into question in the course of investigations designed to answer a specific problem: namely, which is the best method of assessing the statistical significance of the index when methods such as chi-square cannot be used?

It can be seen from the expected ratio equation (E) given in expression (3) above, that Criswell has based the index on the binomial distribution. Indeed, in 'Sociometric Measurement and Chance' (1944), Criswell stated that '. . . in predicting the theoretical choice distributions . . . use was made of the expansion of the binomial, $(q + p)^n$.'

The binomial distribution, essentially, describes the probability of a particular number of outcomes produced in a succession of Bernoulli trials. A Bernoulli trial is the very simplest probability distribution, with only two event classes. In a sociometric item, for example, the individual selected either is, or is not, a member of the same group as the subject. The important point to note is that both a Bernoulli process (i.e. a series of Bernoulli trials) and the binomial distribution assume either sampling independently with replacement, or, in the existence of an infinite number of events within the sample space – so that the basic probabilities do not change over the trials made.

As regards a sociometric item, the binomial distribution, strictly speaking, should only be used when the subject is invited to select one, and only one, individual from the sample space (class, school, etc.). Then, the problem of replacement does not occur. However, in both Criswell's 1939 study and the present research, subjects were asked to select two individuals; that these individuals were different children was, at the very least, implicit in the wording of the question.

In fact, sociometric items such as that included in the present study should, strictly, be based on a hypergeometric distribution; or more correctly, the distribution resulting from the summation of a series of hypergeometric distributions. The hypergeometric distribution assumes random sampling from a finite space without replacement, the probabilities changing for each observation made. Here, each subject would perform a hypergeometric trial, and it is necessary to sum each resulting distribution for all the subjects in a particular group, before a final probability of outcome is reached.

At this stage of the reasoning two further problems require resolution. What are the expressions for the mean, and variance of a sum of hypergeometric distributions? At what stage, in terms of size of sample space and sub-group, do these expressions produce results which approximate to those resulting from application of the binomial distribution?

The answer to the first problem is furnished by Fellers (1957) in the chapter of his book dealing with random variables. If the size of a particular group in a test population is defined as a random variable with a hypergeometric distribution, then the mean and variance can be obtained by direct computation.

Fellers also shows that as the sample space approaches infinity, the binomial increasingly approximates to the hypergeometric distribution. Thus, 'for large populations, there is practically no difference between sampling with or without replacement'. Conversely, Hays (1973) demonstrates by example that for small test populations, or for populations in which one particular group is small, then 'the sampling scheme adopted (binomial or hypergeometric) makes a real difference in the probability of a given result.' In other words, as the size of the population or group increases, the discrepancy between the probabilities resulting from sampling with or without replacement decreases.

However, the problems remain of determining the size of the test population and sub-group required for the hypergeometric to approach the binomial, and of which method to use for assessing statistical significance.

In order to answer the first of these problems, a computer programme was written which calculated the mean and variance for both the binomial and hypergeometric distributions, together with the associated probabilities, for samples of varying population and sub-group sizes. Having done this, it was a simple matter to calculate the absolute differences between the means and variances of the two distributions.

The results of this direct computational approach supported what would be expected theoretically; namely, that for small samples, or samples with skewed groups, the variance of the binomial distribution was larger than that of the hypergeometric (which would affect the outcome of significance testing). The means of the two distributions were found to be the same, and so Criswell's expected ratio equation is, in fact, correct. Thus, for such samples, basing the estimation of probability on the binomial distribution, produces conservative results.

It was decided, therefore, that for large, non-skewed samples ($N \geq 100$) the probability estimation could be based on the binomial distribution. Of course, with samples of this size, the binomial also approximates to the normal distribution and so chi-square can legitimately be used for significance testing.

Unfortunately, large samples bring with them their own theoretical problem, albeit less serious than using the wrong distribution. The hypergeometric distribution assumes that each event in the sample space should have the same probability of occurrence. This means, here, that every child in the test population should have an equal chance of being chosen. Clearly, this may not be the case if the test population is large, especially if the children belong to different classes within the school.

Furthermore, it is not legitimate to combine smaller categories where the above holds, in order to increase numbers, unless each category is of exactly the same size and sub-group composition. If this is not the case, then what is being combined may not be equal in terms of initial probabilities. Such a situation could only be rectified by estimating the exact probabilities, and then devising a weighting scheme before addition. However, if the first stage of this process is carried out, significance testing can take place then, making the second stage redundant.

For small test populations, or samples with very uneven sub-group sizes, the probabilities and significances are based on the sum of hypergeometric trials as suggested by Fellers (1957).

Thus, Criswell's claim that the index produces measures comparable for different populations to which the same sociometric test was given, even though these populations varied in size and the percentage of each race present can only be regarded with suspicion.

Finally, and more obviously, Criswell Indices should only be calculated for those groups which have at least one more member than there are selections. Otherwise, given that an individual cannot choose himself or herself, an out-group orientation is forced. In the present research, the children had two choices for each sociometric question, and therefore, an index was calculated only when there were at least three children in an ethnic grouping.

Comparing parents and children

The possible relationship between parental attitudes and the magnitude of their children's enthnocentricity was approached in two ways. First, the parents were classified according to their responses to certain 'key' questions. These 'parental types' served as the independent variables for a series of analysis of variance procedures, with their children's ORPS scores (see above) as the dependent variables. Since the analysis of variance procedure requires the explanatory variables to be independent of one another, the results were based on the adjusted deviation about the mean.

The second approach was purely descriptive. We identified the children in each ethnic group in the upper and lower deciles of the own-race preference scale in order to see if their respective parents were characterized by contrasting sets of attitudes.

References

Adam, B.D. 1978: Inferiorization and 'self-esteem'. *Social Psycholgy* 41, 47–53.

Adorno, T.W., Frenkel-Brunswick, E., Levinson, D.J. and Sanford, R.N. 1950: *The authoritarian personality*. New York: Harper.

Allport, G.W. 1954: *The nature of prejudice*. Cambridge, Mass.: Addison-Wesley.

Allport, G.W. and Kramer, B.M. 1946: Some roots of prejudice. *Journal of Psychology* 22, 9–39.

Allport, G.W. and Postman, L. 1947: *The psychology of rumour*. New York: Holt.

Amir, Y. 1969: Contact hypothesis in ethnic relations. *Psychological Bulletin* 71, 319–42.

Anwar, M. 1980: *Votes and policies: ethnic minorities and the general election* London: Commission for Racial Equality.

Aronson, E. 1972: *The social animal*. San Francisco: Freeman.

Aronson, E., Stephan, C., Sikes, J., Blaney, N. and Snapp, M. 1978: *The jigsaw classroom*. Beverley Hills, Calif.: Sage Publications.

Asch, S.E. 1946: Forming impressions. *Journal of Abnormal and Social Psychology* 41, 258–90.

Asher, S.R. and Allen, V.L. 1969: Racial preference and social comparison processes. *Journal of Social Issues* 25, 157–66.

Aucott, J., Cox, H., Dodds, A. and Selby, D. 1979: World studies on the runway: one year's progress towards a core curriculum. *The New Era* 60, 212–19.

Bagley, C. and Coard, B. 1975: Cultural knowledge and rejection of ethnic identity in West Indian children in London. In Verma, G. and Bagley, C. (eds.), *Race and education across cultures* (London: Heinemann), 322–31.

Bagley, C., Mallick, K. and Verma, G. 1979: Pupil self-esteem: a study of black and white teenagers in British schools. In Verma, G. and Bagley, C. (eds.), *Race, education and identity* (London: Macmillan) 176–91.

Bagley, C., Verma, G., Mallick, K. and Young, L. 1979: *Prejudice, self-esteem and prejudice*. Farnborough: Saxon House.

Banks, W.C. and Rompf, W.J. 1973: Evaluative bias and preference behaviour in black and white children. *Child Development* 44, 776–783.

Barker Lunn, J.C. 1970: *Streaming in the primary school*. Slough: National Foundation for Educational Research.

Barnes, D. 1977: *Communication and learning in small groups*. London: Routledge & Kegan Paul.

Baxter, P. and Sansom, B. (eds.) 1972: *Race and social differences*. Harmonsworth: Penguin Books.

Beloff, H. (ed.) 1980: *A balance sheet on Burt*. Leicester: British Psychological Society.

Berger, P.L. 1966: Identity as a problem in the sociology of knowledge. *European Journal of Sociology* 7, 105–15.

Berkowitz, L. 1962: *Aggression: A social-psychological analysis*. New York: McGraw-Hill.

Berry, J.W., Kalin, R. and Taylor, D.M. 1976: Multiculturalism and ethnic attitudes in Canada. Unpublished paper, Queen's University – Kingston, Ontario.

Billig, M. 1978: *Fascists: A social psychological view of the National Front*. London: Academic Press.

Billig, M. and Tajfel, H. 1973: Social categorization and similarity in intergroup behaviour. *European Journal of Social Psychology* 3, 27–52.

Bindman, G. 1980: The law, equal opportunity and affirmative action. *New Community* 7, 248–60.

Bird, C., Monachesi, E.D. and Burdick, H. 1952a: Infiltration and the attitudes of white and negro parents and children. *Journal of Abnormal and Social Psychology* 47, 688–99.

Bird, C., Monachesi, E.D. and Burdick, H. 1952b: Studies of group tension, 3. The effect of parental discouragement of play activities upon the attitudes of white children towards negroes. *Child Development* 23, 295–306.

Blake, R.R. and Mouton, J.S. 1961: *Group dynamics: key to decision making*. Houston: Gulf.

Bogardus, E. 1933: A social distance scale. *Sociological and Social Research* 17, 265–71.

Borges, J.L. 1970: Funes the memorious. In *Labyrinths*, 87–95. Harmonsworth: Penguin Books.

Brittan, E.M. 1976: Multiracial education 2. Teacher opinion on aspects of school life. Part one: changes in curriculum and school organization. *Educational Research* 18, 96–107.

Bruner, J.S. 1964: The course of cognitive growth. *American Psychologist* 19, 1–15.

Bruner, J.S., Goodnow, J.J. and Austin, G.A. 1956: *A study of thinking*. New York: Wiley.

Bruner, J.S. and Olver, R.R. 1963: The development of equivalence transformations in children. In Wright, J.C. and Kagan, J. (eds.), *Basic cognitive processes in children*. Monograph of the Society for Research in Child Development 28, 125–43.

Bruner, J.S., Olver, R.R. and Greenfield, P.M. 1966: *Studies in cognitive growth*. New York: Wiley.

Bunton, P.L. and Weissbach, T.A. 1974: Attitudes towards blackness of preschool children attending community controlled or public schools. *Journal of Social Psychology* 92, 53–9.

Burt, C. 1966: The genetic determination of differences in intelligence: a study of monozygotic twins reared together and apart. *British Journal of Psychology* 57, 137–153.

Christie, R. and Jahoda, M. (eds.) 1954: *Studies in the scope and method of 'The Authoritarian Personality'*. New York: Free Press.

Clark, K.B. 1955: *Prejudice and your child*. Boston: Beacon Press.

Clark, K.B. and Clark, M.P. 1939a: The development of the consciousness of self and the emergence of racial identity in negro preschool children. *Journal of Social Psychology* 10, 591–9.

Clark, K.B. and Clark, M.P. 1939b: Segregation as a factor in racial identification of negro preschool children: a preliminary report. *Journal of Experimental Education* 8, 161–3.

Clark, K.B. and Clark, M.P. 1940: Skin colour as a factor in racial identification in negro preschool children. *Journal of Social Psychology* 11, 159–69.

Clark, K.B. and Clark, M.P. 1947: Racial identification and preference in negro children. In Newcomb, T.M. and Hartley, E.L. (eds.), *Readings in social psychology* (New York: Holt, Rinehart & Winston) 169–78.

Commission for Racial Equality 1977: *Urban deprivation, racial inequality and social policy*: a report. Her Majesty's Stationery Office.

Coopersmith, S. 1975: Self-concept, race and education. In Verma, G. and Bagley, C., *Race and education across cultures* (London: Heinemann) 145–67.

Coser, L.A. 1956: *The functions of social conflict*. Glencoe, Ill: Free Press.

Criswell, J.M. 1939: A sociometric study of race cleavage in the classroom. *Archives of Psychology* 33, 1–82.

Criswell, J.M. 1943: Sociometric methods of measuring group preferences. *Sociometry* 6, 398–408.

Criswell, J.M. 1944: Sociometric measurement and chance. *Sociometry* 7, 415–21.

Daniel, W.W. 1968: *Racial discrimination in England*. Harmonsworth: Penguin Books.

Davey, A.G. 1968: The Tristan da Cunhan children's concepts of equivalence. *British Journal of Educational Psychology* 38, 162–70.

Davey, A.G. 1973: Teachers, race and intelligence. *Race* 15, 195–211.

Davey, A.G. 1976: Attitudes and the prediction of social conduct. *British Journal of Social and Clinical Psychology* 15, 11–22.

Davey. A.G. 1980: *Racial awareness and prejudice in young children*. SSRC Data Archive, University of Essex.

Davey, A.G. and Pushkin, I. 1980. *A study of racial awareness and prejudice in young children: a report*. Boston Spa: British Library Lending Division.

Davie, R., Butler, N. and Goldstein, H. 1972: *From birth to seven*. London: Longman.

Department of Education and Science 1973: *Statistics of education*. London: Her Majesty's Stationery Office.

Department of Education and Science 1974: *Educational disadvantage and the needs of immigrants*. London: Her Majesty's Stationery Office.

Department of Education and Science 1977: *Education in schools: a consultative document*, Cmnd. 6869. London: Her Majesty's Stationery Office.

DeVries, D. and Slavin, R. 1978: Team-games – tournaments: a research review. *Journal of Research and Development in Education* 12, 28–38.

Dickens, L. and Hobart, C. 1959: Parental dominance and offspring ethnocentrism. *Journal of Social Psychology* 49, 297–303.

Dixon, B. 1977: *Catching them young 1: sex, race and class in children's fiction*. London: Pluto Press.

Douglas, J.W.B. 1964: *The home and the school*. London: MacGibbon & Kee.

Durkheim, E. 1964: *The rules of sociological method*. New York: Free Press.

Durojaiye, M.O.A. 1969: Race relations among junior school children. *Educational Research* 11, 226–8.

Durojaiye, M.O.A. 1970: Patterns of friendship in an ethnically mixed junior school. *Race* 12, 189–200.

Ehrlich, H.J. 1973: *The social psychology of prejudice*. New York: Wiley.

Epstein, R. and Komorita, S.S. 1966: Childhood prejudice as a function of parental ethnocentrism, punitiveness and outgroup characteristics. *Journal of Personality and Social Psychology* 3, 259–64.

Epstein, Y.M., Krupat, E. and Obudho, C. 1976: Clean is beautiful: the effects of race and cleanliness on children's preferences. *Journal of Social Issues* 32, 109–18.

Fellers, W. 1957: *An introduction to probability theory and its applications*. 2nd ed. Vol. 1. New York: Wiley.

Fielding, G. and Evered, C. 1980: The influence of patients' speech upon doctors: the diagnostic interview. In St Clair, R.N. and Giles, H. (eds.) *The social and psychological contexts of language* (New Jersey: Lawrence Erlbaum Associates) 51–72.

Figueroa, P., 1981: Race and cultural differences: some ideas on a racial frame of reference. Mimeo. Paper presented at Third International Conference on Intercultural Issues. University of Bradford, 1981.

Foner, N. 1977: The Jamaicans: cultural and social change in Britain. In

Watson, J. L. (ed.), *Between two cultures*. (Oxford: Basil Blackwell) 120–50.

Fox, D.J. and Jordan, V.B. 1973: Racial preference and identification of black, American Chinese, and white children. *Genetic Psychology Monographs* 88, 229–86.

Frenkel-Brunswick, E. 1948: A study of prejudice in children. *Human Relations* 1, 295–305.

Frenkel-Brunswick, E. 1949: Intolerance of ambiguity as an emotional and perceptual personality variable. *Journal of Personality* 18, 108–43.

Fromm, E. 1941: *Escape from freedom*. New York: Rinehart.

Futcher, S. 1972: West Indian foster children. *Social Work To-day* 29 June, 4–6.

Gergen, K. 1967: The significance of skin colour in human relations. *Daedulus* 96, 390–407.

Giles, H. and Powesland. P. 1975: *Speech style and social evaluation*. London: Academic Press.

Gill, D. 1982: Geography in a multicultural society. *World Studies Journal* 3, 5–18.

Glendenning, F. 1971: Racial stereotypes in history books. *Race To-day* February, 52–4.

Goodman, M.E. 1952: *Race awareness in young children*. Cambridge, Mass.: Addison-Wesley (Republished: New York: Collier, 1964).

Green, B.F. 1954: Attitude measurement. In Lindzey, G., *Handbook of Social Psychology* Vol. 1 (Cambridge, Mass.: Addison Wesley) 335–69.

Greenwald, H. and Oppenheim, D. 1968: Reported magnitude of self-misidentification among negro children – artifact? *Journal of Personality and Social Psychology* 68, 95–106.

Gregor, A.J. and McPherson, D.A. 1966a: Racial attitudes among white and negro children in a deep-South standard metropolitan area. *Journal of Social Psychology* 68, 95–106.

Gregor, A.J. and McPherson, D.A. 1966b: Racial preference and ego identity among white and Bantu children in the Republic of South Africa. *Genetic Psychology Monographs* 73, 217–54.

Grossak, M. 1957: Group belongingness and authoritarianism in southern negroes. *Phylon* 18, 261–6.

Haavelsrud, M. (ed.) 1976: *Education for peace: reflection and action*. London. IPC Science and Technology Press.

Halsey, A.H. 1972: *Educational priority*, Vol. 1. Her Majesty's Stationery Office.

Halsey, A.H., Sheehan, J. and Vaizey, J. 1972: Schools. In Halsey, A.H. (ed.), *Trends in British society since 1900* (London: Macmillian), 148–91.

Harris, D.B., Gough, H.G. and Martin, W.E. 1950: Children's ethnic attitudes: 2, relation to parental beliefs. *Child Development* 21, 169–82.

Hartley, E.M., Rosenbaum, M. and Schwartz, S. 1948: Children's use of ethnic frames of reference. *Journal of Psychology* 26, 367–86.

Hartman, P. and Husband, C. 1974: *Racism and the mass media*. London: Davis-Poynter.

Hatch, S. 1962: Coloured people in school text books. *Race* 4, 63–72.

Hays, W.L. 1973: *Statistics for the social sciences*. 2nd ed. New York: Holt, Rinehart & Winston.

Heater, D. 1980: *World studies: education for international understanding in Britain*. London: Harrap.

Hester, H. and Steedman, C. 1983: *Language in the multicultural primary classroom: work in progress*: London: Schools Council.

Hicks, D.W. 1980: *Peace studies in the 1980s: some preliminary notes*, mimeo. Centre for Peace Studies, St Martin's College, Lancaster.

Hicks, D.W. n.d. *Racial justice, global development or peace: which shall we choose in school?* World Studies document 6. University of York: World Studies Teacher Training Centre.

Homans, G.C. 1950: *The human group*. New York: Harcourt Brace.

Horowitz, E.L. 1936: The development of attitude toward the negro. *Archives of Psychology* No. 194. Columbia University.

Hraba, J. and Grant, G. 1970: Black is beautiful: a re-examination of racial preference and identification. *Journal of Personality and Social Psychology* 16, 398–402.

Husband, C. 1975: Racism in society and the mass media: a critical interaction. In Husband, C. (ed.), *White media and black Britain* (London: Arrow Books) 15-38.

Husband, C. 1977: News media, language and race relations: a case study in identity meintenance. In Giles, H. (ed.), *Language ethnicity and intergroup relations* (London: Academic Press), 211–40.

Husband, C. 1979; Social identity and language in race relations. In Giles, H. and Saint-Jacques, B. (eds.) *Language and ethnic relations* (Oxford: Pergamon Press) 179–95.

Jahoda, G. 1959: Development of the perception of social differences in children from 6 to 10. *British Journal of Psychology* 50, 159–75.

Jahoda, G., Thompson, S.S. and Bhatt, S. 1972: Ethnic identity and preference among Asian immigrant children in Glasgow. *European Journal of Social Psychology* 2, 19–32.

James, W. 1905: *Textbook of psychology*. London: Macmillan.

Jelinek, M.M. and Brittan, E.M. 1975: Multiracial education: 1. inter-ethnic friendship patterns. *Educational Research* 18, 44–53.

Jencks, C. 1973: *Inequality: a reassessment of the effect of family and schooling in America*. London: Allen Lane.

Jensen, A.R. 1969: How much can we boost IQ and scholastic achievement? *Harvard Educational Review* 39, 1–123.

Johnson, D. and Johnson, R. 1975: *Learning together and alone*. Englewood

Cliffs, NJ: Prentice-Hall.

Jones, C. 1977: *Immigration and social policy in Britain*. London: Tavistock.

Jones, J.S. 1981: How different are human races? *Nature* 293, 189–90.

Juel-Nielson, N. 1965: Individual and environment: a psychiatric-psychological investigation of monozygous twins reared appart. *Acta Psychiatrica et Neurologica Scandinavica. Monograph supplement* no. 183.

Kagan, J.S. 1969: Inadequate evidence and illogical conclusions. *Harvard Educational Review* 39, 274–7.

Kahn, R.L. and Cannell, C.F. 1957: *The dynamics of interviewing*. New York: Wiley.

Katz, D. 1960: The functional approach to the study of attitudes. *Public Opinion Quarterly* 24, 163–204.

Katz, D. and Braly, K.W. 1933: Racial stereotypes of 100 college students. *Journal of Abnormal and Social Psychology* 28, 280–190.

Kawwa, T. 1968: Three sociometric studies of ethnic relations in London schools. *Race* 10, 173–80.

Kelvin, P. 1969: *The bases of social behaviour*. London: Holt, Rinehart & Winston.

Kirp, D.L. 1979: *Doing good by doing little*. Berkeley: University of California Press.

Laishley, J. 1975: The images of blacks and whites in the children's media. In Husband, C. (ed.), *White media and black Britain*. (London: Arrow Books) 69–89.

Le Page, R.B. 1981: *Caribbean connections in the classroom*. London Institute of Linguists Educational Trust.

Lester, A. and Bindman, G. 1972: *Race and law*. Harmonsworth: Penguin Books.

Lewontin, R.C. 1974: The analysis of variance and the analysis of causes. *American Journal of Human Genetics* 26, 400–11.

Little, A. and Kohler, D. 1976/77: Are race relations getting worse? *Community Relations Commission Journal* Dec/Jan 10–11.

Little, A. and Willey, R. 1981a: *Multiethnic education: the way forward*. London: Schools Council.

Little, A. and Willey, R. 1981b: *The task facing the schools*. Mimeo. Goldsmiths College: University of London.

Liu, W.H. 1977: The evolution of Commonwealth citizenship and UK statutory control over Commonwealth immigration. *New Community* 5, 426–47.

Loehlin, J.C., Lindzey, G. and Spuhler, J.N. 1975: *Race differences in intelligence*. San Francisco: Freeman.

Louden, D.M. 1978a: Conflict and change among West Indian parents and their adolescents in Britain. *Educational Research* 20, 44-53.

Louden, D.M. 1978b: Self-esteem and the locus of control: some findings on immigrant adolescents in Britain. *New Community* 6, 218–34.

Lyle, W.H. and Levitt, E.E. 1955: Punitiveness, authoritarianism and parental discipline of grade school children. *Journal of Abnormal and Social Psychology* 51, 42–6.

McCarthy, J. and Yancey, W.L. 1971: Reply to Washington by McCarthy and Yancey. *American Journal of Sociology* 77. 590–1.

Madge, N. 1976: Context and expressed ethnic preference of infant school children. *Journal of Child Psychology and Psychiatry* 17, 337–44.

Marsh, A. 1970: Awareness of racial differences in West African and British children. *Race* 11, 289–302.

Melamed, L. 1968: Race awareness in South African children. *Journal of Social Psychology* 76, 3–8.

Miller, N.E. 1941: The frustration-aggression hypothesis. *Psychological Review* 48, 337–442.

Milner, D. 1973: Racial identification and preference in 'black' British children. *European Journal of Social Psychology* 3, 281–96.

Milner, D. 1979: Does multi-racial education work? *Issues in Race and Education* 23, 2–3.

Milner, D. 1981: Racial prejudice and social psychology. In Turner, J. and Giles, H. (eds.) *Intergroup behaviour* (Oxford: Blackwell), 102–43.

Minard, R.D. 1952: Race relations in the Pocahontas coal field. *Journal of Social Issues* 8, 29–44.

Moore, C.L. 1976: The racial preference and attitude of preschool black children. *Journal of Genetic Psychology* 129, 37–44.

Morland, J.K. 1958: Racial recognition by nursery school children in Lynchburg, Virginia. *Social Forces* 37, 132–7.

Morland, J.K. 1962: Racial acceptance and preferences of nursery school children in a southern city. *Merrill-Palmer Quarterly* 8, 271–80.

Morland, J.K. 1963: Racial identification: a study of nursery school children. *American Catholic Sociological Review* 24, 231–42.

Morland, J.K. 1966: A comparison of race awareness in northern and southern children. *American Journal of Orthopsychiatry* 36, 22–31.

Morland, J.K. 1969: Racial awareness among American and Hong Kong Chinese children. *American Journel of Sociology* 75, 360–74.

Mosher, D.L. and Scodel, A. 1960: Relationship between ethnocentrism in children and ethnocentrism and child-rearing practices of their mothers. *Child Development* 31, 369–76.

Nash, N. 1962: Race and the ideology of race. In Baxter and Sansom 1972, 111–22.

Newman, H.H., Freeman, F.N. and Holzinger, K.J. 1937: *Twins: a study of heredity and environment*. Chicago: Chicago University Press.

Norburn, V. and Wright, J. 1982: Policies on racism: what parents think. *Where* 182, 20–5.

Orive, R. and Gerard, H.B. 1975: Social contact of minority parents and their children's acceptance by classmates. *Sociometry* 38, 518–24.

Osgood, C.E., Suci, G.J. and Tannenbaum, P.H. 1957: *The measurement of meaning*. Urbana: University of Illinois Press.

Parekh, B. 1978: Asians in Britain: problem or opportunity? In Commission for Racial Equality, *Five Views of Multi-racial Britain*. (London: CRE), 36–55

Pettigrew, T.F. 1958: Personality and socio-cultural factors in inter-group attitudes: a cross-national comparison. *Journal of Conflict Resolution* 2, 29–42.

Pettigrew, T.F. 1978: Placing Adam's argument in a broader perspective. Comment on the Adam paper. *Social Psychology* 41, 58–61.

Pettigrew, T.F., Allport, G.W. and Barnett, E.V. 1958: Binocular resolution and the perception of race in South Africa. *British Journal of Psychology* 49, 265–78.

Plowden, Lady, 1967: *Children and their primary schools: a report of the Central Advisory Council for Education (England)*. London: Her Majesty's Stationery Office.

Porter, J.D.R. 1971: *Black child: white child: the development of racial attitudes*. Cambridge, Mass.: Harvard University Press.

Pryce, K. 1979: *Endless pressure*. Harmonsworth: Penguin Books.

Pushkin, I. 1967/1983: A study of ethnic choice in the play of young children in three London districts. Unpublished Ph.D. thesis, University of London. Published in part in Pushkin, I. and Norburn, V. 1983: *Ethnic preferences in young children and in their adolescence in three London districts*. Human Relations, 36, 309–44.

Pushkin, I. and Veness, T. 1973: The development of racial awareness and prejudice in children. In Watson, P. (ed.), *Psychology and race* (Harmonsworth: Penguin Books), 23–42.

Racial Discrimination. 1975: Cmmd. 6234. Her Majesty's Stationery Office.

Radke, M., Sutherland, J. and Rosenberg, P. 1950: Racial attitudes of children. *Sociometry* 13, 154–71.

Radke-Yarrow, M. and Lande, B. 1953: Personality correlates of differential reactions to minority group belonging. *Journal of Social Psychology* 38, 253–72.

Radke-Yarrow, M., Trager, H.G. and Miller, J. 1952: The role of parents in the development of children's ethnic attitudes. *Child Development* 23, 13–53.

Razran, G. 1950: Ethnic dislikes and stereotypes: a laboratory study. *Journal of Abnormal and Social Psychology* 45, 7–27.

Rex, J. and Tomlinson, S. 1979: *Colonial immigrants in a British city*. London: Routledge & Kegan Paul.

Richardson, S.W. and Green, A. 1971: When is black beautiful? Coloured and white children's reactions to skin colour. *British Journal of*

Educational Psychology 41, 62–9.

Rogers, C.R. 1951: *Client-centered therapy*. Boston: Houghton-Mifflin.

Rokeach, M. 1956: Political and religious dogmatism: an alternative to the authoritarian personality. *Psychological Monographs* 70, 1–43.

Rosenberg, M. and Simmons, R.G. 1972: *Black and white self-esteem: the urban school child*. Washington, DC: American Sociological Association.

Rosenhan, D.L. 1973: On being sane in insane places. *Science* 179, 250–8.

Rowley, K.G. 1968: Social relations between British and immigrant children. *Educational Research* 10, 145–8.

Runnymede Trust 1980: *Britain's black population*. London: Heinemann.

Salmon, P. and Claire, H. 1984: (forthcoming). *Classroom collaboration*. London: Routledge & Kegan Paul.

Sattler, J. 1970: Racial 'experimenter effects' in experimentation, testing, interviewing and psychotherapy. *Psychological Bulletin* 73, 137–60.

Scarman, Lord. 1981: *The Brixton disorders, 10–12, April 1981*. London: Her Majesty's Stationery Office.

Schofield, J.W. 1981: Complementary and conflicting identities: images and interaction in an interracial school. In Asher, S.R. and Gottman. J.M. (eds.), *The Development of children's friendships*. (Cambridge: Cambridge University Press), 53–90.

Scodel, A. and Austrin, H. 1957: The perception of Jewish photographs by non-Jews and Jews. *Journal of Abnormal and Social Psychology* 54, 278–80.

Seeleman, V. 1940: The influence of attitude upon the remembering of pictorial material. *Archives of Psychology* 258.

Selby, D. 1980: The purple armband experiment: an experiential unit in discrimination. *The New Era* 61, 218–21.

Selby, D. 1983: World Studies: towards a global perspective in the school curriculum. The Social Science Teacher (in press).

Selby, D and Cox, H. 1978: Living and learning in the global village: aims and plans at a new school. *The New Era* 59, 134–9.

Sharan, S. 1980: Cooperative learning in small groups: recent methods and effects on achievement, attitudes and ethnic relations. *Review of Education Research* 50, 241–71.

Sharan, S. and Sharan, Y. 1976: *Small group teaching*. Englewood Cliffs, NJ: Educational Technology Publications.

Shields, J. 1962: *Monosygotic* twins. London: Oxford University Press.

Sherif, M. 1966: *Group conflict and cooperation: their social psychology*. London: Routledge & Kegan Paul.

Sherif, M. and Sherif, C.W. 1953: *Groups in harmony and tension*. New York: Harper & Row.

Siegel, S. 1956: *Nonparametric statistics for the behavioural sciences*. New York: McGraw-Hill.

Simmons, R.G. 1978: Blacks and high self-esteem: a puzzle. *Social Psychology* 41, 54–7.

Singleton, L.C. and Asher, S.R. 1979: Race integration and children's peer preferences: an investigation of developmental and cohort differences. *Child Development* 50, 936–41.

Smith, D.J. 1974: *Racial disadvantage in employment*. London: Political and Economic Planning.

Smith, D.J. 1976: *The facts of racial disadvantage. A national survey*. London: Political and Economic Planning.

Smith, D.J. and McIntosh, N. 1974: *The extent of racial discrimination*. Broadsheet 547, London: Political and Economic Planning.

Springer, D. 1950: Awareness of racial differences by preschool children in Hawii. *Genetic Psychology Monographs* 41, 215–270.

Stevenson, H.W. and Stewart, E.C. 1958: A developmental study of racial awareness in young children. *Child Development* 29, 399–409.

Stone, M. 1981: *The education of the black child in Britain*. London: Fontana.

Storm, M. and Richardson, R. 1980: *Development education: education for life in a changing world*. London: University of London Institute of Education.

Street-Porter, R. 1978: *Race, children and cities*. Milton Keynes: Open University Press.

Sumner, W.G. 1906: *Folkways*. New York: Ginn.

Tajfel, H. 1969: Cognitive aspects of prejudice. *Journal of Social issues* 25, 79–97.

Tajfel, H. 1974: Social identity and intergroup behaviour. *Social Science Information* 13, 65–93.

Tajfel, H. (ed.) 1978: *Differentiation between social groups, studies in the social psychology of intergroup relations*. London: Academic Press.

Tajfel, H. 1981: Social stereotypes and social groups. In, Turner, J. and Giles, H. (eds.), *Integroup behaviour* (Oxford: Blackwell), 144–67.

Tajfel, H., Flament, C., Billig, M. and Bundy, R. 1971: Social categorization and intergroup behaviour. *European Journal of Social Psychology* 1, 149–78.

Tajfel, H. and Jahoda, G. 1966: Development in children of concepts and attitudes about their own and other nations: a cross-national study. *Proceedings of the 18th International Congress of Psychology*, Moscow, Symposium 36, 17–33.

Tajfel, H., Jahoda, G., Nemeth, R., Rim, Y. and Johnson, N. 1972: Devaluation by children of their own national and ethnic group: two case studies. *British Journal of Social and Clinical Psychology* 11, 235–43.

Tajfel, H., Nemeth, C., Jahoda, G., Campbell, D. and Johnson, N. 1970: The development of children's preferences for their own country: a cross-national study. *International Journal of Psychology* 5, 245–53.

Tajfel, H. and Turner, J. 1979: An integrative theory of intergroup conflict. In Austin, W. and Worchel, S. (eds.), *The social psychology of intergroup relations* (Belmont, California: Brooks-Cole), 33–47.

Tajfel, H. and Wilkes, A.L. 1963: Classification and quantitative judgement. *British Journal of Psychology* 54, 101–14.

Teplin, L.A. 1977: Preference versus prejudice: a multi-method analysis of children's discrepant racial choices. *Social Science Quarterly* 58, 390–406.

Thomas, K.C. 1978: Colour of tester effects on children's expressed attitudes. *British Educational Research Journal* 4, 83–90.

Titmuss, R.M. 1976: *Commitment to welfare*. London: Allen & Unwin.

Townsend, H. and Brittan, E.M. 1972: *Organization in multiracial schools*. Slough: National Foundation for Educational Research.

Townsend, H. and Brittan, E.M. 1973: *Multiracial education: need and innovation*. Schools Council Working Paper 50. London: Evans/-Methuen Educational.

US War Department Information and Education Division. 1947: Opinions about negro infantry platoons in white companies of seven divisions. In Newcomb, T.M. and Hartley, E.L. (eds.), *Readings in social psychology* (New York: Holt), 542–6.

Vaughan, G.M. 1964: The development of ethnic attitudes in New Zealand school children. *Genetic Psychology Monographs* 70, 135–175.

Vaughan, G.M. 1978: Social change and intergroup preference in New Zealand. *European Journal of Social Psychology* 8, 297–313.

Veness, T. and Brierley, D.W. 1963: Forming impressions of personality: two experiments. *British Journal of Social and Clinical Psychology* 2, 11–19.

Vernon, P.E. 1979: *Intelligence: heredity and environment*. San Francisco: Freeman.

Vygotsky, L.S. 1962: *Thought and language*. New York: Wiley.

Ward, S.H. and Braun, J. 1972: Self-esteem and racial preference in black children. *American Journal of Orthopsychiatry* 42, 644–7.

Webber, R. and Craig, J. 1978: *Socio-economic classification of local authority areas*. London: Her Majesty's Stationery Office.

Weinreich, P. 1979: Cross-ethnic identification and self-rejection in a black adolescent. In Verma, G. and Bagley, C. (eds.), *Race, education and identity* (London: Macmillan), 157–75.

Williams, B. 1962: The idea of equality. In Laslett, P. and Runciman, W.G. (eds.), *Philosophy, politics and society*. Second series (Oxford: Blackwell), 110-131.

Wilson, A. 1981. Mixed race children: an exploratory study of racial categorization and identity. *New Community* 9, 36–43.

Winkley, D. 1981: Multicultural policy and practice: a view from Grove

Junior School. *Education 3-13* 9, 12–16.

Wiseman, S. 1964: *Education and environment*. Manchester: Manchester University Press.

Young, L. and Bagley, C. 1979: Identity, self-esteem and evaluation of colour and ethnicity in young children in Jamaica and London. *New Community* 7, 154–69.

Index